Praise for *The High Road to China*

'There is no more entertaining or informative account . . . Teltscher's account of Bogle's long stay with the Panchen, based in part on his vivid letters to his sisters, makes this book soar'

Jonathan Mirsky, *Literary Review*

'A splendid and fascinating account of early British attempts to establish contact with Tibet and China in the 1770s'

Patrick French, *Sunday Times*

'This enthralling book tells the story of Bogle's amazing adventure with extraordinary skill'

Good Book Guide

'Bogle's refreshing readiness to accommodate himself to Tibetan ways, and to reflect critically, from the perspective of the mountains and the plateaux, on his own society make a thought-provoking contrast with the pompous stridency of Britain's later ventures into China and Tibet . . . Unfailingly interesting and thorough'

Julia Lovell, *Guardian*

'Bogle caused a sensation in the Himalayas. When he approached the palace of the ruler of Bhutan, his route was lined with spectators all craning to catch sight of this weird, white-faced alien with tight clothes and funny hair . . . Fascinating'

Hilary Spurling, *Observer*

'For Tibetans and Han Chinese these two meetings that Teltscher recreates have a very real political significance . . . Raises issues that powerfully inform our understanding of one of the prickly issues of our time'

Fraser Newham, *Asia Times*

THE
HIGH ROAD TO CHINA

George Bogle, the Panchen Lama
and the First British Expedition to Tibet

KATE TELTSCHER

BLOOMSBURY

First published in Great Britain in 2006
This paperback edition published 2007

Bloomsbury Publishing Plc
36 Soho Square
London W1D 3QY

www.bloomsbury.com/kateteltscher

A CIP catalogue record for this book
is available from the British Library

ISBN 978 0 7475 8547 3

10 9 8 7 6 5 4 3 2 1

All papers used by Bloomsbury Publishing are natural,
recyclable products made from wood grown in well-managed
forests. The manufacturing processes conform to the
environmental regulations of the country of origin.

Typeset by Hewer Text UK Ltd, Edinburgh
Printed in Great Britain by Clays Ltd, St Ives plc

Maps by John Gilkes

For Julian,
whose idea it was,
and for Jacob and Isaac,
who grew with the book

CONTENTS

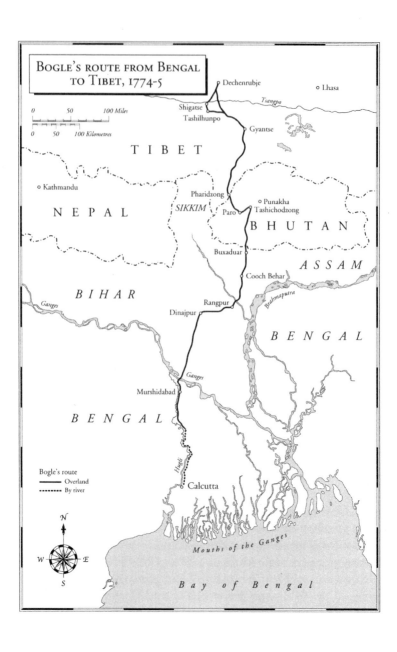

BOGLE'S ROUTE FROM BENGAL
TO TIBET, 1774-5

o Dechenrubje   o Lhasa

Tsangpo

Shigatse
Tashilhunpo   o Gyantse

0   50   100 Miles

0   50   100 Kilometres

T I B E T

o Kathmandu

N E P A L

Pharidzong
SIKKIM   o Punakha
Paro   Tashichodzong

B H U T A N

Buxaduar

A S S A M

Cooch Behar

B I H A R

Ganges

Brahmaputra

Rangpur
Dinajpur

B E N G A L

Ganges

Murshidabad

B E N G A L

Bogle's route
——— Overland
▪▪▪▪▪ By river

Hugli

o Calcutta

N

W   E

S

Mouths of the Ganges

B a y   o f   B e n g a l

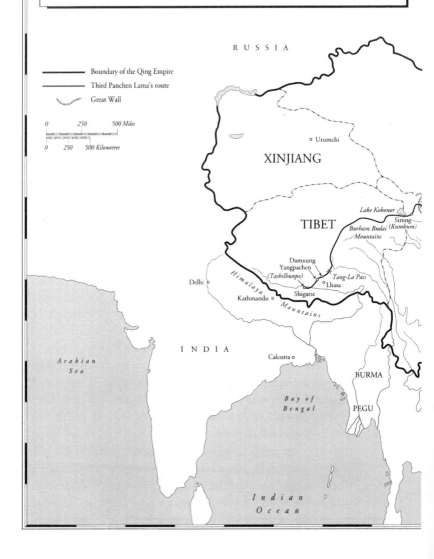

THE QING EMPIRE, SHOWING THE PROBABLE ROUTE OF THE THIRD PANCHEN LAMA FROM SHIGATSE TO PEKING, 1779-1780

RUSSIA

——— Boundary of the Qing Empire

——— Third Panchen Lama's route

∿∿∿ Great Wall

0   250   500 Miles

0   250   500 Kilometres

o Urumchi

XINJIANG

Lake Kokonor

TIBET

Sining
(Kumbum)

Burham Budai
Mountains

Damxung
Yangpachen
(Tashilhunpo)

Tang-La Pass

Delhi o

H i m a l a y a

o Lhasa

Shigatse

Kathmandu o

M o u n t a i n s

I N D I A

Calcutta o

Arabian
Sea

BURMA

Bay of
Bengal

PEGU

Indian
Ocean

LIST OF ILLUSTRATIONS

Colour Plates

Freer Gallery of Art, Smithsonian Institution, Washington DC Purchase – anonymous donor and Museum funds, F2000.4.

11. Detail of Complete Map of the Resort Palace at Chengde. Library of Congress, Washington DC, G7824.C517A3 1890. G8 Vault Shelf.

12. Rubbing taken from an impression of a painting of a Sal tree by the Qianlong Emperor, © The Field Museum, A100689-A.

Line Drawings: Chapter Headings and Part Openers

Prologue: Statue of lion at Peking, William Alexander, in George Staunton, *An Authentic Account of an Embassy from the King of Great Britain to the Emperor of China*, 1798.

Part 1: J. Redaway, after William Daniell in Hobart Caunter, *The Oriental Annual*, 1837. School of Oriental & African Studies Library, London.

Chap 1: Government House, Calcutta, Thomas Daniell, *Views of Calcutta*, 1788.

Chap 2: 'Mr. Bogle', Francis Younghusband, *India and Tibet*, 1910.

Chap 3 'Hindoo fruit boat', Reginald Heber, *Narrative of a Journey through the Upper Provinces of India*, 1828.

Chap 4: 'Capta Castle Bootan', engraved by J. Cousen, after William Daniell, in Hobart Caunter, *The Oriental Annual*, 1837. School of Oriental & African Studies Library, London.

Chap 5: 'Palace at Tassisudon Bootan', engraved by J. B. Allen after William Daniell, in Hobart Caunter, *The Oriental Annual*, 1837. School of Oriental & African Studies Library, London.

Chap 6: The Residence of Lam' Ghassa-too', James Basire, after Samuel Davis, in Samuel Turner, *An Account of an Embassy to the Court of the Teshoo Lama in Tibet*, 1800.

Chap 7: 'Guard House near Tassisudon', engraved by W.J. Cooke, after William Daniell, in Hobart Caunter, *Oriental Annual*, 1838. School of Oriental & African Studies Library, London.

Part II: The Grand Monastery at Tashilhunpo, Sarat Chandra Das, *Journey to Lhasa and Central Tibet*, 1902.

Chap 8: Statue of Amitabha, William Rockhill, *The Land of the Lamas*, 1891.

Line Drawings: Integrated Images

Chap 2, p.23: Map of Tibet by Jean Baptiste Bourguignon d'Anville, 1735.

Chap 4, p.52: 'Near Buxaduar Bootan', engraved by W.J. Cooke, after William Daniell, in Hobart Caunter, *Oriental Annual*, 1837. School of Oriental & African Studies Library, London.

Chap 4, p.55: James Basire, after Samuel Davis, in Samuel Turner, *An Account of an Embassy to the Court of the Teshoo Lama in Tibet*, 1800. School of Oriental & African Studies Library, London.

Chap 4, p.58: James Basire, after Samuel Davis, in Samuel Turner, *An Account of an Embassy to the Court of the Teshoo Lama in Tibet*, 1800. School of Oriental & African Studies Library, London.

Chap 5, p.68: MSS Eur E226/77, p.92. APAC, British Library, London.

Chap 21, p. 242: 'The Yak of Tartary', engraved by De la Motte, after George Stubbs, in Samuel Turner, *An Account of an Embassy to the Court of the Teshoo Lama in Tibet*, 1800. School of Oriental & African Studies Library, London.

Chap 21, p.248: 'His Excellency, the Earl of Macartney', William Alexander, in George Staunton, *An Authentic Account of an Embassy from the King of Great Britain to the Emperor of China*, 1798.

AUTHOR'S NOTE

In this book I have used 'Peking' for 'Beijing' and 'Calcutta' for 'Kolkata' because these names were current among the British in the eighteenth century.

PROLOGUE

In August 1780, at the imperial palace of Chengde, just north of the Great Wall of China, a meeting took place between two of the most exalted figures on earth. The Qianlong Emperor presided over the world's largest, richest, most populous unified empire. The Third Panchen Lama was the spiritual head of the Tibetan Buddhist faith. To those who witnessed the encounter, they were more than human. Living enlightened beings, they touched the divine. All power – secular and sacred – was concentrated in the audience chamber where they sat enthroned, side by side on a golden dais, engaged in conversation.

The Panchen Lama had undertaken the year-long journey from central Tibet to attend the Qianlong Emperor's seventieth-birthday celebrations. The festivities were to last some five weeks and spread throughout the palace complex and grounds. Also invited were scores of Mongol princes, there to witness the spectacle of imperial piety and munificence. For above all else, the Qing court knew how to put on a good show. The Panchen Lama officiated at the ceremony for the Long Life of the Emperor, dispensed multiple blessings and, in private, initiated the Qianlong Emperor into Tantric mysteries. During his visit, there were banquets in a great Mongolian tent erected in the Garden of Ten Thousand Trees. Seated at tables covered in yellow satin, the Emperor and Lama dined off plates of gold, the other guests off silver. The between-course entertainment consisted of magic shows, wrestling matches, acrobatics and operatic scenes staged by the court eunuchs. Three weeks into the festivities, there was a grand firework display. Pyrotechnic gardens bloomed, fiery dancers twirled and, in a final dazzle, the Chinese characters for 'Place of All Happiness' blazed through the darkness.

In quieter moments, there were opportunities for the Lama and Emperor to discuss affairs of state. On one occasion, when the dancing boys had been dismissed, the Lama begged leave to raise a matter with the Emperor. Following the dictates of friendship, he felt bound to mention the country of Hindostan (northern India), situated to the south of Tibet. The Governor of Hindostan and he were friends, he said, and it was his wish that the Emperor too would enter into friendship with the Governor. Such a small request, the Emperor courteously replied, was easily granted. What was the Governor's name? How large his country and how great his forces? To answer, the Lama summoned a humble member of his entourage, a Hindu trading monk called Purangir who knew the country well. Hindostan was far smaller than China, Purangir said, and its army numbered some three hundred thousand. The Governor was called Mr Hastings. So it was, the story goes, that the name of the British Governor General, the head of the East India Company in India, reached the ears of the Manchu Emperor.

When I first read the account of this conversation, I was intrigued by the possibilities that it raised. In the late eighteenth century the British longed to open relations with the Emperor of China. But the imperial court was utterly inaccessible to European traders, who were confined to seasonal trading at the southern port of Canton. Some twenty years earlier, a British merchant who had attempted the journey to Peking to present a petition to the Emperor had been stopped a hundred miles short of the Forbidden City – and punished with three years' imprisonment. China then, as now, appeared a most alluring market to Western companies. All the more so because European traders were banned from entry and commerce was subject to strict regulation. British merchants fantasised about the day when China's trading rules might be relaxed and a huge potential market and corresponding profits unleashed. The first step would be to open amicable relations with the imperial court. To the eighteenth-century British reader, the commendation of Mr Hastings to the Emperor would have sounded like the answer to a merchant's prayer.

But what possible reason could the Panchen Lama have for raising the subject of the East India Company with the Qianlong Emperor? In China foreigners were generally viewed with suspicion and traders, according to Confucian tradition, occupied a lowly social status. Could the Panchen Lama really be suggesting that the Qianlong Emperor should enter into friendly correspondence with a British commercial body? The Panchen Lama claimed to be motivated by considerations of friendship alone, but what kind of friendship could exist between a great incarnate Lama and a British trading company? And what, in the midst of this unlikely scenario, was the role of Purangir, the trading monk? Why should a Hindu be in the service of the Panchen Lama? It was from Purangir's reports that the British learnt of the encounter at Chengde. He seemed to be in the pay of two powers: both serving the Panchen Lama and reporting back to the British. Perhaps he had fabricated the whole scene.

To answer these questions, I started to trace the connections built up over six years between three very different worlds: British-ruled Bengal, the Qing empire, and Tibet under the Panchen Lama. In the 1760s and early 1770s, Britain became for the first time a truly imperial power. The conclusion of the Seven Years' War (1756–63), the conflict that raged across the globe between Britain, Prussia and Hanover on one side, and France, Austria, Russia, Sweden, Saxony and Spain on the other, catapulted Britain to the possession of a vast overseas domain. By the terms of the Treaty of Paris of 1763, Britain acquired great swathes of territory in Canada and the Floridas, and a host of West Indian islands. Two years later, the Mughal Emperor granted the East India Company the right to collect the revenues of Bengal, transforming the trading company into effective ruler of the richest province in India. This sudden access of power was at once intoxicating and troubling. Britain had conclusively thrashed its European rivals and gained an immense empire; but the nation had to pick up the bill for the military expenditure, and learn how to defend and administer its far-flung and diverse colonial possessions.

In India the problems of new power quickly became apparent. Less than a decade after the Company had become *de facto* ruler in Bengal, the province was laid low by war, famine, excessive taxation and official corruption. Burdened by military and administrative expenses, the Company itself was barely solvent. With no product to sell to the Chinese, it poured the revenues from Bengal into the tea trade at Canton. There was an unquenchable demand in Britain for tea, and China was the only supplier. Tea was by far the most significant of the East India Company's imports, and the annual purchase of tea at Canton was seen as a great drain on Company reserves of silver. By 1772 the most important commercial body in Britain was on the verge of bankruptcy. If the East India Company were to go under, the shock waves would threaten the whole British economy.

Qing imperial power, by contrast, was at its zenith. Under Qianlong, a series of ruthlessly successful military campaigns had doubled the extent of the empire, expanding thousands of miles westward. Much like the British in India, the Qing controlled their empire through a diverse group of subordinate local rulers. A policy of cultural incorporation allowed the Qing to integrate the many different conquered peoples into their empire. In the mid-eighteenth century, the Qing moved on Tibet. Abolishing the institution of secular government, the Qing declared a Chinese protectorate over the country and vested full temporal authority in the Dalai Lama. In order to secure the loyalty of the Tibetan and Mongol peoples, Qianlong and his predecessors lavished patronage on Tibetan Buddhism, building temples, commissioning works of scholarship and honouring high incarnates.

The dynasty was far less accommodating to Europeans (other than the Jesuits, the dominant Catholic mission in China, who were valued at court for their artistic and technological skills). Strictly segregated, banned from entering the interior and from learning Chinese, European traders were kept at a very safe distance from the Chinese population. From the Qing point of view, foreigners were potentially disruptive. Attracted by the superabundance of China, they came to purchase Chinese goods. But the purchase of tea at Canton was not particularly important in economic terms (the British share represented less than 15 per cent of the annual crop of tea). In any case, economic exchange did not feature high in the Qing concept of trading relations. According to the official view, it was a mark of imperial bounty that foreigners were granted the privilege of engaging in one-way trade.

How were the British to find a way through this impasse? No direct approach to the Qing court was possible, so the Company had to pursue a more circuitous route. In the Panchen Lama the British saw a possible advocate with Peking. This book tells the story of the attempt to reach the Qianlong Emperor's ear. It is a narrative of ambition and intrigue that ranges from Scotland to Bengal, and from Tibet to China. The book traces two extraordinary journeys across some of the harshest and highest terrain in the world: the first British mission to Tibet, and the Panchen Lama's state visit to China. The key players were men of wide vision, curiosity and daring: the Panchen Lama and his young Hindu envoy, Purangir; Warren Hastings and his young Glaswegian envoy, George Bogle.

In addition to crossing mountains, these travellers crossed cultures. Crucial to this process was Purangir, the trading monk: master negotiator, intermediary and cultural translator. Through his epic journeys, the rulers of Tibet, Bengal and China could gather information and correspond with each other. When viewed from the vantage point of Canton, the China of this period looks impenetrable and isolated, but, by adopting a Tibetan perspective, the last quarter of the eighteenth century appears a unique moment of cultural collaboration.

As eager to gather information as to negotiate, Bogle recorded his findings in extensive journals and private correspondence. As soon as I started to read Bogle, I was beguiled. By turns playful, penetrating, self-deprecating and shrewd, his observations light up the mission with their engaging detail. Here was the voice that I wanted to sound throughout my book. Although I had worked for many years on eighteenth-century British accounts of India, I had never come across a writer like Bogle. His Tibetan journals and letters had none of the cultural arrogance commonly found in travel writing of the period. In Bogle's accounts I discovered a captivating freshness and delight in the Tibetan way of life. He was the first European to depict Tibet as an innocent mountain stronghold, a place of simple happiness. Indeed

Bogle prepared the ground for the later myth of Shangri-La, the most enduring of all Western fantasies of Tibet.

But the real focus of Bogle's account was the Panchen Lama. I became fascinated by the relationship between the young Scot and the Tibetan Incarnate. Their encounter was a meeting of two worlds, a moment of mutual discovery. It stands out in the history of encounters between Europeans and non-Europeans because it was neither violent nor exploitative. Both the Panchen Lama and Bogle were eager to cultivate each other, both were equally keen to learn. If there were moments of incomprehension and misrepresentation, there were many more of shared understanding and pleasure. In the process of explaining the world to each other, a remarkable friendship was born.

Would the bonds of friendship stretch all the way to Peking? Could conversations over yak-butter tea influence the commercial policies of the richest empire on earth? The Governor General gambled on the possibility. The Panchen Lama might be able to persuade the Qianlong Emperor to look favourably on the British. Perhaps the great Incarnate would save the East India Company from financial collapse. Tibet just might offer a high road to China.

Hoop bridge in Bhutan

I

Bengal & Bhutan

1774

THE PANCHEN LAMA'S LETTER

The mansions of Esplanade Row glared white in the sun. By late March the Calcutta heat had set in and the wide avenues offered little shade. At this time of year the British preferred to travel even the shortest distance by palanquin, hoisted on the shoulders of four Indian bearers. Swaying to work in a reclining position, George Bogle passed the houses of senior merchants, all gleaming porticoes and colonnades. As the bearers turned into the courtyard, Government House swung into view. Outsized adjutant-birds, waiting for carrion, struck ungainly poses along its balustrade. Dismissing the palanquin, Bogle escaped from the light into his office in Government House.

Since his arrival in Calcutta in 1770 as a lowly writer or clerk, Bogle had proved himself adept at climbing the ranks of the East India Company. The Company was still in its infancy as the ruling power in Bengal. In the previous decade and a half, it had fought and intrigued its way to dominance until, in 1765, the Mughal Emperor had granted it the right to collect revenue in the region. The years since had been full of administrative upheaval as the trading body remade itself in the image of government. There were plenty of opportunities for a resourceful and well-connected young man. By 1774, at the age of twenty-seven, Bogle held three posts simultaneously: as secretary to the Select Committee, he was privy to all secret political business of the Presidency; as registrar to the Diwani Adalat or Court of Appeals, he exercised legal authority; and, as private secretary to the Governor, he was on intimate terms with the most important man in Bengal. But, for all his application and talent, Bogle had yet to make either his fortune or his mark.

As he settled at his desk, Bogle turned his attention wearily to his papers. Lately, with his various commitments, he felt as if his life were dominated by work. There had been a rush in Company business, as always before the departure of one of the ships bound for London. The six-month sailing season was the busiest part of the year, when 800-ton East Indiamen, laden with cotton piece goods, raw silks and saltpetre, left Calcutta for Britain every month or so. With all the dispatches to prepare, Company servants had to extend their working hours beyond the usual three in the morning to an extra hour and a half in the evening.

Over the past week, most of Bogle's spare time had been spent on correspondence to his family in Scotland. He had found himself staying up two nights in a row to finish his letters before the packet closed. Writing to his sisters, he filled pages with accounts of Calcutta life, his social circle and its diversions. But he also devoted considerable space to family reminiscence. The purpose of these anecdotes, he told his sister Mary, was to 'convince both my Friends and me that I am the identical same Person I was in the days of yore, which the jumbling of Chaises & the Rolling of Ships with all the Variety of Faces and greater variety of Characters which I have met with and indeed played myself . . . is very likely to give one some doubts of'.[1] After four years in Bengal, Bogle feared that the exercise of colonial power might have transformed him out of all recognition.

The flow of traffic outside had increased. There was the constant slow progress of bullock-drawn hackeries and heavily laden porters. Occasionally a rich European's carriage spun past, each horse attended by a running groom. Esplanade Row led directly down to Chandpaul Ghat on the River Hugli, connecting the government buildings with the port on which the city's wealth was founded. In the harbour lay all manner of vessels: country ships trading between Bengal, Bombay and China, barges transporting indigo and opium, and budgerows ferrying passengers to Indiamen anchored downriver. The river approach to Calcutta was dominated by Fort William, an immense octagonal fortress, the very latest in siege technology. The city, still new and expanding, was one great emporium, drawing all kinds of people to work as traders, artisans, labourers and servants. The British were in a tiny minority: fewer than 200 Company servants in Calcutta, although backed by a formidable military presence. There were Bengalis, Gujaratis and Parsis, Portuguese, Armenians, Greeks, Arabs and African slaves. Each community tended to live in its own district, but the greatest divide was between the spacious affluence of central and south Calcutta – White Town – and the cramped lanes of Black Town to the north, where the occasional Indian-owned mansion stood out against the mass of mud and straw huts. Amid such diversity, the couple making their way that morning down Esplanade Row would have attracted little attention. But then travelling unobtrusively numbered among the particular skills of Purangir, the young Hindu trading monk (*gosain*), and Paima, his Tibetan companion.

Purangir, the *gosain*, had journeyed through much of India and the countries to the north. He had climbed the Himalayan passes into Bhutan and Tibet and spoke Tibetan and Mongolian fluently. A celibate devotee of the god Shiva, Purangir belonged to the Giri, one of the ascetic lineages of the monastic order the Dasnami, reputedly founded in the ninth century by Shankara Acharya. With their network of monasteries, the *gosain*s controlled much of the commerce of North India, specialising in luxury items such as silk and gems. As holy men, they enjoyed special trading privileges and exemption from certain custom dues. Their monasteries (*math*) doubled as trading posts. From their commercial activities, they branched out into banking and moneylending. In some cities, like Benares, *gosain*s were the principal traders and property owners. The *gosain*s' commercial success was backed by considerable military might. They possessed sizeable armies that sold their services to regional rulers and defended trade routes. This made them virtually unassailable. In some cities, *gosain*s controlled municipal life, and in central India one *gosain* commander even established his own small state.[2]

The annual pilgrimage circuit presented *gosain*s with the opportunity to combine piety with profit. Travelling by little-used routes, they dealt in 'articles of great value and small bulk', carrying coral, pearls and diamonds northwards and returning with musk and gold dust.[3] They supplied the Tibetan market with the precious stones used to decorate religious images and fashion jewellery for both sexes. The gems were secreted about their person, tied in cloths around the waist or hidden in their hair. Ranging from the pearl fisheries of southern India to sacred Mount Kailash in western Tibet, the *gosain*s travelled in groups, sometimes protected by armed guards. But for all their riches – and perhaps to avoid unwelcome attention – they lived and dressed simply. Purangir took just one meal a day, slept on the ground and generally wore a red loin cloth and a tiger skin thrown across the shoulder.[4]

Their extensive travels enabled *gosain*s to branch into yet other professions. Local rulers regarded them as valuable informants. They could gather news and political intelligence, provide geographical and commercial information and supply curiosities from distant lands.[5] Endowed with linguistic skills, knowledge of routes and local customs, *gosain*s were also recruited as diplomatic agents, carrying letters between states and principalities. Since they had, in theory, rejected worldly ambition along with caste and class affiliations, they were trusted as negotiators.[6]

Purangir was currently in the service of Lobsang Palden Yeshé, the Third Panchen Lama of Tibet.[7] The young *gosain* had impressed the Lama as much by the quality of his information as by his initiative. He was intelligent, persuasive and only twenty-five years old. When the occasion arose to send an envoy into the hot plains of Bengal – a climate considered fatal to Tibetans – the Lama's choice fell on Purangir. Tall, well-built and energetic, he was likely to survive the rigours of the journey. His devotion to Shiva did not present a barrier to the Panchen Lama, who seems to have regarded *gosain*s as the inheritors of a Buddhist Tantric tradition.[8] At his monastery in Tibet the Panchen Lama supported around 150 of them. In return for a monthly food allowance, the *gosain*s supplied the latest news, rumour and gossip. Leaning out of a palace window, the Panchen Lama would quiz them daily on the situation of neighbouring states.

The Panchen Lama then enjoyed religious and political pre-eminence throughout Tibet and the surrounding region, a position built up during the childhood of the Eighth Dalai Lama. In the mid-eighteenth century the Manchus had tightened their hold over Tibet by establishing a Chinese protectorate and outlawing secular rule. All temporal and spiritual authority was henceforth vested in the Dalai Lama, the head of the Gelugpa monastic order. But the Seventh Dalai Lama had died in 1757 and his reincarnation was a child. A regent was appointed to oversee the government in Lhasa, under the supervision of two Manchu residents or *ambans*. During this period of regency the Panchen Lama, the second most significant Incarnate in the order, had managed to establish himself as the dominant figure in Tibet.

The Panchen Lama was the abbot of Tashilhunpo monastery and a renowned teacher in the Kalachakra tradition with a devoted following. But his interests lay as much in the realm of diplomacy as of scholarship. He was not prepared to be bound by the rulings of the Lhasa regent and the Manchu *ambans*. Indeed his prestige and authority far outweighed theirs. In a gesture of independence, the Panchen Lama managed to conduct his own external relations. He was the first Tibetan Lama to enter into sustained diplomatic contact with Indian powers and often acted as a mediator in regional disputes.

Skirting Government House, Purangir and Paima arrived outside the handsome building that formed the Governor's offices and residence. First they needed to satisfy the gatekeepers that they had business with the Governor. The British corresponded with a number of Indian princes and relied on a network of local informants, trading partners and moneylenders. There were always queues of petitioners, spies and go-betweens waiting to see the Governor. The two men were ushered into the entrance hall by one of the army of servants who staffed the house. The Governor, Warren Hastings, like all high Company officials, lived in a style unimaginable in Britain. Everything was on a grand scale: the neo-Palladian architecture, the vast establishment and lavish hospitality. There were many opportunities to make a fortune in Bengal – both more and less corrupt – and many ways to spend it. Although not among the most rapacious or ostentatious of Company servants, Hastings certainly had an eye for profit and a taste for splendour. The Governor's residence was opulently furnished in the European style, its walls hung with damasked silk. Purangir and Paima waited uncomfortably as their message was transmitted up the line of command, from *dewan* (steward) to *munshi* (interpreter) to secretary to reach the Governor at last.

Warren Hastings received the news of their arrival with a quickening of attention. An impetuous man of considerable intellect, he was always alert to new opportunities. After nearly twenty years' service in India, he was not unfamiliar with the art of the diplomatic manoeuvre – one of the chief means by which the British had acquired power in Bengal. From mercantile beginnings, he had honed his political skills as resident at the court of Murshidabad where he had helped to depose the Nawab of Bengal. Capable of acting with ruthless calculation, Hastings was also a reflective man whose interests ranged across Indian culture and the natural world. He wrote poems and translations, botanised and built up a menagerie. In Britain he proposed the establishment of a chair in Persian at Oxford University, and in India patronised research into Hindu and Muslim law, literature and philosophy. His aim was to learn as much as possible about all aspects of the provinces subjected to British rule. Both political operator and gentleman scholar, Hastings resolved these apparent contradictions in the desire to establish a secure hold on the newly acquired Company territories in India.

The region to the north of Bengal was currently of some interest to him. Just over a week before he had given directions to accept peace proposals offered by the Bhutanese to end hostilities over the small border state of Cooch Behar.[9] This was a conflict that had developed soon after Hastings's arrival as governor in Calcutta. The Bhutanese had long claimed the right to appoint the rulers of Cooch Behar, and in 1771 a succession dispute had erupted.[10] The Bhutanese Desi or ruler, Zhidar, had invaded Cooch Behar and installed his own candidate on the throne. The ousted Raja of Cooch Behar had appealed to the East India Company for help in being reinstated. The military assistance which Hastings offered, 'from a love of justice and desire of assisting the distressed', had certain conditions attached: the Raja must pay for the operation, and the British would thereafter gain control of his state and receive over half its annual revenue.[11] With these points agreed, Hastings dispatched a company of troops in April

1773 to expel the invaders. Now that the Bhutanese had retreated to their mountains with the loss of three border forts, Hastings was quite prepared to come to terms. He had achieved his aim of adding the state of Cooch Behar to Company possessions and extending British territory to the Himalayan foothills.[12] But of the regions beyond those foothills he had a much shakier knowledge. Perhaps these envoys could provide some useful information.

Finally admitted, Purangir and Paima at last encountered the man whom they had travelled so far to see. Hastings was then in his early forties, spare and balding, somewhat reserved in manner and plain of dress. Purangir delivered his patron's greetings, and placed before the Governor the Panchen Lama's presents and letter. Inside the handsome wooden chests lay sheets of gilded leather, stamped in black with the Russian imperial eagle, Tibetan woollen cloth and Chinese silks. Nestling amid the fabric were bags of musk, purses of gold dust and ingots of gold and silver.[13] The Panchen Lama's letter had been translated into Persian, the language of diplomatic communication in India. As the Bengal Secret Department later reported to the Company Directors in London, the Lama's letter was 'a Curiosity of no common sort . . . replete with Sentiments that do credit to both his Ecclesiastical and Political Character'.[14]

The letter opened with formulaic greetings, then proceeded to the issue that had recently been occupying Hastings. Making the inflated claim that the Bhutanese were Tibetan subjects, the Panchen Lama took it upon himself to mediate in the conflict over Cooch Behar. In acting as a peace-maker, the Panchen Lama was living up to the ideal expected of all high lamas. Blaming Zhidar for his 'Criminal Conduct in committing Ravages & other Outrages' along the British borders, the Panchen Lama nevertheless requested that the Governor 'treat him with Compassion and Clemency'. Hostilities should be brought to an end, he wrote, since it was 'evident as the Sun' that the Company army had been victorious. The Lama represented himself as a simple holy man: 'As to my Part I am but a Fakeer & it is the Custom of my Sect with the Rosary in our Hands, to pray for the Welfare of Mankind & for the Peace and Happiness of the Inhabitants of this Country and I do now with my Head uncovered, entreat that you may cease all Hostilities.' His letter, however, was not without the gentlest of threats: 'should you persist in offering further molestation to the Dah's [Desi's] country it will irritate both the Lama & all his Subjects against you.'[15]

Since Hastings had already embarked on peace negotiations, he could afford to agree graciously to the Lama's request. What interested him more was the commercial opening which the envoys' arrival represented. Hastings was himself answerable to the Company Directors in London, who were primarily interested in the balance sheet. The complexities of the diplomatic and political situation in Bengal were completely lost on the Directors, many of whom had never served in India themselves. The slow communication between London and India made it impossible for them to exert any effective control over the activities of Company servants; nevertheless they sent regular sets of instructions to the Governing Councils in India. Poorly informed and largely impotent, London struggled to keep up with developments on the ground as twenty million Bengalis were subjected to Company rule. Attracted to territorial power by the prospect of enhanced revenue through taxation, the Company found itself ill equipped to deal with its new military and administrative responsibilities. Above all, the expenses of war crippled its finances and brought it to the verge of bankruptcy.

Six years previously the Court of Directors had recommended gathering intelligence on trade in Nepal and Tibet. Their suggestion was that Tibet might provide an entrance for British goods into the immense Chinese market, a route that would avoid the restrictions placed on Company trade at Canton. Various means of redressing the imbalance of the trade in Chinese tea were under investigation; just the previous year Hastings had established a Company monopoly in the cultivation of opium, a crop sold to private traders to smuggle into China. A more respectable method might be found in establishing commercial links with Tibet. The gifts sent by the Lama offered evidence of Tibetan wealth and craftsmanship, and the Russian and Chinese goods included suggested that Tibet was at the heart of central Asian trading networks. The idea of extending Bengal's commerce northwards had been proposed twice in recent years to the Court of Directors in London by Hugh Baillie, a returned Company servant.[16] Until now, however, such initiatives had proved abortive. The Gurkha conquest of Nepal of 1769 had effectively blocked all trans-Himalayan trade. But here was an opportunity to open a channel of communication, to respond to the Panchen Lama's embassy with one of Hastings's own. A mission to Tibet, a country which few Europeans and no Briton had ever visited, now seemed a tantalising possibility.

With characteristic decisiveness, Hastings presented the Panchen Lama's letter to the Bengal Council the same day. With the Council's approval, he responded positively to the Lama's proposals and suggested in his turn a general treaty of friendship and commerce between Bengal and Tibet. Purangir and Paima were summoned and consulted at length about the distance and hazards of the journey, the nature of the country, its people, government, customs and commerce. From them Hastings learnt that the Panchen Lama (or Teshu Lama, as the British termed him, from the Tibetan 'Tashi', referring to the Panchen Lama's seat at Tashilhunpo) was in charge of the government and held in great veneration, that he lived in a state of celibacy and believed in the transmigration of the soul. The Lama's dress, they told Hastings, was most singular: '[u]pon his head he wears a cap of a purple colour, over his loins, a kind of petticoat, which reaches to his feet and is tied with a girdle round his waist; over his shoulder is thrown a short jacket of silk, which reaches down to his waist, and leaves both arms bare.' His diet was 'the flesh of goat, sheep, also ghee, curd, milk, vegetables, fruits'.[17] Tibet, Purangir and Paima said, had mines of gold, silver and all kinds of metal. The craftsmen and artisans – carpenters, smiths, masons and weavers – were skilled and there was a buoyant foreign trade. The country supplied horses, woollen cloth and precious metals in exchange for shawls and spices from Kashmir, porcelain, tea and silk from China, and clothes, coral and pearls transported by Nepali traders.[18]

Encouraged by Purangir's assurances, Hastings proceeded to make arrangements for a mission. Once a peace treaty with the Bhutanese had been signed, the route through Cooch Behar was secured, and Hastings could apply to Bhutan for the necessary passports for a mission. There remained only the issue of whom to send. The envoy would have to cross the formidable barrier of the Himalaya with only the sketchiest of maps, to conduct negotiations with little knowledge of local protocol or politics. The mission was an exercise in commercial and cultural reconnaissance, an opportunity to learn about a new and unfrequented region. There were no set directives, precedents or phrasebooks. The man Hastings chose would have to trust to the guidance of Purangir and his own gifts of improvisation. The ideal candidate would combine the skills of an adventurer, diplomat, geographer, anthropologist and spy. These were not qualities for which the penpushers of the Company were famed. Who could possibly possess the necessary energy, understanding, tact and audacity?

Just over a month after Purangir's and Paima's arrival in Calcutta, Hastings informed the Bengal Council of his decision. He had appointed his young Scottish private secretary, George Bogle, as the first British envoy to Tibet. 'I readily accepted of the Commission,' Bogle wrote to his father. 'I was glad of the Opportunity which this Journey through a Country hitherto unfrequented by Europeans would give me of shewing my Zeal for the Governor's Service, at the same time that it gratified a Fondness I always had for travelling, and would afford me some Respite from that close and sedentary Business, in which I had for some years been engaged.'[19]

PRIVATE COMMISSIONS TO MR BOGLE

There were lists and accounts everywhere. The trade samples and gifts for the mission were to be paid for by the treasury. From the Company warehouses Bogle had assembled bolts of broadcloth, intricately printed chintzes, muslins and *kingcob*s – rich gold brocades. A string of pearls had been purchased for presentation to the Panchen Lama. There were matching mirrors, clocks, cutlery and glassware; compasses, thermometers, spy-glasses and all the apparatus required for scientific demonstrations: microscopes, prisms and even an electrifying machine to surprise onlookers with small electric shocks. Everything was of the best quality and designed to delight and intrigue – a parade of Bengali and British artistry and ingenuity. How else to seduce a nation other than with a tempting display of luxury goods, scientific instruments and mechanical toys? The mission must impress. As the newly established power in Bengal, the Company would not countenance the discreet methods of the Panchen Lama's diplomacy. Bogle's embassy would be conducted with a certain style.

Hastings had directed Bogle to choose a companion for his travels. Casting his mind over his Bengal acquaintances, Bogle had proposed an old family friend, Alexander Hamilton, an assistant surgeon and fellow Scot. Hamilton was hardy, energetic and good company, 'a fine agreeable fellow and very active'.[1] Six feet tall, he was as well built and solid as Bogle was spry and diminutive. While Hamilton was in charge of the expedition's medical supplies, Bogle had to organise the retinue of attendants. He had already dispatched his most valued servant, Govindram, to accompany Purangir and Paima as part of the advance party. With a guard of Indian troops or sepoys, they were to make their way to the border province of Cooch Behar. There they would make arrangements for the ongoing journey. Bogle and Hamilton would meet up with them en route. But there were all the other servants for his steward to engage: twenty-two bearers (to carry palanquins in relay), thirteen armed *peon*s, twelve *harkara*s or messengers, six torchbearers (for travel by night), two *chubdar*s (silver stick bearers) to announce the embassy's importance, not to mention overseers, serving men, cook, and tent-pitcher. Sixty-three servants in all, Bogle calculated, and five more for Hamilton.

Bogle had been learning as much as he could about the countries he was to visit. First there was the problem of nomenclature: Tibet was sometimes called Bootan. These names appear to have been used interchangeably. 'Bootan' did not refer to the country that we now know as 'Bhutan', rather it was an alternative name for Tibet.[2] To Europeans, Tibet was famous for its inhospitable terrain and climate, its sheer inaccessibility. The vast Himalayan range formed a frontier between the familiar plains of Bengal and the remote plateaux of Tibet. For Bogle, the mission was 'a new and untrodden Path', full of the allure of adventure.[3]

The Governor had prepared a report for him, a 'Memorial relative to Tibet', based on the scarce materials available on the region. 'Tibet is a cold, high, mountainous country,' it began.[4] The European idea of the geography of the region was derived from Du Halde's monumental *General History of China* (1736), compiled from the accounts of Jesuit missionaries. The text was accompanied by maps prepared by D'Anville based on information gathered by Jesuits at Peking over the period 1708–18. The Kangxi Emperor, who valued the cartographic skills of the missionaries, had invited the Jesuits to conduct a general survey of his empire. The section on Tibet was contributed by two lamas whom the Jesuits had trained as surveyors and then dispatched to the Outer Regions. Fixing their measurements by astronomical observations, the lama surveyors started in the north-eastern corner of

Map of Tibet by Jean Baptiste Bourguignon d'Anville, 1735

Tibet and continued to Lhasa, then on to the Himalayan sources of the Ganges. From the resulting map, ridged all over with the symbols for peaks, Hastings could see how the great rivers of south and east Asia – the Indus, the Sutlej, the Brahmaputra, the Mekong, the Yellow River and the Yangtze – all had their sources in Tibet. Deducing from this that it must be the highest land in the continent, he proposed a comparison with Quito in the Andes. As the prompt for geographical musings, the map might serve well; as a practical tool for orientation, it was sadly lacking. But it was the best map available, so a copy was packed up for Bogle.[5]

Over the previous century and a half, a handful of Jesuit and Capuchin missionaries had undergone the rigours of the journey from

India and China into Tibet. Some went in search of lost Christians, following Marco Polo's reports of Nestorian Christian communities in Cathay (Northern China), others in pursuit of converts. Of the various attempts to establish missions in Tibet, none had really prospered; it was not long before they either met with hostility or ran out of funds. The harvest of souls had been far from plentiful: the Capuchin mission to Lhasa of 1716–33 managed to make only thirty-five converts.[6]

From the few accounts published, the Governor learnt a confused history of Tartar and Chinese invasions, but remained unclear whether China still possessed power in the region. What, Hastings wanted to know, was the precise nature of the relationship between China and Tibet? The details available on the Dalai Lama were equally sketchy: identified when young by various signs, he was believed to be an incarnation of the Buddha, and so greatly revered that 'his excrements' were 'sold as charms at a great price among all the Tartar tribes of this religion'.[7] Of the customs of the people, Hastings considered their marital arrangements the most intriguing. Was it true, he wondered, that to guard against hereditary succession, as soon as a new chief of a Tibetan tribe was chosen, he was separated from his wife and family? And what about their traditions of cohabitation? 'It is said that in Thibet it is very common for a Lady to have several Husbands,' wrote Hastings. 'I should wish much to know if this practice obtains in all the ranks of society and whether those husbands who all have intercourse with one woman have not likewise other women that are their wives, with whom likewise they hold an intercourse in common.'[8] In addition to his official diplomatic duties, it would be Bogle's job to attempt to answer the Governor's scholarly questions and satisfy his wide-ranging curiosity.

The commission gave Bogle the chance to secure the Governor's favour and build a reputation. A successful outcome, he imagined, would be a sure way to preferment. Indeed this appointment was the culmination of an assiduous campaign to cultivate Hastings. Early on in his career, Bogle had realised that the guiding principle of advancement in the East India Company was 'interest', that is, having friends in the right places. Letters of recommendation from influential contacts were the first step towards lucrative posts in Bengal. The connections of his brother Robert had initially secured Bogle a writership with the Company, and had then gained him introductions to men like Colonel Lauchlin Macleane, Commissary General of the Army, in whose house he was now living, and John Stewart, Secretary to the Bengal Council and Judge Advocate General. In fact it was Stewart who had first brought him to the Governor's attention.

Hastings soon discerned Bogle's many qualities. His sharp intellect was complemented by an affable manner. Quick to learn, he was also trustworthy and good-humoured. And he was Scottish. In a period when many Englishmen deeply resented the Scots, Hastings showered them with patronage. Throughout the British Empire, Scots played an extremely significant role, eagerly pursuing opportunities for advancement in the colonies that were denied them at home; but in Bengal nearly half the new writers appointed under Hastings were Scottish. In Calcutta Bogle kept happening on acquaintances from home. Hastings's inner circle or 'family' of confidants and advisers was largely made up of young Scottish men, a group he would term his 'Scotch guardians'.[9]

As the youngest son of a prominent Glasgow trading family, Bogle was well equipped with the commercial and political connections that Hastings particularly valued. His father, also George, was a member of the set of merchants who had made huge fortunes importing American tobacco and sugar, cultivated in part by slave labour. The profits of Bogle's American ventures were invested in other concerns: companies that exported goods back to America and the Caribbean, and another that manufactured dyestuffs for the local textile industry. During his youth, Glasgow was in its heyday, one of the most prosperous and elegant cities in Britain. The city's wealth was based on its geographical position; the Clyde ports offered a much quicker and cheaper voyage to Virginia and Maryland than the English ports, undercutting the sailing time by two to three weeks. Glasgow became, in effect, a great warehouse, storing and processing American tobacco and sugar for sale all over Britain and the Continent. The leading merchants, later dubbed the 'Tobacco Lords', were a tight network of interrelated families who lived in great splendour. They owned city mansions and grand country estates, parading their wealth in lavish furnishings or ploughing it into schemes of agricultural improvement. They were showy dressers, sporting curled wigs, cocked hats, scarlet cloaks and gold-headed walking canes. Among their ranks was John Glassford of Dougaston, at the time the wealthiest merchant in Europe.

The merchant elite had close links with the landowning classes. Bogle's mother, Anne Sinclair, came from an aristocratic background. Her father was Sir John Sinclair, a direct descendant of James I and II of Scotland; and her mother, Martha Lockhart, was the daughter of Lord Castlehill. Her dowry included the estate of Whiteinch near Glasgow. Of the nine children borne by Anne Sinclair, two died in infancy, to leave four daughters – Martha, Mary, Elizabeth and Anne – and three sons – Robert, John and George, the youngest. George had barely entered his teens when his mother died, and from then on the household was managed by the sisters. The eldest, Martha, married an apothecary, Thomas Brown, and moved to London, but the trio of unmarried sisters – Mary, Elizabeth and Anne – remained at home with their ageing father.

In his advancing years, increasingly incapacitated by gout, George Bogle senior contented himself with overseeing his estate and farms. The family seat was at Daldowie, five miles east of Glasgow. His own father had purchased the land in 1724, and he himself had built the house to accommodate his growing family. Following the practice of many of the Tobacco Lords, the Bogles acquired a coat of arms and added the name of their estate to their surname. The Bogles of Daldowie lived in fine style. Their mansion, situated on a rise above the River Clyde, overlooked nearly 150 acres of gardens and woodlands, with a stockyard, dovecote and riverside walks. The handsome villa was a rural retreat from the business interests and civic duties that dominated the working week. From the late 1730s, George Bogle senior rose to positions of considerable influence in various Glasgow institutions. He repeatedly served terms of office as lord rector of Glasgow University, becoming actively involved in the administration of the university and its library. He was also Dean of Guild, the head of the body that represented the mercantile interests in the city.[10] Both widely read and devout, he was a staunch supporter of the Moderate group in the Church of Scotland. His letters demonstrate

that distinctive mix of commercial canniness and Presbyterian seriousness which one contemporary observer considered characteristic of
Glasgow: 'The chief objects that occupied the minds of the citizens
were commerce and religion; the chief means of acquiring importance
among them were wealth and piety.'[11]

An educated man himself, the elder George Bogle devoted some
care to the education of his sons. While it was not necessary for a
merchant to pursue a full course of study, some university education
was considered desirable. In his youth, George senior had combined
study at the University of Leiden with travels in northern Europe, and
his sons attended Glasgow and Edinburgh Universities for varying
periods of time. The youngest, George, studied logic at Edinburgh
University for six months, from the age of fourteen. After eighteen
months learning the family business in London, he transferred to a
private academy in Enfield to pursue a more practical course of
mercantile education. Then, following a six-month visit to the south
of France as the companion of a sick friend (who died in pursuit of a
cure at Toulouse), George returned to join his brother Robert in
London.

For three years George worked at his brother's firm of Bogle &
Scott, trading in American tobacco and exporting goods to plantation
stores in Virginia. During this period, Robert was his closest friend
and mentor, instructing him in the ways of the market and the world.
In their frequent conversations, Robert loved to hold forth on the
issues of the day. In later life, he was a great pontificator and writer of
letters to the government. His second cousin recalled that in middle
age Robert was 'a man of much information and of much speculation,
the results of which he did not fail to impart often to the ruling powers
. . . In society, with a great deal of kindness and *bonhomie*, he was yet
tedious, from the long lectures on mercantile and political subjects –
for he did not converse when he entered upon these, but rather
declaimed – which he was in the habit of delivering in the most
humdrum and monotonous manner.'[12] Perhaps Robert only grew
boring with age. George, at least, referred affectionately to the hours of
companionable 'Crack' with his brother.[13] But by 1769 George was
beginning to think of a break with Robert and the family business.
Weighing up the possibility of a career with the East India Company

in either China or India, he eventually opted for Bengal. Robert could supply him with the necessary letters of introduction and, as he explained optimistically to his father, 'the Climate & Society are very good, the Chance or rather Prospect of gaining an Independence is great and I go out with every Advantage I could wish.'[14]

In the event, it proved the right time to leave the family business. Three years later the affluent comfort of the Bogles, along with that of many other merchants and financiers, was abruptly shattered. It all started on 10 June 1772 when Alexander Fordyce, a Scottish partner in a London banking house, suddenly absconded to France. Fordyce was a speculator on a grand scale; he made and then lost a substantial fortune on the stock market. In an attempt to make good his losses, he dealt heavily in fictitious bills. At the time, bills were the main means of conducting commercial transactions; they were notes demanding payment at a later date, drawn by one firm on another. They could be endorsed and passed on and go into circulation. The entire system relied on trust; a bill would be accepted only if drawn on and endorsed by creditable firms and individuals. Once confidence was undermined, panic spread and the whole chain of credit collapsed.[15] This is what happened in June 1772. Fordyce's debts – rumoured to be between £350,000 and £550,000 – forced the closure not only of the bank for which he worked, but of ten more in the following fortnight. Observing the wreckage, Samuel Johnson blamed the crisis on the general climate of fear: 'such a general distrust and timidity has been diffused through the whole commercial system that credit has been almost extinguished and commerce suspended.'[16] There were runs on the banks and money grew scarce. Fordyce's firm had particular links with Scotland and on 25 June the Ayr Bank, which supplied two-thirds of the banknotes in Scotland, also stopped payment. Fordyce himself became the focus of much anti-Scottish sentiment. Crowds turned out to jeer when he appeared before the bankruptcy commissioners, and the press gleefully reported his humiliation. Forced to surrender all that he owned, Fordyce had to turn out his pockets for his last remaining possessions: a snuff box and a handful of coins.[17]

Not since the South Sea Bubble of 1720 had the financial world been so rocked. The shock waves were felt in Amsterdam and across

northern Europe. Scores of businesses across Scotland and England
were declared bankrupt, among them the firm of Bogle & Scott. The
suddenness and violence of the crash reduced those involved to
despair. Robert detailed the personal repercussions in a long and
dramatic letter to his brother in Bengal:

It was impossible to withstand the Torrent every Connection we had
was gone so that we were under a necessity of submitting to the general
Calamity . . . The Distress I was under it is impossible for any Pen to
describe . . . I took a Fever I lost my Reason and on the second Day
after we stopt my Servant, who was attending me, having gone [out] of
the Rooms about 5 o'Clock in the morning, thinking me asleep – I got
up & jumped out of our two Pair of Stairs Windows into the Court –
such a Fall must have inevitably put a Period to a Life which at that
Time I had no Inclination to preserve, had not the Goodness of
Providence interposed & saved me in a most miraculous Manner – My
servant returned just as I was going over, catched hold of my shirt,
which altho it gave way & did not prevent my Fall, yet it broke the
Force, & altho I was a good deal hurt I was not thought dangerously so
– My Back had got a great Strain which confined me to Bed for two
Months.[18]

In the months of recuperation that followed, Robert had much time to
contemplate the workings of Divine Providence. He 'called on the
Assistance of Religion & Devotion & gained the most perfect
Tranquility & Resignation'. With this new-found conviction, he
reflected on the wretchedness and evil produced by riches (although
'a Competency', he conceded, was a necessity).[19]

When he had recovered sufficiently, Robert's first move was to take
out a Commission of Bankruptcy and then to look into the family's
state of affairs. The business finances were so entwined with his
father's that the whole family was drawn into difficulties. Daldowie,
the much loved family home, was under threat, although Robert was
determined that it should not be sold during his father's lifetime. The
family estates were put into trust. The only member who might be
able to secure the family's future was the youngest, thousands of miles
away in Bengal. Robert wrote to inform George of the state of affairs:

> When you last heard from me, the Prospect was very different – our Business was flourishing, our Credit was strongly founded . . . In that situation the Prospect was that your Fortune could be of Use to none but yourself as our Business afforded the appearance of supporting my Father [and] all his Family in a life of Affluence. But in an Hour all is blasted, & we must again (like Sisiphus) ascend this Hill from which we have been hurled down Headlong.[20]

With a single letter, all sense of security was shattered. As he read his brother's cramped script, George learnt of the collapse of his family's fortunes, his brother's suicide attempt and his new financial responsibilities. He told Robert, 'my Heart was agitated successively by a Thousand different Passions – Grief Regret Gratitude – took possession of it by Turns.'[21] The decision not to sell the estate was quite right, George affirmed. He too would take his part in the Sisyphean labour of debt repayment: 'My Father's Situation is distressing beyond Measure – You desire me to inform you of my own Situation and how far you think I can assist you in your Schemes of relieving Daldowie – There is one thing you may depend upon, that my whole attention will be turned towards this Point, and I have hopes of succeeding so as to assist you.'[22] From then on, remitting money home became a prime object. There was now a new urgency to George's career.

But it was easier to spend than to save in Calcutta. A culture of excess characterised British life in the city. A modest dinner for two might consist of 'soup, a roast fowl, curry and rice, a mutton pie, a fore quarter of lamb, a rice pudding, tarts, very good cheese, fresh churned butter, fine bread, excellent Madeira'; drinking was on a heroic scale, dress flamboyant, and the stakes for gambling high.[23] Junior servants were criticised by the Court of Directors for their large establishments and deep debts.

The hectic pace of consumption in Calcutta was a kind of show staged for Indian observers, a parade of economic dominance (which, ironically enough, owed much to Indian moneylenders). It was also a retreat from the boredom of colonial existence, a frenzied forgetting of the distance of home and the proximity of death. For the mortality rates of East India Company servants were alarmingly high; around half of those who travelled to Bengal were buried there. Within a year of their arrival, both of the writers who shared Bogle's first lodgings were dead. The British fell victim to multiple diseases: cholera, malaria and dysentery. The most dangerous months were April to October; to mark the end of the killing season, the British inhabitants met to celebrate their survival at a gathering called the 'Reunion'.

Troubling reports of the extravagance of Company servants had reached Robert and his father. Did George understand the importance of moderation? Although he tried to live economically, Bogle replied, Calcutta was expensive and it was important to avoid a reputation for stinginess.[24] One outlay that Bogle did not mention to his family was the cost of keeping a concubine. It was common practice among the British to purchase the attentions of a *bibi*, or Indian mistress. A somewhat later handbook, *The East India Vade-Mecum*, suggested that £60 a year would cover the expense, 'which must certainly be considered no great price for a bosom friend, when compared with the sums laid out upon *some* British damsels'.[25] The women were unlikely to have had much choice in the matter; a few were from noble families hoping to secure political advantage from such an alliance, but most were servants or slaves who entered British households as children or were transferred between Englishmen.[26] At the outset of the relationship, a contract would sometimes be drawn up specifying a monthly rate for the *bibi* with allowances for clothes, jewellery, betel and tobacco and the employment of a couple of female servants. Some *bibi*s maintained their own establishment, others were part of the household. Sadly, we have no clear record of Bogle's domestic arrangements.

Bogle's letters home reveal a constant concern with his own future and the progress of his career. Rank in the Company was calculated on length of service. Initially Bogle had been content to play the long game, waiting for a position to fall vacant (which, with the high mortality rates, happened quite frequently), but after he learnt of Robert's bankruptcy he began to seek openings more actively. The first opportunity was presented by the arrival of one of Robert's connections, Colonel Lauchlin Macleane, with a brief to procure supplies for the Company forces. 'I fondly flatter myself,' Robert wrote, 'that your Connection with Mr Mcleane may prove very useful to you, he is a Man of great Enterprize, very aspiring & sanguine, he has acquired a great deal of Money & lost it over & over again so that at present I believe he is immensely behind hand . . . his present aim is to make money to discharge the whole without any Distinction – If your Appointment under him takes place, I would advise your Duty by assiduity & application to the Business but I by all means dissuade you from entering into large Engagements for him by lending Money, by being Security or otherwise.'[27]

Well might Robert warn Bogle of the dangers of trusting Macleane in money matters. A doyen of the political underworld, of great charm and few scruples, Macleane had been the under secretary and personal financial agent to the Earl of Shelburne who, as secretary of state for the Southern Department, handled European and American affairs. Macleane was the architect of a grand scheme speculating in East India shares which had come crashing down. Macleane lost £90,000 and Shelburne had covered a third of his debts. An appointment in India was procured in 1772 as the quickest route to meet his creditors' demands. Macleane came out to join John Stewart, his friend and former protégé. Stewart had himself been ruined by Macleane's share scheme, but now held the post of secretary to the Bengal Council – a man with the ear of the Governor. The two men shared a far from respectable past. When they first met, Stewart had just served a prison sentence for debt. While in gaol, he had made the acquaintance of his mistress, Anne Bailey, a seaman's wife and haberdasher-turned-prostitute. The relationship between the three of them became increasingly entangled as Macleane involved Stewart in his dubious share dealings, securing him a post in Shelburne's ministry, and Bailey gave birth to a son who bore both their names (for whom Stewart accepted paternity and Macleane paid maintenance).[28]

On arrival in India, the charismatic Macleane swiftly charmed the Governor. 'No man living ever won so much of my confidence in so short an acquaintance,' Hastings later wrote.[29] In characteristic fashion, Macleane busied himself in making friends and promoting his own interests. Bogle, for one, was seduced. Macleane, he assured his sister Elizabeth, did not deserve his bad reputation: 'his Character my Dear Bess is very different from that you have received – He is warm hearted and friendly to the greatest Degree, attached to his Party and of a bold and liberal way of thinking beyond almost anything I ever met with.'[30] Macleane had decided that his post as commissary general of the Army in Bengal lacked sufficient scope; he set about redefining his role, requesting additional powers and an expanded staff. He needed a deputy; would Bogle be interested? Coming just a few months after the news of Robert's bankruptcy, the offer was indeed tempting. Bogle was flattered by Macleane's attentions and excited by the prospect of making money. But he was also worried about abandoning Hastings's inner circle; he would forgo the chance of promotion in the Governor's service and risk losing all the interest that he had so painstakingly cultivated. It was Hastings's response to the scheme that put an end to the matter. Bogle wrote to his brother: 'I find that the Governor is not willing that I should leave him, and his pleasure must be to me a Law.'[31]

Bogle's sense of loyalty and desire to conciliate his patron paid off. Only a few months later, the Governor rewarded him with the post of envoy. In his official letter of appointment, Hastings laid out the terms of his commission to Tibet (or 'Bootan', as he termed it): 'The Design of your Mission is to open a mutual and equal Communication of Trade between the Inhabitants of Bootan and Bengal, and you will be guided by your own Judgement in using such means of Negotiation as may be most likely to Effect this Purpose.'[32] Bogle was instructed to deliver a letter and presents from Hastings to the Panchen Lama. He was to carry trade samples and find out about Tibetan products. In the course of his travels, he was to enquire into routes between Bengal and Tibet and the neighbouring countries, and to gather information on the manners of the people, their government and methods of revenue collection. Periodically, he was to report his findings and the progress of his negotiations to the Governor. But, beyond these general instructions, everything was left to Bogle's own discretion. The length of his stay, the extent of his expenses, whether or not to establish a British residency in Tibet – all these were matters for Bogle to decide. That Hastings allowed Bogle such latitude is both a measure of the trust which he placed in his envoy and a gauge of the depth of British ignorance of Tibet.

Hastings was hungry for knowledge of the region. The British in Bengal were then engaged in gathering all kinds of information – political, legal, economic, geographical, historical, cultural and social. Hastings encouraged Company servants to acquire Indian languages and pursue scholarly research into the peoples and the lands that they occupied. The contemporary Indian observer and historian Ghulam Hussain Khan Tabataba'i described the Company officials' habits of interrogation and annotation:

the English commenced acquiring a knowledge of the usages and customs of the country: for it was a standing rule with them, that whatever remarkable they heard from any man versed in business, or even from any other individual, was immediately set in writing in a kind of book composed of a few blank leaves, which most of them carry about, and which they put together afterwards, and bind like a book for their future use.[33]

In his 'Private Commissions to Mr. Bogle', Hastings even specified how Bogle should take notes. Bogle was directed to:

keep a Diary, inserting whatever passes before your observation which shall be characteristic of the People, their Manners, Customs, Buildings, Cookery, the Country, the Climate, or the Road, carrying with you a Pencil and Pocket-Book for the purpose of minuting short Notes of every Fact or Remark as it occurs, and putting them in Order at your Leisure while they are fresh in your Memory.[34]

Hastings hoped that Bogle's journal would be of as much interest to the gentleman reader as to the Company servant. To this end, the Governor plied him with questions: what countries lay between Lhasa and Siberia, between China and Kashmir? Could Bogle find out about the course and navigation of the Brahmaputra river? And in what particular art or science did the Tibetans excel? Hastings also wanted live specimens of the flora and fauna of the region. Could Bogle arrange to send down one or more pairs of shawl goats (which bore the finest wool) and the same number of cowtail cattle (yaks) for his menagerie? Some fresh ripe walnuts for seed, and medicinal plants like rhubarb and ginseng would also be most welcome. The desires of the amateur botanist and collector mingled with those of the souvenir-hunter. Bogle was to keep his eyes open for any 'Curiosities, whether natural productions, Manufactures, Paintings, or what else may be acceptable to Persons of Taste in England'.[35]

Bogle added Hastings's instructions to the piles of documentation that he had already accumulated. He packed supplies of pens, pencils, blotting paper and ink, reams of paper and stacks of notebooks. He instructed his servants to lay out twenty shirts and twenty pairs of stockings, ten pairs of breeches and ten waistcoats, twelve short drawers and two long drawers. He would make do with two pairs of shoes, one blue suit, his Portuguese cloak and a pair of boots. There were travelling chairs and a table. For meal times, he had two sets of cutlery and crockery, tablecloths, salt-cellars and candlesticks. He would take his hookah to smoke after dinner and borrow a chess set from Macleane for diversion in the evenings. There were certain comforts that a gentleman could not do without.

At their final meeting, the Governor promised Bogle that, whatever the outcome of the mission, he could depend on his continued favour and protection. These were reassuring words; the coming months presented only uncertainty and challenge. As Hastings wrote to the Court of Directors, 'the great Length of the Journey & the natural difficulties which Mr. Bogle has to encounter from the severity of the Climate & the rudeness of the Country will make it a long while before we shall hear from him.'[36] A shrewd judge of character, Hastings prized Bogle's ready under-standing, energy and determination. If anyone could rise to the physical, intellectual and personal demands of the mission, then George Bogle could. Eager as Hastings was to send Bogle on his way, he could not see him leave without regret. He had grown fond of his young private secretary. Before they parted, Hastings placed a small object in Bogle's hands; it was a diamond ring, a token of his friendship and pledge of his remembrance.

3

LAZY, LOLLING PALANKINS

The party set off in the summer of 1774. It was the worst time of year to embark on a journey. By 20 May, 'the thermometer was often above the Degree of Blood Heat', the sun almost vertical in the sky, and the monsoon only a few weeks away.[1] As the boatmen pulled on their oars, hoping for a favourable wind to fill the sail, Calcutta receded into the distance. Bogle and Hamilton's budgerows negotiated their way through the busy river traffic. Heavy, square-sailed barges with a crew of up to twenty oarsmen, budgerows had a long cabin, pierced with windows. Passengers were accommodated in comfort, but the boatmen sweated it out in the sun. The Hugli was notoriously difficult to navigate, with its shifting sandbanks and changeable course. There was always the danger of running aground or getting caught in the eddies. All budgerows were equipped with a long bamboo pole to avoid colliding with sandbanks. At times, the rowers would have to disembark to haul the vessel upstream with a track rope, and the sail was continually being hoisted and lowered as the character of the river and the winds changed. In a few weeks the monsoon-swollen river would break its banks and the fields would be flooded, ready for paddy cultivation. But now the Hugli was at its most shallow, a thick carpet of silt making it navigable for only part of its course.

Travel in Bengal was everywhere easiest by water. The province was

cut through with rivers; as James Rennell, the Surveyor General of
Bengal pronounced, 'every part of the country, has, even in the dry
season, some navigable stream within 25 miles at farthest; and more
commonly, within a third part of that distance'.[2] People and goods
moved along the waterways rather than the roads (which were often so
poorly maintained that pack animals had to be used instead of carts).
The rivers were not only a means of communication but also the source
of Bengal's wealth. The annual inundation, extending over the plains,
brought irrigation and fertility to the soil. These low-lying areas were
perfect for growing rice, and the higher ground suited cotton, sugar
cane, pulses, oil seeds and mulberry to raise silkworms.[3]

It was the cotton cloth and fine silks which attracted foreign
merchants to Bengal. Fifteen miles upstream from Calcutta, the
budgerows passed Serampore, a small Danish settlement built snugly
around the Governor's residence. Then came the French port of
Chandernagore, stretching for a mile along the left bank, with its
ruined fort a reminder of the British assault on the town of 1757.
Although the French were no longer a military threat in India, and the
two nations had been at peace for a decade, the British still viewed them
with suspicion and prevented them from fortifying their settlement.
The Dutch captain, Jan Splinter Stavorinus, reported that when the
French dug a ditch around the town, ostensibly for drainage purposes,
the British believed it to be defensive, and hastily dispatched some
troops to fill it up again.[4] The last of the European settlements along the
Hugli was the Dutch Chinsura. From the river, the most visible
buildings were Fort Gustavus, with its battery of twenty-one guns,
and a small white church with a steeple (but no resident clergyman). On
special occasions – and for a handsome fee – the chaplain from Calcutta
could be persuaded to officiate.[5] Although in comparison to Calcutta,
these European enclaves were sleepy outposts, Bogle envied their
standard of living: 'You will think it very odd,' he wrote to his brother,

> that in this Country where we are Sovereigns, and the French, Dutch,
> and Danes hold only little settlements, in a manner by our permission
> – that they should be better served, and Cheaper by half, than we are,
> that their Towns should be much neater, provisions Cheaper, and at
> this present moment when there is no such thing as geting a Baker,

that is good for anything in Calcutta – Chandernagore, and Chinsura, the French & Dutch Settlements, are supplied with the finest Bread, and in the greatest Plenty.[6]

The river journey came to an end some seventy miles from Calcutta at the village of Mirzapur; there was no going beyond this point in the dry season. The party disembarked to continue by road to the city of Murshidabad. By now the heat was beginning to take its toll. 'Having set out from Calcutta at the hottest Season of the year,' Bogle told Robert, 'we had suffered greatly from the Heat; being obliged to travell chiefly during the Night; and take Shelter in the Day time under a Tamarind or Banyan Tree.'[7] Bogle and Hamilton were installed in 'lazy, lolling Palankins', comfortably upholstered with mattresses and cushions.[8] They were accompanied by a train of torchbearers, servants, porters and bullocks laden with provisions and luggage. In an attempt to beat the rains, they proceeded as quickly as possible. The teams of palanquin bearers were replaced in relays. This was hard physical labour, jogging along with the palanquin at a steady four miles an hour, while Hamilton and Bogle rested. To ease the effort, the bearers grunted rhythmically or improvised songs which made fun of the palanquin's occupant. A later traveller attempted an English translation of one such song:

> Oh, what a heavy bag!
> No; it's an elephant:
> He is an awful weight.
> Let's throw his palkee down –
> Let's set him in the mud –
> Let's leave him to his fate.
> No, for he'll be angry then;
> Ay, and he will beat us then
> With a thick stick.
> Then let's make haste and get along,
> Jump along quick.[9]

The bearers, like the coolies and the boatmen, were drawn from the lowest ranks of society. Most of the Calcutta bearers came from Orissa.

Higher up the social scale were the craftsmen and cultivators who lived
in the villages through which the party passed. In the flaring torch-
light, the servants could just make out the village houses, built of
bamboo, thatch and mud. Many of these communities were devoted to
the export cloth industry. The women spun raw cotton at home and the
men worked as weavers, dyers or embroiderers. As the group neared
Murshidabad, the villagers were more likely to be employed in silk
production, cultivating mulberry and silkworms or winding silk.[10] But
both the silk and cloth industries, indeed the whole region, were still
recovering from the devastation of four years previously.

Murshidabad had been one of the areas worst afflicted by a famine that
had descended upon Bengal and Bihar in 1770. The previous year, the
rains had failed. The region's reserves of food and money were already
diminished by the ruinous rate of Company taxation. Although the
British belatedly started to distribute food in Calcutta, the activities of
some Company servants and their Indian associates exacerbated the
famine. Individuals were accused of enforcing monopolies on rice and
other staples, of stockpiling, profiteering, and buying up grain at fixed
prices.[11] In the countryside, villagers sold off first their cattle, then their
tools and finally, in desperation, their children. To support themselves,
they ate their seed grain and the forbidden flesh of animals, then leaves
and grass. By August 1770, when Bogle had first arrived in Calcutta, the
city was full of the emaciated and the dying:

> There were men employed to pick up the Dead Bodies in the Streets,
> and throw them into the River, and from the 1st to the 9th of last
> Month no less than twelve Hundred Carcasses were found – in the
> streets of Calcutta – that had died not of Pestillence, or Sickness, but
> absolutely of Hunger . . . I have seen them myself, take off the Turban
> from their Heads, Bind it about their Eyes, when their Hands were so
> feeble as hardly to be able to Perform that last Office, and resign
> themselves to Death without a single Complaint or Groan.[12]

The situation was yet worse in Murshidabad, where people were
dying at the rate of 500 a day. 'The scene of misery that intervened,

and still continues, shocks humanity too much to bear description,'
wrote the British Resident, at the height of the famine. 'Certain it is,
that in several parts, the living have fed on the dead.'[13] Those who did
not actually starve to death were killed instead by diseases which
overcame the weak and emaciated. In the area around Murshidabad,
smallpox took hold. 'Whole villages and whole towns were swept
away by these two scourges,' lamented Ghulam Hussain, 'and they
suddenly disappeared from the face of the earth.'[14] In all, perhaps a
third of the Bengal population lost their lives and many of the
survivors turned vagrant.

As a response to the part played by the British in the famine,
Company servants were banned from trading in grain in 1773
(although individuals found ways of evading this restriction, as they
did many of the regulations). Company servants were allowed to
engage in internal commerce or trade within Asia on their own
account. Indeed the right to trade in a private capacity was a clause in
the writer's covenant. Although salaries in the Company were relatively modest, there were endless ways to make a fortune: private
trade, bribes and perquisites (the casual profits attached to a post, later
abbreviated to 'perks'). Moral standards were none too high, as Bogle
confided to Robert:

> One of the greatest Checks upon a Man that wants to increase his
> Fortune by unfair Means, in Europe, is the Odium that he is liable to
> draw upon himself, and be despised, and shunned by all his Acquain-
> tances, but that is not the case here, and several People keep the best
> Company, and are exceedingly well regarded, who are great Rogues,
> not only from Suspicion, but even by their own Confession, and have
> been obliged to refund Money that they had unjustly taken away,
> either by extortion, or in cheating People that employed them.[15]

An appointment in the East Indies was generally regarded in
Britain as a speedy path to riches. In the early years of British rule
in Bengal, it was possible for the less than scrupulous to acquire vast
fortunes. So general was British greed that Ghulam Hussain termed it
a 'custom . . . which every one of these emigrants holds to be of divine
obligation; I mean, that of scraping together as much money in this

country as they can, and carrying it in immense sums to the kingdom of England'.[16] After the collapse of the family business, Bogle's cousin and former associate William Scott wrote with news of an acquaintance, newly returned from India, 'with an immensity, some say Seventy thousand & he only went out about ten years ago'. India presented the most tempting of prospects. 'One woud realy imagine,' Scott continued, 'that the Golden Age reigns with universal Sway, on the other Side of the Cape & that in these Regions it rains Gold and Silver Rupees.'[17] Such fantasies were fed by newspaper reports of the spectacular fortunes amassed by 'Nabobs', former Company servants who purchased great landed estates and parliamentary seats on their return to Britain. Although Nabobs were attacked in the press and on the stage as greedy, corrupt and extravagant, combining all the worst excesses of the *nouveaux riches* with the supposed venality and decadence of the East, they also attracted envy and emulation.

Posts in the East India Company were much coveted by the sons of merchants and professionals, and in demand too among the gentry and aristocracy. Newly appointed writers of sixteen imagined that they could retire at forty to live as gentlemen.[18] Families used their influence with the Directors to gain writerships, and Directors used patronage to buy support in their annual elections. Political pressure was also exerted; Bogle's friend, Alexander Elliot, gained his post after the Prime Minister had intervened on behalf of his father, Sir Gilbert Elliot, Treasurer of the Navy and a confidant of the King. One of the ways that Scottish interests were tied to those of England after the Union of 1707 was through the distribution of East India Company posts. The promise of a Company writership could be used as a bribe or reward for political loyalty.[19]

The most important contact a writer could make on arrival in India was a *banian*, an agent who managed his household, engaged servants, arranged for financial loans and provided an entrée into local trade. The *banian* acted as an indispensable intermediary who, in the words of a contemporary writer, combined the roles of 'interpreter, head book-keeper, head secretary, head broker, the supplier of cash and cash keeper and in general also secret keeper'.[20] This close collaboration with the British afforded the *banians* themselves many opportunities to make fortunes through trade and land revenue management. Until the practice was abolished in 1773, Company servants could grant their *banian*s tax exemption on trade in certain goods and, in return, earn a commission of up to 25 per cent. During his first year in Calcutta, Bogle wrote to Robert about engaging a new *banian*: 'I have taken one who serves a particular friend of mine. He is very clever & a man of Property – and as the Gentleman he is now with may probably go home in a year or two – I may then perhaps have him all to myself, which would be of great service to me, if I should then find it proper to carry on any extensive concerns.'[21] But Bogle was cautious about entering into private trade. Although the potential profits were high – twice if not three times those of a British merchant's – so too were the risks. More importantly, following the famine, commercial prospects were far from good.

It was the economic, rather than the humanitarian, consequences of the famine which most exercised the Company Directors in London. With such a high level of mortality, local industries went into a sharp decline and land revenues fell. The financial difficulties of the Company were aggravated by the means by which its servants remitted their fortunes back home. Bills of exchange were issued in India to be drawn on the Company in London; but by 1771 it became clear that the Company had insufficient funds to honour the bills. The credit crisis of 1772 (which wrecked the Bogle family business) exacerbated the situation. The Company was placed under increased pressure to meet its obligations and, at the same time, found it difficult to receive payments on its sale of Indian goods. Following reports of profiteering during the famine, there were calls for a parliamentary inquiry into the activities of Company servants. East India stock plummeted and the Company, finding itself close to bankruptcy, turned to the government for support. The loan of nearly £1.5 million came with the requirement that the Company be subject to extensive reorganisation. The resulting Regulating Act, passed in 1773, radically restructured the Company both in London and in India.[22]

The repercussions of these reforms had yet to reach Calcutta at the time of Bogle's departure, but the financial imperatives were clear. Hastings was under great pressure from the Directors to find new sources of income. When the opportunity arose to open up trade relations with the countries to the north, he gladly embraced it. Tibet, with its mines of gold and silver, was a tempting prospect. Bogle was well aware that Hastings had considerable hopes for a profitable new commercial venture riding on his mission.

The city of Murshidabad, which the party now entered, was the seat of the Nawabs of Bengal, embellished with palaces, forts, public buildings, mosques and pleasure gardens; but the place held little attraction for Bogle. He had travelled there two years previously as an assistant to Hastings on an official tour. On his first visit, he had been less than impressed: 'it is an old decayed Town,' he wrote to his sister Martha, 'it never was a handsome one and now from the great Change of things is going fast to ruin.'[23] Murshidabad had for seventy years been the capital of the province, a flourishing administrative and commercial centre, at the heart of the Bengal silk trade, with a rich court culture. But in recent years the city's wealth, prestige and population had drained away. This was partly the result of the famine – which nearly halved the number of inhabitants – and partly the effect of British policy: Murshidabad's decline was Calcutta's gain.

Following the British victory at Plassey in 1757, Bengal had become a virtual client state. At Plassey, the Company had defeated Siraj ud-Daula, the Nawab of Bengal, by conspiring with a rival court faction; over the next seven years, the Company installed and deposed a succession of rulers. Early in his career, as resident of Murshidabad, Hastings had been involved in one such coup. But the Nawab that he backed, Mir Kasim, was himself deposed and subsequently defeated at the battle of Buxar (1764). The following year, the Mughal Emperor acknowledged British dominance by transferring the *diwani* of Bengal, Bihar and Orissa from the Nawabs to the East India Company. The *diwani* conferred the right to collect the revenues of the provinces in return for an annual tribute to be sent to the Emperor. The Nawabs were left with the post of *nazim*, responsible for justice and nominally in charge of law and order and defence, but without an effective army. The reduction of Murshidabad was now complete. The Nawab's court, much diminished in size and grandeur, had to survive on an allowance granted by the Company.

On his first visit, Bogle had been received by Mubarak al-Daula, the Nawab (or Nabob, as the British termed him). Nothing about the meeting lived up to received notions of oriental splendour. 'I expected to have seen a fine Magnificent Palace, where so many wealthy Princes had resided but was sadly disapointed,' Bogle reported to his sister; 'it is low built without any Regularity & Stone & Wood are mixed together which has a bad Effect.'[24] The whole party, including the Governor, took off their shoes as a mark of respect. They were then conducted through dark rooms, where the furniture was shrouded in white sheets, to reach the Nawab's presence. After ceremonial greetings and the formal exchange of compliments, the British guests were presented with perfume and betel. 'The Nabob,' wrote Bogle, 'gave us these with his own hands – God bless me says you how you were honoured – I did not consider myself honoured at all – The Nabob himself is about 15 Years, of a very puny Constitution, extremely debauched even at that age – he possesses no power but over his own Servants, and all his Grandness is in State and Pageantry.'[25]

Bogle reaches for commonplaces to characterise Mubarak al-Daula. In European eyes, Muslim rulers were deeply degenerate and self-indulgent; their harem upbringing was supposed to encourage vice from an early age. For Bogle, physical and moral debility rendered the Nawab unfit to govern – a convenient enough conclusion, since curtailing the Nawab's influence was precisely Hastings's aim. On instruction from London, the Governor had taken direct responsibility for the collection of the Bengal revenues. The Nawab's deputy, who managed tax collection for the British, was arrested on trumped-up charges. Hastings relocated the government treasury and revenue offices from Murshidabad to Calcutta, and cut the Nawab's allowance and the number of his dependants in half. As Mubarak al-Daula was still a minor, he could offer little effective opposition. Munni Begum, Mubarak al-Daula's stepmother, was appointed the Nawab's household manager and guardian. The choice of a female guardian, living in purdah, was calculated to limit the influence of the position.[26] The Company was resolved 'to suffer no person to share in the management of the Nawab's domestic affairs, who from birth, rank, personal consideration, or from actual trust, may have it in his power to assist his master with the means or even to inspire him with hopes of future independence'.[27] Following Hastings's tour, the Nawab was reduced to a mere figurehead, and the capital of Bengal transferred from Murshidabad to Calcutta.

Departing from Murshidabad, Bogle's party was ferried across the Ganges to head north to the town of Dinajpur, site of a Company 'factory' or fortified trading post. They travelled through flat grasslands, rustling with reeds and bamboo. In recent years, the district had become notorious for dacoits or armed robbers. These gangs attracted the dispossessed and unemployed, those who had suffered from the upheaval caused by the famine and the introduction of Company rule. The British, however, understood dacoity as sheer lawlessness and treated dacoits with extreme severity: the penalty for convicted dacoits was execution, and for their families enslavement.[28] But the gangs were unlikely to attempt anything against a large government deputation like Bogle's. At the major towns along the way, Bogle and Hamilton were received by factory chiefs, collectors and assistant collectors, who arranged for supplies, cash and porters, as required. At Rangpur, further to the east, Bogle decided to give his entourage a more official air by ordering uniforms for his servants.

Around Rangpur, the building material was mainly bamboo – woven into mats for house walls, fences, even bridges. The land was completely level, stretching monotonously into the distance. But at daybreak, before the sun raised a mist, the Himalayan foothills were briefly visible, darkly etched on the horizon. The whole region was regarded as dangerous by the Company. Groups of armed monks or *sannyasis* regularly passed through the area on pilgrimage. As holy men, they were eligible for support from the villages en route. The activities of the *sannyasis* filled the Company with horror. British notions of law and order were affronted by the sight of armed bands of naked holy men roving through the countryside. The situation became worse in the years of scarcity following the famine when the *sannyasis* mounted direct attacks on Company warehouses and treasuries, and then melted away into the countryside. Such guerrilla tactics proved particularly difficult to counter. So great a problem did these activities appear to the British that in 1773 Hastings outlawed all *sannyasi* movement in Company territory. He even inserted a clause in the recently concluded treaty with Bhutan prohibiting the Bhutanese from offering shelter to them.

Some form of protection against *sannyasi* attack may have been offered to Bogle's party by Purangir, the Panchen Lama's agent. As a *gosain*, he may have had contact with the *sannyasis*, since they were members of the same monastic order, the Dasnami.[29] Whether or not Purangir exerted his influence in this respect is unclear, but Bogle would have been reassured to meet up with him and Paima at the town of Cooch Behar, some three hundred miles north of Calcutta. Charles Purling, the Collector at Rangpur, had organised the necessary passports for the onward journey into Bhutan, and supplied Bogle with large reserves of ready cash to cover the mission's expenses. After consultation, Bogle fixed on a method of conveying mail to and from Calcutta as he proceeded on his travels. Letters addressed to Bogle should be sent to Lieutenant Williams in Cooch Behar who would forward them through the network of Bhutanese runners. In the mountains there would be no use for palanquins, so Bogle sent the teams of bearers back to Calcutta. It was then that the rains set in.

For several days it poured. The whole area was one low-lying plain, and when it rained the rivers and creeks would flood to form wide marshlands, and even the wells would overflow. Frustrated at their arrested progress, Bogle was impatient to be off. At the first break in the weather, on 8 June, the party started out again along sodden roads. The newly green countryside was alive with birdsong and the croaking of frogs. After four miles they found themselves in uninhabited wetlands close to the border. It was a ten-mile thicket 'formed of Reeds, Brushwood, and long Grass closely interwoven', noted Bogle, 'Frogs, watery Insects, and dank air: one can hardly breathe'.[30] The exhalations of swamps were thought to breed fever; many of the troops sent by Hastings the previous year to Cooch Behar had in fact succumbed to malaria. Emerging at last on to firmer ground among forest trees, the party reached the river that formed the frontier with Bhutan, and were ferried across in canoes lashed together. 'I was now arrived at the foot of that Chain of Hills which stretch along the northern Frontier of Bengal, and seperate it from Thibet,' Bogle wrote to his father. 'As none of the Company's Servants, and I might almost say no European, had ever visited the Country which I was about to enter; I was equally in the Dark as to the Road, the Climate, or the People, and the imperfect Account of some religious Mendicants who had travelled through it, however unsatisfactory, was the only Information I could collect.'[31] From here on, Bogle was in sketchily charted territory.

PERPETUAL ASCENDING AND DESCENDING

The first night across the Bhutanese border was spent on a bamboo floor above a stable. Chichakotta was a small settlement with little to offer. Its fort had been destroyed the previous year in an unequal encounter between the British, equipped with the latest firelocks and cannon, and the Bhutanese, armed with antiquated matchlocks, swords and bows. After a determined defence, the Bhutanese had been driven back to the hills, fighting all the way. But a year later, with the peace treaty signed, the Bhutanese received the British delegation in quite different manner. By government order, Bogle's party was to be given food and lodging, and supplied with porters and horses at villages along the way to the capital fortress of Tashichodzong. As Bogle later reported, 'The best House in every Village was allotted me for my Quarters, and the best provisions which the Country afforded, were prepared for my supper.'[1]

At Chichakotta, the house assigned to Bogle was raised on stilts and constructed entirely of bamboo. 'It had much the look of a bird cage, and the space below being turned into a hog sty contributed little to its pleasantness,' Bogle archly observed.[2] But the evening was convivial: 'The head man of the Village, and some of the neighbours got Tipsy with a Bottle of Rum – a female peddlar sojourned with him; good features & shape, fine teeth, and Rubens Wife's Eyes; whole

Dress one Blanket wrapped round her, and fastened over the Shoulders with Silver Skewers. Drank rum too – Men, Women, and Children sleep higldy pigldy together.'[3] The impromptu party, fuelled by alcohol and alluring glances, was Bogle's introduction to Bhutanese hospitality. It augured well for the mission: Bogle enjoyed informal society and had resolved to be affable on his travels. He later explained that he was concerned to give a good impression of the national character. The previous year's war had demonstrated the martial prowess of the British, Bogle wrote, now he wanted to gain the people's confidence and goodwill.[4]

As the first envoy to the region, Bogle saw himself as the representative of his nation (which, for these purposes, he identified as English). His aim was to be the ideal gentleman: plain-dealing, unaffected and sociable. He was aware that he was on display; his conduct, his manners – even his body – were subject to scrutiny. He joked that he was hardly built for the job: 'This Idea, of being shown as a Specimen of my Countrymen has often given me a world of Uneasiness, and I dont know that I ever wished so heartily to have been a tall personable Man, as upon this Occasion. It was some Comfort to have Mr. Hamilton with me, and I left it entirely to him to give a good Impression.'[5] But perhaps Bogle's frame, slight by European standards, served him well: his appearance would have been as unthreatening as his manner.

Bogle's sense of being watched may have been prompted by his own habits of observation. Following the Governor's instructions, Bogle was always alert, always recording. On his arrival in Bhutan, he took a large sheet of paper, and folded it into twelve – 'duodecimo size' – to fit into his pocket.[6] He jotted down notes as he went. When one page was full, he would unfold the paper to go on to the next. Sometimes the pencil would break, and he would have to wait for the next resting place to sharpen it, then try to recall the details of what had passed. As he progressed, the notes extended to cover the whole sheet; but with the frequent opening and refolding, the constant rubbing in his pocket against crumbs of bread and seeds of trees, the script grew faded and in parts illegible. It was only later that he would attempt to reconstruct the narrative in his ink-written journal.

Bogle had an eager audience for his journal in Hastings. The

Governor was motivated both by scholarly curiosity and by the
thought that, as Bogle's patron, he might in due course gain credit
from its publication. There was an enormous appetite for travel
literature among the British reading public. Books of travels were
usually printed as large folio editions or multi-volume collections that
would handsomely furnish a gentleman's shelves; but they also
increasingly appeared in cheap editions and were often extracted in
the periodical press. Those who could not afford to purchase the more
expensive volumes might borrow them from the new circulating and
subscription libraries. Accounts of voyages were required reading for
anyone who wanted to keep up with the intellectual debates of the
day. By the 1770s it was not uncommon for travellers to contribute
papers to that great forum of scientific discussion, the Royal Society in
London. Furnishing the material for a new science of mankind, travel
writers aspired to a degree of scientific precision in their descriptions
of distant lands and peoples. Scottish philosophical historians plundered travel accounts for empirical evidence to support their theories
on society and the differences between peoples. Writers such as Adam
Smith, Adam Ferguson and William Robertson all turned to travel
literature to substantiate their claims about human development and
the progress of civilisation.

The travel book most in demand that year was John Hawkesworth's
recently published *Voyages* which related Captain Cook's exploration
of the Pacific. The narrative of navigational, cartographic and astronomical triumph was interspersed with descriptions of idyllic islands
and freely available women. With its winning combination of
adventure, science and sex, the book went through numerous editions
and helped to establish Cook as a national hero.[7] To Hastings's mind,
the fashion ignited by South Seas exploration would serve Bogle well.
The Governor later outlined his hopes in a letter to his protégé:

> I feel myself more interested in the success of your Commission than in
> Reason perhaps I ought to be, but there are thousands of men in
> England whose good will is worth seeking, and who will listen to the
> story of such enterprizes in search of knowledge with ten times more
> avidity than they would read Accounts that brought Krores [tens of
> millions] to the National Credit, or descriptions of Victories that

slaughtered thousands of the National Enemies. Go on and prosper –
Your Journal has travelled as much as you, and is confessed to contain
more Matter than Hawkesworth's three Volumes.[8]

Redefining the expedition as a search for knowledge (rather than
trade), Hastings cast Bogle in the role of philosophical traveller. The
comparison with Cook flattered Bogle with a vision of national
celebrity. Even as he jotted down his observations, he would have
felt the burden of Hastings's expectations and have been aware of a
potential audience for his journal far wider than that of the Calcutta
government.

Leaving Chichakotta early the next morning, the party headed for the
Himalayan foothills. Although nearly twenty miles away, the ridge
seemed to loom overhead. As they approached the mountains, Bogle
carefully noted the change in the country and climate. Evergreens started
to grow among the bamboos and plantains, and clear streams now
coursed beside the road. It was early afternoon when they reached the
hills, and the real walking began. The path, gentle at first, soon grew
steep and narrow, as it zigzagged its way up the thickly wooded hillside.
The ascent continued for four miles, with great chunks of marble
breaking up the path. At times there would only be a thin ledge
skirting a precipice. 'What a Road for Troops,' exclaimed Bogle in his
diary.[9] The distant thunder of waterfalls reached them from the gorge
below. When thirsty, they would stop at wayside fountains to drink from
bamboo pipes. The Bhutanese travelled equipped with sieves to strain
floating vegetation, insects and stray leeches from the spring water.

Evening saw their arrival at the pass of Buxaduar, one of the
eighteen *duar*s or 'gates' that provided a point of entry into the hills.
Naturally fortified by deep ravines, the village of Buxaduar could
accommodate a garrison if necessary. It was well placed to defend the
route into Bhutan; the single-file path on the hillside opposite was
easily within bowshot range. The official then in charge received
Bogle with customary greetings, the first of many such ceremonies,
involving the presentation of a white scarf (*khatag*) and gifts of butter,
rice, milk and tea. In all his dealings with government representatives,

View near Buxaduar, Bhutan

Bogle followed the advice of Purangir, who acted as interpreter and negotiator. With his linguistic expertise and local knowledge, the *gosain* was an invaluable navigator through the complexities of Bhutanese politics and protocol.

The party stayed a day at Buxaduar, while arrangements were made to engage porters. Most of the porters hired at Cooch Behar had abandoned the expedition along the way. In Bhutan, a system of taxation operated whereby the people were required to contribute compulsory labour to the government (*ulu*). Among other forms of manual labour, the *ulu* included the transport of loads and the supply of food, lodging and horses for touring officials. Bogle and Hamilton benefited from this system throughout their trip. At Buxaduar they were supplied with a couple of Tangun ponies, valued in the mountains for their sturdiness and sure-footed determination. The horses were led by the bridle, while the rider held on to the peak of the wooden saddle; but the going was frequently so steep that Bogle and Hamilton had to walk more often than ride. As the party progressed, relays of porters transported their baggage from one village to the next. As Bogle noted, all members of the community were involved:

Neither sex, nor youth, nor age exempt them from it. The burden is fastened under the arms upon their backs, with a short stick to support it while they rest themselves. Naturally strong, and accustomed to this kind of labour, it is astonishing what loads they will carry. A girl of eighteen travelled one day 15 or 16 miles, with a burden of 70 or 75 pounds weight. We could hardly do it without any weight at all.[10]

From Buxaduar, the route lay across the mountain of Pichakonum. The temperature dropped steadily as the group climbed the rough marble steps cut into the mountainside. 'Midday was cold and chilly,' Bogle wrote in his diary. 'There were very high precipices, but they were not frightful because they were covered with trees. I indulged in the pleasure of tumbling down stones.'[11] Bogle's boyish enjoyment would have contrasted with his companions' reverence for the landscape. His high-spirited pastime might well have offended those who carried his baggage. To the Bhutanese, certain mountains, rivers, rocks and trees were either the homes of gods or manifestations of gods themselves. A later traveller was told to speak only in whispers at the top of Pichakonum, for fear of provoking the elements to a torrential downpour.[12] The cult of deified nature long predated the introduction of Buddhism to Bhutan by the Tibetan king, Songsten Gampo, in the seventh century. Indeed Tantric Buddhism managed to absorb many elements of the older shamanic religion including the worship of sacred mountains. This capacity for assimilation, combined with the spread of various Tibetan Buddhist schools, contributed to the wholesale conversion of the country by the twelfth century. Scrambling up to the peak of Pichakonum, Bogle was arrested by the sight of hosts of Buddhist prayer flags, long white strips inscribed with the mantra *om mani padme hum* ('Hail, the jewel in the lotus'), flapping devotion to the winds.

As he reached the summit, Bogle's exuberance gave way to a moment of reflection. He turned back to survey the view. In the distance, the plains stretched out to the horizon, a great expanse of woods and fields, threaded with rivers and dotted with villages. He could make out the plumes of smoke drifting up from household fires. This was the flat familiar landscape of rural Bengal. But in the foreground the land changed abruptly, folding into deep valleys and steep hills. All around Bogle, the slopes were densely forested, a luxuriant, rustling green. And behind, to the north, great mountains reared into the clouds.

The panorama prompted Bogle to a series of musings on the nature of the land and its people that announced his ambition as philosophical traveller. The sudden transition from one landscape to another might account for differences in the characteristics of the Bengalis and Bhutanese, he speculated in his journal. Following ideas first proposed by the French philosopher Montesquieu and taken up by many writers on India, Bogle argued that a people's temperament and aptitudes derived from the climate and physical features of their country. So, he suggested, the heat and fertility of Bengal produced a 'weak and thin-skinned' people, incapable of exertion, while the chilly mountain terrain gave the Bhutanese a 'constitution more robust and hardy'.[13] The contrast drawn in Bogle's journal between the two locations and peoples turned Pichakonum into something more than a mountain pass; it became a moment of transition, the point of entry into a new world.[14]

Bogle may have based his theories on his sense of the shortcomings of his Bengali attendants. In his private correspondence he complained that his Indian servants could not adapt to the new environment. Writing to John Stewart, he grumbled, 'Your Bengalees may do very well for plain Ground but they are not made for the Ups and Downs of this World. One half fell sick and the other wanted to be so.'[15] Bogle combined the colonial stereotype of the lazy Indian servant with the belief that the Bengali constitution was unsuited to Bhutan. The party's progress through the mountains slowed as Bogle coaxed, berated and tended to his staff: 'I was obliged to shorten the Stages: to give some their Dismission; and what with Blankets, Boots, Drugs, Good words, and Bad words, I have brought the remainder thus far.'[16] The event that most affected Bogle and Hamilton was the defection of their cook, 'an uxorious Man . . . his Wife enticed him away.'[17] The cook's place was supplied by the *hooka-burdar*, promoted from tending hookahs to preparing dinner. But the new cook's skills were sadly limited. Lamenting his own lack of culinary knowledge, Bogle requested a friend in Calcutta to forward a copy of Mrs Glasse's *The Art of Cookery Made Plain and Easy* (which included recipes for curry and pilau).[18]

Cascade of Minzapeezo

The environment and altitude might not have suited his servants, but Bogle was in his element. The climate he found most agreeable; by day he wore a suit of broadcloth, and at night slept wrapped in his Portuguese cloak. The party covered some fifteen or twenty miles of ground each day. Often the ascent was so steep that the road consisted of steps carved out of the rock face, but each resting place revealed a new and spectacular view. Sometimes it poured with rain, swelling the Pachu-Chinchu river into grand waterfalls that crashed over boulders, sending up great clouds of spray. Bogle related the rigours of the route to his sister Bess:

Our Path went winding round the Sides of the Mountain – seldom broad enough for two Horses to pass easily – perpetual Ascending and Descending, and you may judge of the Nature of the Country, when I tell you we travelled above 100 Miles without seeing a valley. Nothing but the Deepest and most abrupt Glens, with the River Patchoo Tchentchoo galloping through them, and a few Villages scattered here and there on the Brow of the Hills with a little spot of Ground cleared about them. At one of these we took up our Quarters every night, and always met with the best Reception the place would afford. Who could be so unreasonable as desire more?[19]

In his enthusiasm for the outdoor life, Bogle anticipated by at least a decade the fashion of walking for pleasure. In this period in Britain, only the lower classes went about on foot. Although he did not share a Romantic sense of the sublimity of nature, Bogle – like Wordsworth and Coleridge – relished the physical exertion of walking and admired simple country ways. In a letter to John Stewart, he even fantasised about life as a wandering holy man, unencumbered by possessions or duties, on the road to China: 'if Ever I forfeit the Company's Service,' he mused, 'I will turn Facquier.'[20]

As he progressed, Bogle began to adapt to local custom. He grew Bhutanese-style whiskers. 'I wish you could have the Honour of seeing my Mustachoes, which I have been fostering and Nursing with so much Care ever since I came among these Hills,' he wrote to his sister Annie; 'I assure you when well slicked down with Pomatum, they cut a very respectable Figure.'[21] He also began to learn Dzongkha, the official language of Bhutan. This task was far from easy, as he confided to his friend David Anderson: 'the very Pronunciation is a Matter of Difficulty, which is not diminished by the Berwickshire R which I inherit from my mother.'[22] In attempting to master the language, Bogle was not only hoping to ease communication, but also to free himself from dependence on interpreters and further his diplomatic ends. Here Bogle was following the approach adopted by his patron; for Hastings, language learning and cultural enquiry were essential tools of government.

Another of Hastings's enthusiasms was botany. In accordance with the Governor's instructions, Bogle noted the changing plant species as they climbed the mountains. As far as the settlement of Chuka, which they reached in mid-June, most of the plants were similar to those in Bengal: plantain, bamboo and jack trees. Then, in the course of a single day's journey, the vegetation changed to varieties familiar from Europe: strawberries and primroses grew by the wayside, roses and brambles in the woods, and forests of fir covered the mountains.

With Hastings's encouragement, Bogle also engaged in a small-scale agricultural experiment. At each stage along the route, he planted a number of potatoes to see if they would flourish in the Bhutanese climate. Although Hastings did not know it, a similar experiment had been conducted the previous year, halfway around the globe. On Cook's second voyage to the Pacific, Peter Fannin, master of the ship *The Adventure*, had transplanted potatoes from the Cape of Good Hope to the soil of Motuara Island, New Zealand.[23] As far as Cook and Hastings were concerned, these acts of transplantation were entirely benign, aimed at introducing a valuable new food source for the population. In this surreptitious way, both Cook and Hastings exported European ideas of agricultural improvement.

Hastings also asked Bogle to collect seeds and cuttings of Himalayan plants for dispatch to Calcutta. In a whimsical conclusion to one of his letters, Hastings represented these horticultural activities as souvenir-hunting, a fair (if illicit) exchange: 'Don't return without something to shew where you have been, though it be but a contraband Walnutt, a pilfered Slip of Sweet Briar, or the Seeds of a Bootea Turnip taken in *Payment* for the Potatoes you have given them *gratis*.'[24]

However, the potato experiment proved less than successful, as a subsequent traveller, following the same route some nine years later, reported. He was shown 'a small specimen of potatoes, not bigger than boys' marbles'. Bogle, he wrote, 'had formed great hopes from the introduction of this vegetable, and they [the Bhutanese] had been taught to call it by his name; but either from ignorance or idleness, they have failed in the cultivation of this valuable root, and the stock is now almost exhausted.'[25]

Along with botanical specimens, Bogle gathered technical information. He was particularly interested in the design of bridges. In a land carved into deep ravines by rivers coursing from their Himalayan sources down to the plains, the construction of bridges was of utmost

importance. Bogle observed that bridges were built either entirely of
wood or entirely of iron. The wooden bridges were the most common,
extending up to seventy feet in length. At Chuka he recorded the
design and dimensions of a great iron-chain bridge suspended across
the racing river. Five parallel chains covered with bamboo matting
formed the walkway and two higher chains, connected to the floor
with matting, provided side protection. As soon as a person or horse
stepped on to it, the whole structure would sway (only one horse was
admitted at a time). The bridge that Bogle described was probably
constructed by the fifteenth-century Tibetan saint Thangtong Gyalpo,
a pioneer of iron-chain bridge building.[26] Even more precarious were
the hoop bridges along the way. Two lengths of rope were attached to
stakes on either side of the river. A couple of rings that slid along the
ropes provided the means of conveyance. Passengers wishing to cross
would sit with legs through the hoops and haul themselves along the
ropes with their hands.

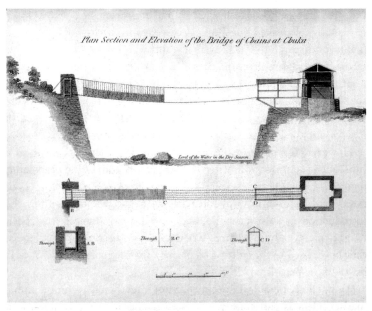

Iron-chain bridge at Chuka

Beyond Chuka, the country began to open out. After days skirting the edge of precipitous gorges, the route now led through wide, cultivated valleys. The road grew more level, allowing Bogle and Hamilton to ride rather than walk. They passed through many more hamlets now, encountering peasants working in the terraced fields. The whole company, and particularly Bogle and Hamilton, would have presented a curious spectacle to the villagers, unused to the sight of Europeans. At night, the party would put up at one of these hamlets, and Bogle and Hamilton would be accommodated in the house of the most substantial villager. The houses were stone built, with thick walls gradually tapering to wooden roofs, weighed down with shingle. The ground floor served as a stable for livestock; the upper floors, extended by wooden balconies, comprised the family's living quarters and altar room, and the attic was used to store fodder and grain. Climbing up a ladder, cut from a single tree-trunk, Bogle and Hamilton would find themselves in a high-ceilinged room, furnished with low tables and a mud stove, where meals were prepared, visitors received and mats rolled out at bedtime. The houses had no chimney, so in the evenings, with the stove burning, a smoky fug would build up. Even so, the nights were getting colder, and Bogle augmented his Portuguese cloak with a double blanket to sleep.

It was in one such house, towards the end of June, that a messenger arrived for Bogle, bearing letters from his family. 'I was just sat down with Mr. Hamilton to our Currie and Rice,' wrote Bogle to Annie, 'when in came a Boot [a Bhutanese] with the Pacquets of Europe Letters. They spoiled my supper, and he got all the Currie and Rice to himself.'[27] Bogle avidly read all the domestic news, some of it a year out of date. In addition to the normal delay of colonial correspondence (the voyage between Britain and India could take up to six months), the mail was further slowed down by the complex system of forwarding. Letters for Bogle passed through the hands of John Stewart in Calcutta, Lieutenant Williams in Cooch Behar and the Governor at Buxaduar.

His relatives were all in good health, Bogle learnt, but Annie informed him of the death of a family servant, and his father of the sudden demise of a family friend. As usual, his father's letters were full of advice on career advancement and pious exhortations to a virtuous life. 'The very High favour you are in my Dear George with the Governor and others in High rank and Offices if managed with prudence and Discretion will be of an unspeakable advantage to you in preferring you to Higher promotions,' his father wrote. But George must always remember to conduct himself with the utmost propriety: 'your fair Character if supported with truth, uprightness and Integrity will make you beloved by all who have any Connection with you.'[28] His brother Robert, he read, had embarked on a new venture to pay off the family's debts. The best prospects for quick profit seemed to lie in the slave-worked plantations of the West Indies. Robert's attention had turned to the island of Grenada, acquired by the British from the French a decade previously. With his business associates he had purchased a third share in a sugar plantation, and had left London – the scene of his financial and personal collapse – to manage the estate.

The arrival of letters from home filled Bogle with a sense of nostalgia, made all the more intense by Robert's departure for the West Indies. He read and reread the packet of letters, 'I will not tell you how often,' he wrote to Bess.[29] Letters were now all that held the family together, an emblem both of connection and of separation.[30] 'We are scattered over the Face of the Earth,' he exclaimed to his sister, 'and are united only by Hope and a tender Remembrance.' For Bess, he painted a sentimental picture of their various activities: 'while you are passing chearful Evenings at Daldowie; while Robin with his Negroes (and happy are they that are under him) is planting his Sugar Canes and while I am climbing these rugged Mountains, there is a secret Virtue like a Magnet which attracts us together and chears or solaces us in every situation.'[31] In Bogle's letter, plantation labour is recast as gardening, slaves are happy Negroes, and his Himalayan mission a pleasure excursion. But the political realities of his own situation would soon become all too apparent.

As the party neared the Bhutanese capital, a messenger arrived from the opposite direction bearing three letters, the first addressed to Bogle, the second to Purangir, the third to Hastings. They were from the Panchen Lama, who was responding to news of Bogle's arrival in Cooch Behar. The report of Bogle's presence was the first that the

Lama had heard of the mission, for the British had not considered it necessary to inform him of their intention to send a deputation or ask permission to enter Tibet. With some anticipation, Bogle struggled to make out the Persian script. Once past the formulaic expressions of goodwill, Bogle realised that this was not the hoped-for letter of courteous welcome. Having travelled nearly 450 miles by boat, palanquin, pony and foot, he was being told that his journey was in vain. Tibet, the Lama wrote, was subject to the Emperor of China who ruled that no Mughal, Hindustani, Afghan or European should enter the country. The customs of China were very different from those of Hindostan. If the Emperor had been easily accessible, the Lama would have represented Bogle's case to him, but his residence was extremely remote, at a distance of a year's journey. It was with regret, then, that the Lama requested that Bogle should return to Calcutta, without dispute.

5

THE FIRST EUROPEAN IN THESE PARTS

The Manchu Emperor's ruling was not the only barrier to the mission. The Panchen Lama's second letter, to Purangir, presented a new obstacle. The mission could not proceed, wrote the Lama, because the region was suffering from an outbreak of smallpox. The Lama himself had fled the infection, abandoning his seat at Tashilhunpo for the monastery of Dechenrubje, situated further to the north. It was difficult for Bogle to determine what lay behind the Lama's prohibition. Was the epidemic the genuine explanation? Or Manchu imperial displeasure? Perhaps neither. The Panchen Lama clearly objected to his visit, but the reasons offered sounded like pretexts to Bogle. The Bhutanese ruler might be able to shed some light on the Lama's position or perhaps act as advocate on the Company's behalf. Given the recent treaty concluded between Bhutan and the British, he might be persuaded to help. What Bogle needed was a diplomatic ploy to gain some time. He decided to refuse to take delivery of the Lama's third letter, addressed to Hastings, or to accept the gifts of silk and gold dust that accompanied it. To receive the Governor's letter and presents would, in effect, be to capitulate. When the messenger returned that evening, Bogle rejected the letter addressed to Hastings and insisted that he continue to Tashichodzong. He had to follow his original instructions.

With the Panchen Lama's frustrated messenger in tow, Bogle and Hamilton resumed their journey. It was on 28 June that they first caught sight of the Desi's summer residence, the great fortress monastery of Tashichodzong. Built beside the rushing Chinchu river, the *dzong* dominated the long valley. Smaller monasteries perched on the surrounding mountains and villages congregated on the gentler slopes, but the *dzong* stood in near isolation. The heavy whitewashed walls, over thirty feet high, were topped with a red band to mark the building's sacred character. Rows of small windows ran round the outer walls at the same level. The *dzong* was elegantly proportioned, twice as long as it was broad. Rising above the wooden roofs was an inner tower, crowned with a gilt pavilion. The whole complex, comprising offices, apartments, temples, state rooms and storerooms, housed some three thousand men, 'and not', as Bogle noted with regret, 'one woman'.[1]

Tashichodzong was founded in 1641 by Ngawang Namgyel, the first *shabdrung* or monk ruler of Bhutan. The Shabdrung ('at whose feet one submits') was a man of great determination and activity. Ousted from his position as head of the Drukpa monastic order in Tibet, he had arrived in Bhutan as a refugee, and worked his way to supreme power through a combination of religious leadership, political acumen and military success. Over his thirty-five-year rule, Ngawang Namgyel repelled a series of Tibetan invasions and overcame internal opposition to unify the country. The *dzongs*, erected in each of Bhutan's valleys, consolidated his control. Situated on rocky outcrops, with massive stone walls pierced by loopholes, the *dzongs* offered a formidable system of defence of the trade route to India. Bogle and Hamilton were impressed by their impregnable appearance as they journeyed through the country. Within their confines, the sacred and secular arms of the state operated side by side. In the ecclesiastical wing, Drukpa monks provided religious instruction and performed rituals for the welfare of the people; in the civil wing, laymen collected taxes and conducted the business of government. Built by a conscripted local workforce, the *dzongs* asserted a distinctive Bhutanese cultural identity. The Shabdrung laid down a basic design for *dzongs* – as he did for all the country's main building types – in an attempt to differentiate Bhutan's architecture from that of its larger neighbour and rival, Tibet.

So central was Ngawang Namgyel to the stability of Bhutan that his death was regarded as a state secret. On the tenth day of the third month of the Iron-Rabbit Year (1651), the authorities announced that the Shabdrung had entered strict seclusion, and he remained 'in retreat' for more than fifty years. Edicts continued to be issued in his name until 1705 (when he would have been 111 years old). Lamas were renowned for their longevity, but even the most pious might have started to have their doubts by this stage. It was then revealed that the Shabdrung had been reborn in triple incarnation; 'when the Shabdrung went out of his meditation, three rays of light emanated from his body, his speech and his mind', a contemporary recorded.[2] Multiple incarnations of leading religious figures were common in Tibetan Buddhism; indeed the Buddha himself is often represented in multiple form. In the case of the Shabdrung, the reincarnation of his mind took precedence over the others and became known as the Shabdrung and occupied the role of the ceremonial head of state. As with all systems of government based on reincarnation, there were long intervals of regency. Only when the Shabdrung reached the age of eighteen could he take up his position. Until that time, other high-level incarnations were called upon to act as regent. The day-to-day business of running the country was left to the head of the civil administration, the Desi.

At the time of Bogle's visit, the Shabdrung was only seven years old, so the nominal head of state was the Regent, Jigme Senge, but it was with the Desi that Bogle's main business lay. On the mission's arrival at Tashichodzong, the Desi was absent, engaged in religious duties, fifteen miles from the *dzong*. By his orders, the party was lodged in one of the few buildings close to the fortress. Constructed around a square courtyard, it could accommodate the whole entourage and provide stabling for the horses. At night the balconies doubled as bedrooms with thick black blankets hung like curtains across the openings. Situated on an outcrop above the river, it afforded fine views along the valley, some five miles in length. Directly beneath the house was a handsome covered bridge across the Chinchu, used by the monks when they filed by the hundred down to bathe in the river. The valley was densely cultivated; rows of willows lined the riverbanks, and orchards of peach, apple and pear grew among grain and rice fields.

Beyond, the ridged mountains were covered with small firs, aspen and birch.

The morning that the Desi was expected to return, red-robed monks crammed on to the balconies of the *dzong* an hour in advance, and a band of pipes, drums, long horns and cymbals intermittently blasted out fanfares. The approach of the cavalcade was greeted by two salutes of gunfire. Heading the procession were twelve horses led by grooms, then 120 men in red uniforms, followed by a guard of thirty musketeers and thirty archers; next came a body of richly caparisoned horses and a division of forty riders; a standard announced the Chief Minister, then six musicians heralded the Desi himself. Kunga Rinchen, the Desi, was in his mid-fifties, mounted on horseback, in scarlet cloak and wide-brimmed yellow hat much, to Bogle's mind, like a cardinal. On either side, attendants whisked away flies, and a third followed bearing a white silk umbrella with multicoloured fringe. As he passed, crowds of spectators prostrated themselves. The procession wound its way slowly towards the *dzong*. At the gates, the riders dismounted and took off their hats; the Desi alone remained on horseback.

Kunga Rinchen had occupied the office of Desi for only a year. He had formerly been a monk, the principal of the college of philosophical logic, but had been plucked from these academic pursuits by the regent, Jigme Senge, who saw him as a suitable replacement for the deposed ruler, the deeply unpopular Zhidar. Over his five-year reign, Zhidar had managed to antagonise much of the monastic establishment and, in particular, the regent. Zhidar's ambitious plans of self-aggrandisement and conquest did not go down well with the monks. He had assumed control of monastic affairs and encroached upon the Shabdrung's prerogatives. In an attempt to gain favour with Peking, Zhidar had circulated an imperial seal of office throughout the country – a political gesture which implied a degree of subservience to Manchu authority that offended most of his subjects. He had sought an alliance with Prithvi Narayan, the expansionist ruler of Nepal, and mounted successive invasions against Bhutan's neighbours, and while the country was still suffering from the aftermath of war, he committed one of his most oppressive acts. In 1772 the fortress of Tashichodzong burnt down, and Zhidar ordered its reconstruction by forced labour in just one year. The impressive walls admired by Bogle had been erected at great human cost. But Zhidar did not enjoy his new *dzong* long. In 1773, while engaged in the unsuccessful campaign against British forces in Cooch Behar, he was deposed. Finding his people in open rebellion, he fled Bhutan and claimed refuge with the Panchen Lama. By interceding on behalf of the Bhutanese, the Panchen Lama both satisfied his sense of spiritual obligation and enhanced his status in the region. Traditionally, Tibet regarded Bhutan as its religious dependant, and much as it was the duty of a high lama to come to the aid of his disciple, so in the political realm the Panchen Lama had to offer assistance to an inferior.[3] It was at the request of Zhidar and his Nepali allies that the Panchen Lama wrote the letter to Warren Hastings that prompted Bogle's mission. Ironically, Nepal had encouraged the Panchen Lama to intercede in the hope of curbing British influence in the region. And even the Panchen Lama had not anticipated that the British would send an official deputation. Now, as Bogle sought an audience with Zhidar's successor, that mission appeared in jeopardy.

Bogle's invitation to the *dzong* arrived two days after the Desi's return. Accompanied by servants, he made his way to the fortress – a short walk that provided almost as great a spectacle for the people as the Desi's progress. 'If there is any Pleasure in being gazed at, I had enough of it,' Bogle wrote to Annie. 'Being the first European they had ever seen in these Parts, the windows of the Palace & the Road that led to it were crowded with Spectators. I dare say there were 3,000.'[4] Once inside the gates, they passed through courtyards framed with galleries that reminded Bogle of coaching inns in England, but here the wooden pillars were painted with intricate designs of dragons and flowers. They climbed successive iron ladders into an antechamber, decorated with all manner of weapons: bows and arrows, swords, muskets and coiled cane shields. After half an hour's wait, Bogle was shown into the audience chamber. The Desi was seated on a dais, raised above his officers. Entering, Bogle bowed low three times, the closest his dignity would allow him to come to the required triple prostration. Then, while the court looked on silently, he presented the customary white satin cloth to the Desi, and his servants laid out gifts of spices, samples of Bengali cloth, European mirrors and cutlery. Conducted to a cushion at the opposite end of the room, Bogle gratefully subsided. Servants placed copper trays piled with rice, butter, treacle, tea, walnuts, dates, apricots and cucumbers before him. No longer the centre of attention, Bogle had a moment to collect himself: 'I had now time to get over a kind of Flurry, which the novelty of the Scene, and the Part I had to act in it naturally occasioned,' he told Annie.[5]

To amuse his sister and help her to visualise the scene, Bogle offered a detailed description accompanied by a diagram showing the layout of the room, the props and the positions of the central actors:

– But it is time I should let you know where you are, and make you acquainted with the Company.

In Order to get a clear Idea of the Debe Rajah's Presence chamber you have only to look at this very elegant Plan of it annexed. He was dressed in his Sacerdotal Habit, a Scarlet colloured Satin Mitre on his Head, and an Umbrella, with party coloured Fringes twirling over him. He is a pleasant looking old man; with a smirking Countenance. On each side of him his principal Officers and Ministers to the Number of a dozen were seated upon Cushions close to the Wall and the rest of the Company stood in the Area or among the Pillars. The Pannells of the Room and also the Ceiling were covered with Chineze sewed Landscapes, and different Colloured Sattins; the Pulpit was gilded, and many silver & Gilt vases about it, and the floor all around, was laid with Carpets. At the Opposite End of the Apartment and behind where I sat, several large Chinese Images were placed in a kind of Nich or Alcove, with Lamps of Butter burning before them, and ornamented with Elephants Teeth, little Silver Temples, China ware, Silks, Ribbons, and Gew Gaws.[6]

Among the offerings at the shrine, Bogle was startled to find a print of an English society beauty, Lady Waldegrave, Duchess of Gloucester. Somehow, this fashionable item had made its way from the London print shops, via the Calcutta bazaar, to Tashichodzong. Bogle playfully cast himself in the role of the defender of the lady's honour: 'I must not forget a solitary Print of Lady Waldgrave, whom I had

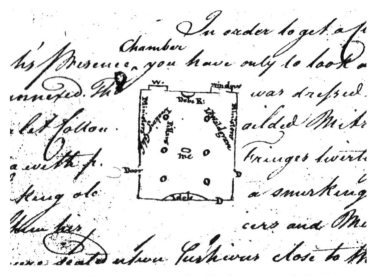

George Bogle's letter to his sister Anne describing his reception at Tashichodzong

afterwards the good fortune to be the Means of rescuing out of the
Hands of these Idols. For it happening to strike some of the Courtiers,
whether the Upholsterer, the Chamberlain, or a Page, I cannot pretend
to say, that Lady Waldgrave would make a pretty Companion to a
Looking Glass I had given the Rajah, she was hung up on one of the
Pillars next the throne, and the Mirror on the other.'[7] Clearly the
Bhutanese elite was as interested in European novelties as the British
Governor was in Himalayan ones.

Through an interpreter, the Desi and Bogle began to exchange
compliments. The Desi hoped that his people had given Bogle every
kind of assistance on his long and arduous journey, and greeted him as
'the first Englishman who had been so far into his Country'.[8] Bogle
responded in kind, thanking the Desi for his gracious hospitality, and
suggesting that they defer business discussions to another occasion.
Meanwhile tea – boiled up with spices and yak butter – was served. As
the silver kettle went the rounds, everyone except Bogle presented
their own wooden cup, 'black enamel in the inside, wrapped in a Bit of
Cloth, and lodged within their Tunick, opposite to their Heart and
next their Skin which keeps it warm and comfortable'.[9] The ceremonial welcome concluded with the presentation of a set of Bhu-

tanese robes to Bogle. 'When we had finished our Tea, and every Man had well licked his cup and deposited it in his Bosom,' Bogle wrote to Annie, 'a water Tabby gown like what Aunt Katty used to wear, with well plated Haunches was brought and put on me; a red Sattin Handkerchief was tied round me for a Girdle.'[10] With his sister in mind, Bogle translated the investiture into domestic terms: crossing cultures turned into cross-dressing. He concluded by wishing that he could have sent the robes as a gift to his old nurse; 'but being without this opportunity, I have converted them into a night Gown, in which I have now the Honour to write you'.[11]

It was at their second meeting some days later that Bogle and the Desi tackled the Panchen Lama's letter of prohibition. What advice could the Desi offer? In raising the matter of Bhutan's relations with Tibet, Bogle inadvertently touched on a sensitive issue. Bhutan regarded its large, domineering neighbour with at best ambivalence, at worst open hostility. For the Bhutanese, Tibet was both the source of Buddhist teaching and a serial invader. The ruling families of Bhutan all traced their pedigrees back to Tibetan nobility, but their ancestors had fled Tibet as political refugees. Although both countries shared a similar system of government, different Tibetan Buddhist orders held power in each state. The Gelugpa order, presided over by the Dalai and Panchen Lamas, ruled in Tibet, while in Bhutan the Drukpa school predominated. In fact, since the time of the first Shabdrung, the Gelugpa order had been banned from establishing monasteries in Bhutan. The Dalai and Panchen Lamas might attempt to influence Bhutanese affairs, but they held no direct authority in Bhutan. By offering shelter and support to the deposed Zhidar, the current Panchen Lama had not endeared himself to the new Bhutanese regime. Little of this would have been clear to Bogle; indeed he had just begun to distinguish the two countries from each other. It was only in his final report that Bogle applied the name Boutan to the country that we now know as Bhutan (in fact the European use of the name originates with Bogle). To Bogle, the Desi simply stated that the Panchen Lama was his 'religious Superior, but their Governments were distinct'.[12] He then reiterated the Panchen Lama's concern about Manchu disapproval of the mission; the Emperor would certainly object to two Europeans entering Tibet. If Bogle persisted with his scheme, the onward journey would be fraught with difficulty and hardship. In short, he would be well advised to turn back.

For Bogle, 'this was ripening the Conversation too fast'.[13] Refusing to accept such an unwelcome conclusion, he begged to inform the Desi of the aims of the mission. The Governor had sent the Panchen Lama a letter, presents and assurances of goodwill because he wished to cultivate friendship with a man of such holy character. It was Bogle's duty to convey these in person. Since the Desi had signed a treaty of amity with the British, he would surely help to remove any obstacles to the mission. 'What would the world say,' asked Bogle, 'if after being sent from the Governor with Tokens of his Friendship to the Teshoo Lama [Panchen Lama], I should be refused Admittance into his Country, and obliged to return with them to Calcutta?'[14] But the appeal to honour and covert threat seemed to have little effect on the Desi. He repeated his advice to return, hinting that the ruling against Europeans arose from suspicion of their motives. Purangir, however, would be welcome to continue into Tibet. 'These discourses inter-mixed with the Ceremonies of the Imposition of Hands &c twice, Beetle-nut, two Cups of whisky, four dishes of Tea and as many graces, spun out the Time,' Bogle wrote. 'The Sun was almost down, and the Priests beginning to repeat their Vespers, I took my leave and retired.'[15]

Over the following weeks, the qualities that Hastings had com-mended in Bogle as peculiarly suited to the role of envoy – his patience, assiduity and moderation of temper – were severely tested.[16] Bogle's days were filled with a succession of meetings with the Desi and his chief officers; similar arguments were rehearsed again and again, on both sides. The Panchen Lama's messenger renewed his suit, and Bogle repeatedly refused to return to Calcutta with the Governor's letter. He would wait until he received further orders. Bogle's mounting frustration would have been fuelled by conversations with Hamilton. By nature forthright and short-tempered, Hamilton had few of Bogle's diplomatic skills. Another letter from the Panchen Lama arrived, this time for the Desi, again denying Bogle entry. 'I could not bear the thought of returning to Calcutta, without fulfilling any of the Ends of my Commission, and before I was furnished with the Governor's orders. Nothing but necessity could justify it,' a grim-faced Bogle wrote. 'The obstacles which the Teshoo Lama threw in my way served only to encrease my Curiosity, and my Desire to Surmount them.'[17]

In order to allay suspicion that he was a spy, Bogle thought it best – at least for the time being – to disregard Hastings's instructions to enquire closely into the country. He tried to give the impression that the British were a pacific people, little concerned with conquest. The East India Company, he asserted, was fully occupied with the management and protection of Bengal and Bihar. These provinces were so productive in terms of trade and revenue that the British did not need to think of expansion. Indeed, the Company resorted to arms only in a defensive capacity. Bogle suspected that the recent history of British military campaigns in Bhutan and some years earlier in Nepal had persuaded both the Desi and the Panchen Lama to the contrary. It was fear of British aggression, he concluded, rather than imperial disapproval that lay at the root of the Lama's prohibition.

The impression conveyed by Bogle's large entourage did not help. 'I had brought up with me a Swarry [cavalcade] more, God knows, from a Consideration of the Company's Honor, than from any vanity of my own,' Bogle wrote. 'I expected too that it would facilitate my views; but I soon discovered that it had quite the Contrary Effect.'[18] A display of magnificence and might was precisely *not* what was required in this situation. The number of his servants also made it difficult for Bogle to establish contact with the Bhutanese. 'If I am to acquire knowledge,' he reasoned, 'I must lay aside the Governor's Deputy, and mix with the People on a more equal footing.'[19] What was more, if there were any substance to the Panchen Lama's concerns about imperial displeasure, an extensive company would attract more attention than a discreet band. Bogle had learnt of the two Manchu residents or *amban*s stationed in Lhasa who monitored the direction of Tibetan policy and reported back to Peking. If the Lama thought that Bogle might escape the *amban*s' notice, he might be less reluctant to admit him. So, after two months' service, twenty of Bogle's attendants were given their dismissal.

About the same time, the seemingly fruitless negotiations and entrenched positions finally started to shift. Bogle managed to extract the promise of a letter in his favour to be sent by the Desi to the Panchen Lama; but the point was conceded with such reluctance that Bogle did not expect much of it. He had higher hopes of a deputation that he intended to send to the Lama. Purangir and Paima were to travel on to the Panchen Lama's monastery, where the *gosain* would act as Bogle's advocate. Bogle had come to rely on Purangir's information and shrewd political advice. 'I think I can depend on his exerting himself on my behalf,' he noted.[20] The mission had, after all, been undertaken on Purangir's assurances, so it was in his interest to see it succeed. There were also certain financial inducements that Bogle hoped would appeal to the *gosain*'s business sense.

For days Purangir remained closeted with Bogle discussing arguments and incentives. On no account should the Panchen Lama be encouraged to write to Peking for imperial approval for the mission. Not only would this incur a long delay, but it would be to invite failure. 'It would be giving me and my Journey an Air of Consequence, which would certainly alarm the Jealousy of that provident Court,' argued Bogle.

> Unable to distinguish objects at 2000 miles distance, their Imagination might magnify them, and forsee a thousand Evils; their Trade ruined, or diverted into new Channels; their Country drained of its wealth; the Empire perhaps invaded. An express Prohibition would probably be the Consequence. For it can hardly be expected, that they who refuse to admit a European into Canton in the Heart of their Government, would allow him to approach their distant Frontier.[21]

Far better to keep the affair quiet; that way even the *amban*s might be none the wiser. Should they get to hear of it, Bogle reckoned, their approval would be easier to gain than Peking's.

If, as Bogle imagined, the Panchen Lama were suspicious of British motives, Purangir would seek to persuade him otherwise, using whatever arguments he thought carried most weight. The British sought only good relations with Tibet, indeed Bhutan's mountainous terrain ruled out the possibility of hostile intent. Friendship with the East India Company, Bogle argued, would boost the Panchen Lama's influence and prestige in the region, allowing him to intervene more effectively in local affairs. The Governor, Bogle said, was a man of great curiosity, who had instructed him to enquire into the customs and manners of the people of Tibet, into the country's flora and fauna, but not to take the slightest interest in military matters, 'considering from the Distance of the Countries, the opposition of the Climate, and other Circumstances, that Bengal had as little to fear from Thibet, as Thibet had from Bengal'.[22]

In addition to this battery of arguments and his own diplomatic finesse, Purangir was to carry a letter from Bogle. Of necessity short – since Bogle composed it in Tibetan, a language he had only just begun to learn – the letter requested permission to enter Tibet. The Governor, Bogle wrote, 'is desirous of cultivating the Friendship of a Man, whose Prayers are offered up for the good of mankind, and whose offices are employed in accommodating their differences. For this purpose am I sent. If I am refused admittance into your presence, my Heart will be cast down, and the Head of the Governor will be covered with Shame.'[23] On Purangir's advice, Bogle requested a passport for no more than four servants. The deputation would have to travel by an indirect route because of the smallpox epidemic, but in less than two months, Purangir promised, Bogle would receive an answer. The fate of the mission depended entirely on Purangir's negotiating skills. On 15 July, 'after drinking a Cordial Dram together, we parted,' wrote Bogle, 'the Messenger, the Gossiene, and Payma set out on their Journey, while I remain quietly at Tassesudden, waiting for their answer.'[24]

MONKISH TO THE GREATEST DEGREE

The day began with the sound of the monks' morning prayers. As the sky lightened, the *dzong* reverberated with massed chanting, horns and drums. In their dark-red robes, the monks sat cross-legged in rows before a towering gilt statue of the Buddha. From time to time, they would bend low towards the altar, touching the floor with their foreheads. This was the first of the three services in the great assembly hall that structured the monastic day. When not engaged in prayer, the monks worked as scholars, craftsmen or artists. The community itself produced numerous objects for devotional use: painted and embroidered banners, intricately traced *mandala*s (geometric representations of the universe) and elaborate costumes for festivals. All these activities took place within the confines of the *dzong*; the monks generally left the precincts just once every eight or ten days to bathe half naked in the river. At nightfall, after evening prayers, the gates were shut fast.

Novices usually joined the monastery as boys aged five or six. Years of study had to be completed before they could take the series of vows that led to full ordination. They vowed to live celibate but, on payment of a fine, could 'retire' to start a family. In a country where the great majority of the population were peasants, to enter monastic life was practically the only route to education and social advancement. So large was the monastic community that most families had members who were monks. Indeed a form of 'monk-tax' operated whereby families were required to devote a male child to monastic life. In return, parents enjoyed both spiritual merit and social prestige.

To Bogle, the life of a monk appeared aimless and joyless. On a couple of occasions, he chose to observe the services in the *dzong* from a gallery 'painted with Festoons of Death's Head and Bones'.[1] The Desi, thinking him interested, invited him to attend 'by Break of Day and at all Hours'; but Bogle's curiosity about religious ritual was strictly limited.[2] There was little obvious occupation. He felt 'fairly buried in these Mountains . . . as much out of the World,' he wrote to a friend in Bengal, 'as if I had paid my Ferry cross the Styx'.[3] His days, he told Bess, were spent paying visits, shooting wild pigeons, botanising in the mountains and playing cards – cribbage and piquet – with Hamilton in the evenings. 'If you want to know how I pass my time,' he wrote to another friend, 'you have only to take my Life in Calcutta and capsize it, not forgetting to add about eight or Ten Cups of Tea with Butter in them a Day.'[4]

Becalmed in Bhutan, Bogle's anxieties over the outcome of the mission and his future career grew. 'At present I have two Causes of Sollicitude,' he wrote to his Calcutta confidant Alexander Elliot, 'the first how this Business will end – the other about all these Choppings & Changes down below – and these two form a Circle for my only Anchor is the Governor's favour and that favour depends on this Business.'[5] During Bogle's absence from Calcutta, major reforms in the administration of the Company required by the Regulating Act of 1773 were to come into force. As far as Bogle was concerned, the most significant of these 'Choppings & Changes down below' were those that affected the status of Hastings. The Governor was to be given the title of governor general, a greatly enhanced salary, and Bengal would take precedence over the other two British Presidencies of Bombay and Madras. But as a check on the Governor General's authority, four new Councillors had been created to make up the governing Council of Bengal. Three of the new Councillors – General John Clavering, Colonel George Monson and Philip Francis – were fresh appointees from England, due to arrive in Calcutta in the next few months. Their presence, as Bogle suspected, would radically affect the Company hierarchy, transforming both Hastings's position and that of his favourites. Where, Bogle fretted, would he fit into the new political landscape?

Then there were the minor inconveniences of daily life. Bogle and Hamilton were still without a trained cook and could not find anyone to do their laundry. The food available was monotonous and little to their taste. The staples were rice, dried beef, pork, dried fish and lashings of yak butter, supplied direct from the *dzong*'s stores. Hoping to liven up their meals, Bogle wrote to Calcutta requesting supplies of alcohol, vinegar and mustard, 'when one has nothing to do, these Matters come to be of Consequence.'[6] By way of return, he engaged porters to carry baskets of green walnuts, peaches and pears to be distributed among his acquaintance in Bengal. Lieutenant Williams, the British officer who handled Bogle's mail, learnt of his domestic plight from the band of dismissed servants who passed through Cooch Behar on their return journey. Responding to the servants' report ('that you can hardly procure any Provisions whatever that's eatable; and likewise that your Cook has left you . . . that you can't procure any body to wash your Cloaths which must be very disagreeable'), Williams sent up a cook, a washerman, soap, supplies of biscuit and two dozen bottles of Madeira.[7]

But, for all the little irritations of life at Tashichodzong, Bogle found himself increasingly at ease in the company of the Bhutanese. 'Among a people where there is not Pre-eminence of Birth and no Finery in dress, there cannot well be much Pride,' he noted in his journal. 'The Booteas seem to have none of it, and live among their Servants and dependents on the most familiar Footing.'[8] The Governor of Tashichodzong invited Bogle to join his household for a picnic and a contest of *dego*, the monks' traditional sport, a cross between bowls and quoit-throwing, aiming stones at a stick driven into the ground. Finding himself outclassed in the *dego*, Bogle went pigeon-shooting instead, but returned for a lunch of hard-boiled eggs, rice, pork and fruit eaten with fingers, seated on the ground. The meal ended with rounds of strong spirits.

Bogle and Hamilton paid several visits to Jigme Senge, the Regent, in his splendid apartment at the top of the *dzong*'s central tower. After the formality of the first meeting, their visits became more relaxed.

Jigme Senge, who had suffered near imprisonment under Zhidar's regime, was then in his thirties – a spare, frail-looking man who, according to Bogle, doted on his lap-dog and pet mongoose. It was his enquiring mind that chiefly attracted Bogle. The Regent, he wrote, 'appears to have more Curiosity than any man I have seen in the Country'.[9] During one of their visits, Hamilton demonstrated the use of a microscope. His attempts to trap a fly to place under the lens caused the Regent some concern lest the insect be killed in the process for, as Bogle explained, monks vowed not to take the life of any living creature.

Small as it was, the fly-catching incident demonstrates the ways in which European technology and Buddhist teaching could collide. Indeed some members of the ecclesiastical establishment regarded the Regent's interest in British manufactures as a dangerous delusion. The retired chief abbot some years later would denounce the Regent's attraction to Western artefacts as a mental aberration, inflicted by demons as a punishment for breaking Tantric rules. He wrote to Jigme Senge, 'barbarian demons have disturbed your mind, to the extent that you are enamoured of the goods of the English.'[10] To enter into commercial relations with a former enemy confused the protective deities, the head abbot warned. No less a figure than the first Shabdrung had appeared to him in a series of visions to prophesy that trade with the British would bring only trouble to the land.[11]

Unaware of the theological arguments against commerce with a former enemy, Bogle felt frustrated in his attempts to find out about Bhutan's trade. Now that the Panchen Lama's messenger had left, Bogle wanted to pursue a more active line of questioning, but made scant progress. 'This Place,' he complained to Hastings, 'is very little favourable to my Commercial Enquiries. It is monkish to the greatest Degree. The Rajah, his Priests, his Officers, and his Servants are all immured, like State Prisoners, within an immense large Palace, and there is not above a Dozen other Houses in the Town.'[12] There was no public market and little economic activity. Communities were largely self-sufficient, most transactions took the form of barter and taxes were paid in kind.

Without Purangir, Bogle had no one to explain and interpret, nobody to help gather information or act as an agent. What was needed was a substitute for the *gosain*, someone who was familiar with the country and the language, but independent of the Desi. Bogle had in mind a Kashmiri merchant whom he had encountered at Rangpur, earlier on his journey. Mirza Settar had impressed Bogle with his sharp intelligence and knowledge of the trade to Tibet. He was extremely well connected, part of the influential Kashmiri trading and banking network in the region. He had offered to accompany the party, but Bogle, wary of offending Purangir, had turned him down. Now, though, there was an obvious need for his services, and Bogle wrote requesting the Governor's permission to send for the merchant.

The lack of apparent trading activity thwarted Bogle in his role as commercial envoy, but it greatly appealed to Bogle the philosophical traveller. In Bhutan, he saw a society free from the ills of civilisation and the corruption of commerce. 'The Simplicity of their manners,' he observed in his journal, 'their slight Intercourse with Strangers, and a strong Sense of Religion, preserve the Booteas from many vices to which more polished nations are addicted. They are strangers to Falsehood and Ingratitude. Theft, and every other Species of Dishonesty to which the Lust of money gives Birth, are little known.'[13] The rigours of life in the mountains also contributed to their qualities; the Bhutanese, Bogle asserted, were 'industrious, faithful, hospitable, honest, grateful, and brave'.[14]

In Bhutan, Bogle seemed to have discovered one of the mountain idylls described by contemporary writers. His vision was clearly indebted to the French philosopher Jean-Jacques Rousseau (whose *Collected Works* Bogle possessed). In the *Discourse on the Origins of Inequality* (1755) Rousseau had famously attacked civilised ways and championed the virtue and happiness of simpler societies. But Bogle's version of Bhutan also drew on sources closer to home, on the ideas circulating among Scottish intellectuals of his youth. Bogle's family connections ensured that he was well versed in the theories of the Scottish Enlightenment: his father had served four years as lord rector at Glasgow University and had taken a particular interest in the university library. Adam Smith, author of *The Wealth of Nations*, held the chair of Logic at Glasgow University – teaching, among others,

George's brother Robert and his friend William Richardson, a poet, critic and playwright, who would become professor of Humanity (Latin) at the same institution.

The Scottish literati were preoccupied, perhaps to a greater extent than other Enlightenment thinkers, with the attempt to define and distinguish primitive and refined societies. Drawing extensively on travel literature, writers like Adam Smith, William Robertson and Adam Ferguson sought to chart human development by dividing society into various stages, usually corresponding to the savage, the barbaric and the polished. This concern was related to the nature of Scottish society itself, split between the sophisticated Lowlands and 'rude' Highlands. To most eighteenth-century Lowland Scots, Highlanders would have appeared barbarous and primitive. The danger that they posed to the state was manifested most obviously in the Jacobite rebellion of 1745–6, when Highlanders rose in support of the Young Pretender, Charles Edward. But with the rebels' defeat at the battle of Culloden, the Highlands suffered ruthless reprisals and the clans were deprived of military power. The Highland way of life, already undermined by the spread of English commercial, political and cultural values, could not recover from the blow. But as Highland culture fell into a decline, so the image of the Highlander grew in stature. Bathed in nostalgia, the literary Highlander became a heroic figure. James Macpherson's forged 'translations' of the Gaelic poems of Ossian did much to promote this image of doomed nobility.

But the Highlander was not confined to Scotland alone. His likeness was found wherever Scottish writers encountered tribal peoples, particularly in North America. Sometimes the parallels returned home: both James Boswell and Samuel Johnson represented Highlanders as native Americans.[15] For his part, Bogle discovered Highlanders in Bhutan. The northerly, mountainous state preserved the martial spirit and independence of the old Highlands. Like the Highland clansmen, Bhutanese peasants owed their chiefs military service and labour dues. Every man was a soldier, 'dressed in short Trouze; like the highland filabeg; woollen Hose, soled with Leather and gartered under the knee; a jacket or Tunick, and over all two or three Striped Blankets . . . They sleep in the open air, and keep themselves warm with their plaids and their whisky.'[16] Sporting the symbols of Highland identity – the philabeg, plaids and whisky – the Bhutanese exhibited manly virtues of resilience and courage. Bogle imagined that they expressed themselves with 'all that loftiness and sublimity of stile used by Ossian, or any other hilly writer'.[17]

Significantly, in Bogle's account, the Bhutanese did not conform to the paradigm of barbarism. According to Bogle, the country was well regulated and, although rebellions were frequent, armed uprisings guaranteed the people's rights rather than threatened the state. Writing to his father, Bogle noted his own surprise at the existence of state institutions: 'So far from that Barbarism which with transalpine Arrogance is too often considered as the Lot of every Nation unknown to Europeans: I found a little State governed by a regular and strict Police, independent by the Situation of the Country, and subject to an elective Government, which though absolute was checked by the free Spirit of the People, unawed by Mercenary Troops, and apt to rebell when treated with Oppression.'[18] In chastising European arrogance, Bogle was following the example of Scottish writers like Adam Ferguson who condemned the habit of taking one's own culture as the sole standard of civility. But Bogle's Bhutan challenged those Enlightenment models of historical progress that clearly demarcated the different stages of society. In Bhutan, the attractions of primitivism – a mountain kingdom untouched by modern commercial greed – were united with the rule of law and an elective government.

It is striking that eighteenth-century European thinkers became preoccupied by ideas of ancient simplicity at the moment that modern consumerism took hold.[19] Not that the myth of primitive innocence was anything new; European culture had long been haunted by the loss of the Golden Age, and as often as writers had proposed the happiness of the savage state, travellers had denied its existence. But commercial expansion – then as now – was accompanied by nostalgia for an older way of life. With the demise of the clans and the spread of commercial values in Scotland, literary works began to celebrate the courage and hardiness of the Highlanders. Ferguson, for one, saw many of the values that had been discarded by modern society embodied in clan life. For it is only when a culture is on the verge of extinction – or has already been destroyed – that it is valued.[20] In his dual roles of philosophical traveller and trade envoy, Bogle exemplified the contradictory impulses of the period. On the one hand, he idealised the Bhutanese, describing them to his father as 'uncorrupted by Trade, or an Intercourse with Strangers'; on the other, he complained to Hastings that the Bhutanese were 'ignorant of all the Advantages which flow from a free and extensive Commerce'.[21] If Bogle found Bhutan an idyll, then the trade that he sought to establish would be unlikely to leave it one. Over time, commerce would awaken new material needs and desires that would gradually erode the hardy self-sufficiency that Bogle so admired.

Did Bogle recognise the contradictions in his roles as East India Company envoy and philosophical traveller? Nowhere in his writing does he acknowledge the conflict. Among the most remarkable features of his journals and correspondence is his ability to keep various, sometimes incompatible, personae in play. This partly testifies to his talent as a letter-writer. One of the great social skills, letter-writing demands that the manner and matter of each letter suit the interests and status of the recipient. This variety of letter-writing voices was one of the qualities particularly esteemed by eighteenth-century critics. Bogle's father commended the fact that George did not repeat himself in a batch of letters written at the same time to his several sisters.[22] Letters to friends and family, critics maintained, should be composed in an easy natural style and engage the recipient's attention.[23] For his pious, widely read father, therefore, Bogle adopted a respectful, serious tone, relating the manners and traditions of the peoples he encountered. In style and content, these letters were very close to Bogle's official journal. His father's replies, written in an increasingly shaky hand, repeatedly enjoined Bogle to attend to the state of his soul while thanking him for remittances sent. For his sister Annie, Bogle adopted a much more playful persona. He liked to represent himself as a hapless wanderer. Responding, for instance, to her imagined question, 'But where are you got to, say you, with your Valleys and your Boots [Bhutanese]?', Bogle suggested that she search out her old school maps to check, for 'it has been by such Turnings and Windings, Ups and Downs, that I have got here that I protest I am as much at a loss as if I had been playing Blind Man's Buff'.[24] In its evocation of shared childhood games, the image of blundering Bogle reasserted familial ties, but was of course sharply at odds with the envoy's actual habits of observation and annotation.

At other moments, Bogle's multiple roles seem notably less innocent. In his dealings with the Desi, he was evidently playing a diplomatic double game. Although he repeatedly reassured the Desi that the British had only pacific intentions in Bhutan, he composed a report for Hastings entitled 'Observations on the proper mode of attacking Bhutan'. In any future military operations, Bogle suggested, the Company should act offensively rather than defensively. It would be best to seize two of the main passes into the country; six companies of troops would be sufficient to garrison them, and supplies could be provided by five more. But, he added, he could see little advantage in a conquest of Bhutan; the difficulties of supplying troops across the mountains would be immense, and the advantages gained would be minimal, certainly not worth the expense and commitment of man-power. Better to be content with the status quo – possession of Cooch Behar and a quiet Bhutan – than embark on a troublesome military venture.[25]

Bhutan proved a more tempting prospect as a market for firearms. A few months into his stay, Bogle informed Hastings that the Bhutanese were keen to purchase up-to-date guns.[26] Although he did not know it, Bogle was not the first European to deal in firearms with the Bhutanese. Nearly 150 years earlier, two Portuguese Jesuits had made the same long journey from Bengal into Bhutan. Like Bogle, Fathers Estevão Cacella and João Cabral were heading for Tibet. Attracted by the stories of Nestorian Christians that had circulated since Marco Polo's day, they intended to join a fellow missionary who had ventured as far as Tsaparang in western Tibet. They followed a similar route to Bogle, travelling through Cooch Behar and Buxaduar into the hills. In April 1627, the two missionaries received a courteous welcome from Nga-wang Namgyel, the first Shabdrung. For two months the Jesuits followed the Shabdrung on his progress around the country, before being accommodated at a monastery, some fifteen miles north of the spot where Bogle was lodged (the fortress of Tashichodzong had yet to be built). In their letters, published only in the twentieth century, the missionaries represented Ngawang Namgyel as a ruler renowned for his gentleness and abstinence, a man of arts and letters.[27] But the Shabdrung was reluctant to allow the missionaries to proceed into Tibet, for this was the territory of one of his enemies, the Desi Tsangpa. In an attempt to dissuade the Jesuits from their journey, the Shabdrung offered them a site in the nearby valley of Paro to build a church. This the missionaries declined, leaving as their only legacy to Bhutan their gifts of firearms and gunpowder. According to the Bhutanese court scribe, 'up to that time guns had not spread [to Bhutan]; and being unfamiliar with them, just to hear their loud noise would inspire fear and terror among the enemy.'[28]

A century and a half later, European firepower remained the implicit threat behind the Company's request for Bhutan's assistance with the mission. At times it came to the surface. When Bogle finally heard from Hastings, in two letters dated 10 August 1774, the Governor suggested that a useful negotiating ploy would be to remind the Desi of what the British might have done in the recent war, had they not exercised restraint. 'You will also urge,' Hastings advised, 'the unfriendly Aspect that this conduct bears so soon after a Cessation of Hostilities which evinced to all the World that my desire was only to live in Peace and Amity with them instead of pursuing those advantages in War which my Superiority in Troops and in Arms put in my Power.'[29] If the Desi were to counter that Company forces could never succeed in subduing Bhutan, Bogle should respond that British troops were suited to the forested, mountainous terrain and climate, 'that our Troops who languish in the Heat of Bengal recover in the Cold and piercing Air of his Country'.[30]

All possible arguments should be deployed to persuade the Desi to aid the mission, the Governor wrote. To Bogle's request that the merchant Mirza Settar join the party, Hastings readily agreed. The Governor was keen to see the venture succeed. 'Having engaged in this Business, I do not like to give it up,' he wrote. The stakes were high for both Bogle and himself. 'We should both acquire a reputation from its success. The well judging World will be ready to class it with the other wild and ill-conceited Projects if it fails.' To Bogle he gave free rein in his dealings with the Desi: 'Make what promises or engagements you please with the Raja, I will ratify them.' Hastings's concluding remarks combined exhortation with a note of caution.

'Leave no means untried,' he began, 'but hazard neither your Person or Health by an obstinate Perseverance.'[31]

Hastings's advice arrived too late to be of any real assistance. The post between Bhutan and Calcutta could take up to three weeks (or a month and a half to receive a reply to a letter); the delay in communication meant that Bogle always had to trust his own judgement. In any case, by the time the Governor's letter arrived, Bogle's situation had changed dramatically.

BLOODY WORK

Seated in his apartment on the upper floor of the monastery, the walls hung with painted silk *thangka*s (cloth paintings), the Panchen Lama had listened to Purangir's arguments with interest. He had quizzed the *gosain* on the motives and disposition of the two foreigners who sought entry to Tibet. The Lama was curious to learn more about the rulers of Bengal. The scores of *gosain*s who visited his monastery kept him informed of the British rise to power and presented him with a stream of European goods and novelties (he still recalled the excitement at court caused by the arrival of the first pair of European spectacles).[1] In recent years he had sent two deputations of monks to northern India to make offerings at Bodh Gaya, the site of the Buddha's enlightenment. Combining devotion with diplomacy, his envoy had opened relations with the ruler of Benares, Chait Singh, who had responded by sending emissaries of his own. They had arrived at the Panchen Lama's court just a few months back with little good to say about the British. Untrustworthy and ambitious, the British used the cover of trade to insinuate themselves into a country. Once established, they gained knowledge of the place only to make themselves masters of it. Much the same story came from the Lhasa Regent. On hearing of the mission, the Regent wrote to warn the Panchen Lama against the two Europeans who had arrived in Bhutan with a large retinue of servants. Europeans were warlike and had a habit of interfering in other people's affairs, the Regent observed. The Panchen Lama, he advised, should find some pretext to turn the two foreigners away, 'either on account of the violence of the smallpox, or on any other pretence'.[2]

The Panchen Lama had complied with the Regent's request, but, as he listened to Purangir, he felt justified in challenging the decision. The relationship between the Regent and the Panchen Lama was not an easy one. Although the Regent was nominally in charge of the government until the Eighth Dalai Lama came of age, the standing of the Panchen Lama was far greater, extending throughout Tibet and the surrounding region. The Regent had to answer to the two Manchu *amban*s stationed at Lhasa, but the Panchen Lama was respected by the Qianlong Emperor himself. While they might consult over policy issues, the Panchen Lama and the Regent both sought to further their own interests.

The British mission offered the Panchen Lama an opportunity to assert his authority over that of the Regent, to conduct foreign policy on his own account. In a letter to Lhasa, the Lama set out his reasons. Unlike the Regent, he had always opposed the military adventures of Zhidar, the former Desi of Bhutan. After Zhidar's defeat, he had been responsible for brokering a peace deal with the British. Now that the British Governor had responded by sending a deputation, it was only fitting that he should receive the envoy. If the Regent should continue to deny the mission entry, any adverse repercussions, any calamity that might befall the country, would be entirely his own fault. Finding no answer to this argument, the Regent was obliged to give way. The British envoys could visit the Panchen Lama, he conceded, on condition that they were accompanied only by a few servants and did not come anywhere near his residence at Lhasa.

On receipt of this reply, the Panchen Lama once again summoned Purangir. There were new orders. Purangir and Paima should retrace their steps to the Bhutanese border. Bogle was to be invited to resume his journey.

Now that Purangir had secured them permission to travel, Bogle and Hamilton were eager to be off. But first they had to wait a month for the merchant Mirza Settar to make the journey up from Rangpur. Since the Lama had issued his invitation, relations between the Desi and Bogle had grown more cordial. On receiving a letter from Hastings, the Desi was pleased to find that the British were interested in cultivating the Bhutanese themselves. Once Mirza Settar had arrived, Bogle was able to learn about an annual trade caravan to Rangpur in Bengal undertaken by agents of the Desi and his chief officers. The Bhutanese sent down ponies, musk, yak tails (for use as fly whisks), coarse-spun blankets and striped woollen cloth. In Rangpur they purchased broadcloth, cottons, dyes and spices that were in turn transported to Tibet, either as tribute or as trading articles. Evidently Bhutan was not the commerce-free idyll of Bogle's musings. If Hastings could guarantee the Bhutanese freedom to trade then, Bogle hoped, the Desi might listen favourably to British requests. More specifically, an agreement on Rangpur might persuade the Desi to allow the passage of British goods through Bhutan and into Tibet.

But all discussion, indeed all normal court business, was suspended in September for the great annual festival, the Thinpu Dromcho. All the district governors were summoned to Tashichodzong to render account of their administration and to attend the spectacular sacred dances that concluded the twenty-day festival. For a week, elaborately masked and costumed monks performed dances that drove out demons, narrated the stories of the faith, and celebrated the triumph of Buddhism. But to Bogle it was just so much whimsical capering; an incomprehensible masquerade of birds, beasts and grotesques.

By October the weather was growing noticeably chillier. Keeping track of the falling temperature, Bogle observed that the thermometer registered below 50°F in the mornings. These days, Bogle went about wrapped in a shawl that had been one of Hastings's parting gifts. Made of fine *pashima* wool, this shawl would have represented one of the luxury products that made Tibet such a tempting trading partner (and functioned as a reminder of Hastings's request for a breeding pair of shawl goats from Ladakh to add to his menagerie). As increased protection against the cold, the Regent presented Bogle with a robe of yellow satin lined with lambskin, and the Desi added a dozen blankets. Bogle and Hamilton were eager to start for Tibet before winter set in and the route became impassable. In a couple of months the Bhutanese court would itself abandon Tashichodzong for the gentler climate of its winter seat at Punakha, two days' journey to the south-east.

But the quiet regularity of court life, seemingly so fixed in routine and ceremonial, was deceptive. Not all of the *dzong*'s inhabitants were content with the current regime; indeed opposition had been growing throughout Bogle's stay. The former Desi, Zhidar, still commanded the loyalty of a band of supporters who argued that his deposition had been unlawful and that he should have held the office for life. It was not appropriate, they maintained, for a *desi* to be deposed by a clerical faction, in his absence, without being heard in his own defence. Moreover, the charges against Zhidar were unfounded. Although he had been accused of exploiting his people by ordering the reconstruction of Tashichodzong in under a year, it was customary to use compulsory labour in state building works. Far from being a warmonger, they argued, Zhidar had actually applied to the Panchen Lama to mediate at the time of the deposition. Zhidar's adherents had come to influence the young Shabdrung who, at the age of seven, had embarked on a hunger strike for the former Desi's restoration. Alarmed at this turn of events, the Desi decided to remove the Shabdrung from his immediate circle and escort him to a neighbouring fortress.

The day following their departure, rebellion broke out. A conspiracy was discovered among Zhidar's party; the plan was for a force of 250 men, led by two former district governors, to attack Tashichodzong. With the aid of monks inside, they would capture the Regent and other high clerics. But the plot was uncovered, several of the monks summarily executed, and the rebels forced to retreat some five miles south to the castle of Simtokha. Strategically sited at a crossroads, guarding all routes to and from the capital, Simtokha was the oldest of the *dzong*s, and much valued for its rich collection of religious artefacts, paintings and statues. Storming the fortress, the rebels found supplies of arms, ammunition, provisions and treasure. Hearing that Simtokha had fallen, some sixty monks made their escape from Tashichodzong to join the rebels.

At the news of the uprising, the Desi immediately returned to Tashichodzong to assemble forces from all over Bhutan. The fighters were not regular soldiers but villagers on military service. They wore loose tunics, draped with cloaks or quilted jackets. Coiled cane shields and helmets of padded cotton or cane were all their armour. They fought with broadswords and six-foot bamboo bows with iron-tipped (sometimes poison-dipped) arrows. A few had antiquated matchlocks that were fired from a crouching position, but the guns were less than reliable, failing to ignite in the wet.[3] Looking out from his window, Bogle could see and hear much of the action. Although the archers concealed themselves to take aim, their tufted helmets gave them away. Each new attack was heralded by war cries, great whoops and howls intended to terrify the enemy and enthuse the combatants. 'The Insurgents approached sometimes almost to the Gates of the Palace,' Bogle wrote to his brother Robin, 'and there was bloody work for some days.'[4]

With Bogle's encouragement, Hamilton offered his services to tend the wounded. His surgical skills were much in demand. 'Your Acquaintance M[r] Hamilton had enough upon his Hands,' Bogle told Robin.[5] Among those he treated was Bogle's cordial picnic host, the Governor of Tashichodzong. With their medical stocks seriously depleted, Bogle wrote to Calcutta to request further supplies. The Regent, with his usual interest in things European, had requested a supply of medicines and dressings from Hamilton; he intended to take over the surgeon's role himself when the doctor departed.

The rebels' base at Simtokha had strong natural defences but was not actually fortified. Rather than destroy the *dzong* and its precious contents by fire, the Desi's army settled down for a siege. There were no wells at Simtokha, so the Desi hoped to reduce the rebel army quickly through lack of water. Supply routes were cut, and several villages, supposed to favour Zhidar, were burnt to the ground. After ten days, with no prospect of relief, the rebels chose a moonlit night to make their escape. A few were captured, but the leaders of the uprising fled over the mountains towards Tibet.

One day after the rebels' flight, Bogle and Hamilton finally set out on their journey. Order had only just been restored, but it was now mid-October, with the first fall of snow capping the mountains, and they could wait no longer. Following the terms of their passport, they were a greatly reduced band. Paima, the Tibetan envoy, and Mirza Settar, the Kashmiri merchant, accompanied them. A guide supplied by the Desi was to conduct them as far as the Bhutanese border. The few Bengali servants who were in attendance 'were amazed in the Morning to see the Tops of the Mountains all white', Bogle wrote to Bess. 'They applied to the Boots [Bhutanese] for an Explanation of this Phenomenon, who told them it was Cloths which God Almighty covered the Hills with in the winter time to keep them warm.' It is unlikely that this fanciful explanation would have satisfied the servants, but their astonishment was even greater, according to Bogle, when they first encountered ice: 'they all agreed not to mention it to their fellow Countrymen on their Return to Bengal, as they were sure it would not be credited.'[6]

An armed escort had been laid on for their passage across the mountains, but, now that the rebels had fled, Bogle and Hamilton took the easier route, riding along the valley bottom, past the recently besieged fort of Simtokha. All around were signs of the uprising. High on the slopes, flames marked the destruction of a village loyal to Zhidar, and at a village close to the *dzong* some of the Desi's forces were taking their ease from a pursuit of the rebels. Seated on a carpet surrounded by his men, the commander invited Bogle to join him for a cup of spirits. The officer was one of the Desi's most trusted ministers, a man of sharp intellect and shrewd judgement. After months spent in the company of monks, Bogle found his company as refreshing as his liquor. A Scottish proverb, with its homely ring and anti-clerical sting, summed up his pleasure in the encounter. 'Of a truth,' wrote Bogle in his journal, 'an Ounce of Motherwit is worth a pound of Clergy.'[7]

Crossing into the narrow valley of the River Pachu, the party journeyed for a couple of days towards Paro, the capital of the province. The countryside grew increasingly populous and fertile. The village women were busy harvesting rice. Before it could be cut, the streams that fed the paddyfields had to be diverted and the plots drained. When it was dry, the grain was built into loose ricks, and finally trodden out by foot. Bhutanese women, Bogle noted in his journal, 'have a hard lot of it – Besides all this [agricultural work], the

Economy of the Family falls to their Share. They have to dress the victuals and feed the Swine . . . not unfrequently one sees them with a Child at the Breast, staggering up a Hill with a heavy Load, or knocking Corn, a Labour scarcely less arduous.'[8] Bogle's interest in the condition of women was typical of eighteenth-century travel accounts; the way in which women were treated was considered a measure of a society's level of civilisation. Bhutanese women appeared to Bogle to lead lives of unremitting toil, unsweetened by amusement or adornment; they engaged in hard labour and drank strong liquor, they mixed freely and washed infrequently. This lack of feminine refinement was, for Bogle, related to Bhutanese neglect of rank: finer feelings grew out of a sense of superiority that was derived from class status. Although he enjoyed the informality of Bhutanese society, Bogle saw the unconstrained behaviour of the women as one of its flaws.

With the harvest in full swing, everyday life appeared little disrupted by the rebellion. But, the first morning at Paro, Bogle was jolted from his sleep by the sound of gunshot and the whoop of war cries. Thinking himself in the midst of another attack, his initial alarm gave way to relief when he discovered that the noise in fact announced a government victory. The head of an executed rebel was being paraded through the streets to the *dzong*. A number of rebels had been captured at Paro, he learnt. They had been variously punished: the leaders were drowned in the Pachu, their followers either imprisoned or released on payment of a fine. At Paro, too, was the armed division that Bogle had encountered on the road. They had given up their pursuit of the rebels and were now heading back to Tashichodzong.

Although it appeared little more than a collection of villages, Paro was the seat of Bhutan's most powerful district governor and the site of the only market in the country. It was famous for its blanket manufacture and metal workshops (which produced both religious statues and high-quality sword blades). The Governor, formerly a monk, was a cousin of the Regent at Tashichodzong. At the overthrow of Zhidar, he had left his monastic retreat to assume authority over the province. When he heard of the deputation's arrival, the Governor invited Bogle to an audience at the *dzong*. After the customary formalities, Bogle was presented with a sample of the local merchandise: yet more blankets – but a necessary provision for the onward journey.

Following the course of the Pachu, the route to the Tibetan border started out gently enough, but then snaked up a steep gorge. It was impossible to ride here and Bogle and Hamilton found themselves clambering over boulders, damp with spray from the river. All around the woods glowed with autumn colours, rendered more brilliant by the white of the snow above. But, as they continued to climb, the trees thinned out. At this altitude, there were no villages, and the last resting place in Bhutan was little more than a rough shelter that reminded Bogle of a stable – though without the luxury of doors. Such accommodation would have appealed even less to Hamilton, who disliked discomfort, and was more disposed to grumble than Bogle. Bundled in blankets round yak-dung fires, the travellers attempted to keep warm as snow fell through the night. The next day's journey took them along icy roads to the hilltop crowned with prayer flags and cairns that marked the Tibetan border.

Lying before them now was the Tibetan plain of Phari, a stony expanse that appeared unimaginably wide after the confined valleys of Bhutan. 'The first Object that strikes you as you go down the Hill into Tibet is a Mount in the Middle of the Plain,' wrote Bogle in his journal. 'It is where the People of Pharidzong expose their dead. It happened, I hope not ominously, that they were carrying a Body thither as we came down. Eagles, Hawks, Ravens, and other carnivorous Birds were soaring about in expectation of their Prey.'[9] With timber in scarce supply and the ground frozen solid for much of the year, sky burial, which originally derived from Zoroastrian rites in Persia, was a practical option among the various methods for the disposal of the dead practised in Tibet. If the ritual filled Bogle with a sense of foreboding, then Pharidzong added to his gloom. 'It is on every account, abundantly bleak, bare and uncomfortable,' he wrote.[10] The fortress, though impressive from the outside, was cramped and shabby within. Some eighty of the rebels from Tashichodzong had taken refuge there, despite demands for their return to Bhutan. The town, a central trading post for Tibetan wool, was huddled round the fortress in an attempt to defy the biting wind. Nobody ventured out at night for fear of the packs of half-wild dogs that roamed the streets. The houses were low and undistinguished, their flat roofs covered with drying straw and fodder. Inside, Bogle was forever bumping his head or colliding with pillars. And there was no such thing as privacy. 'The Doors are full of Holes and Crevices, through which the women and children keep peeping,' he complained. 'I used to give them Sugar Candy, and sometimes Ribbons; but I brought all the Children of the Parish upon my Back by it.'[11]

Paima, on the other hand, was delighted to be in Pharidzong. The Panchen Lama's envoy enjoyed great prestige in the town. Streams of visitors came to pay him their respects, offer gifts and cultivate their connection at court. For the first time, Bogle found himself eclipsed by a member of his entourage. In need of diversion on their final night, he dispatched a servant to request Paima's company for a game of chess. The report came back that he was otherwise engaged. The servant had discovered Paima, seated under a canopy of green silk, splendidly dressed in an outfit that had been presented by Hastings. He was hosting an entertainment for his many acquaintances and their wives – an evening of dance, drink and song.

Six other members of the Panchen Lama's staff joined Paima at Pharidzong to conduct the embassy towards the Lama's residence. All but the servants were supplied with horses, shaggy and unshod, but hardy and reliable. Riding across the gravel of the Phari plain, Bogle observed that one of Paima's servants carried a white scarf tied to a branch. Assuming that this was to announce his own importance, Bogle tried to adopt a suitably dignified posture, sitting upright in the saddle. But, to his amused chagrin, he later learnt that the flag was to honour a far greater personage than the British envoy. Stopping at a pile of stones directly in line with a sheer snow-covered peak, Paima led prayers and made offerings to the great mountain goddess, Tsheringma. The 'Ruler of the Sacred Mountain', Tsheringma both dwelt in and was embodied by the towering Mount Chomolhari, one of the fifty highest peaks in the world. At the climax of the ritual, the flag was planted upon the cairn.

For all its self-deprecating humour, this small incident points to the potential for misunderstanding across cultures. For Bogle there was always the danger that he might misread situations, that he might inadvertently cause offence. Indeed, inappropriate behaviour might offend deities as well as people (and with considerably greater consequences). Tsheringma was not necessarily well disposed towards humans. Like all gods of natural places, she was originally a pre-Buddhist deity who had been conquered in a magical fight by Guru Rinpoche, the great sage who brought Buddhist teaching to the Himalayan region in the eighth century. According to Tibetan belief, the Guru Rinpoche did not destroy the old gods but rather tamed them, converting them into protectors of the Buddhist faith. The gods' continued protection depended on the regular performance of certain rituals. It was to placate Tsheringma that Paima made his offerings; a journey was always a risky undertaking and such rituals warded off misfortune.

The following day took them around the white encrusted shore of a great salt lake, half frozen over. The area teemed with wildlife and waterfowl: hares, antelopes, ducks and geese. Bogle and Hamilton were keen to have some sport, but Paima protested vehemently: both Tsheringma and the local people would be angered by such slaughter. 'We had many long Debates upon the Subject,' wrote Bogle in his journal, 'supported on his side, by plain common-sensical Reasons drawn from his Religion and Customs, on mine, by those fine Spun European Arguments, which serve rather to Perplex than Convince – I gained nothing [by] them, and at length we Compromised the Matter. I engaged not to shoot till we were fairly out of sight of the Holy Mountain, and Payma agreed to suspend the Authority of the Game Laws, in Solitary and Sequestered Places.'[12]

Over the next few days, solitary and sequestered places abounded. Setting out at dawn and continuing always to the north, they rode through empty valleys framed by red-brown crags. 'It is Bareness itself,' Bogle wrote to his Glasgow friend William Richardson, 'and the weather being set in before I travelled through it, I saw it stark naked.'[13] The country was made more desolate still by the numbers of abandoned houses and ruined villages along the way. The area had been ravaged by war and disease, devastated during fighting between Bhutan and Tibet some sixty years previously, and most recently by

the outbreak of smallpox, the same epidemic that had caused the
Panchen Lama to retreat from his seat at Tashilhunpo. With its
alarming mortality rates, smallpox was particularly dreaded in the
region. At one house where Bogle and Hamilton lodged, all fifteen of
its inhabitants had succumbed to the disease. Wherever smallpox
struck, the uninfected would flee and the village would be placed
under strict quarantine. Victims' houses or even whole villages might
be put to the torch in an attempt to arrest the spread of the disease.
With its widely dispersed people, Tibet was visited less frequently by
smallpox than the more densely settled regions of China, but every
decade or so outbreaks would decimate the centres of population. The
Chinese system of childhood inoculation against smallpox was not
widely practised in Tibet, and there was no known remedy.

As they neared the town of Gyantse, the villages grew more
prosperous, hedged against the barren landscape with windbreaks
of willow. The villagers sang as they worked, stacking straw. Bogle
was particularly taken with one family in whose house he stayed. 'The
house belongs to two brothers, who are Married to a very Handsome
Wife; and have 3 or 4 of the prettiest Children I ever saw. They all
came to drink Tea and eat Sugar-Candy. After night came on, the
whole Family assembled in a Room to Dance to their own singing,
and spent two Hours in this Manner with abundance of Mirth and
Glee.'[14] Here Tibetan marital arrangements – so curious to Hastings's
mind that he had proposed them as a particular topic of research –
represented a kind of domestic idyll. 'Our Landlords' Family seemed
to be one of the happiest in Thibet,' affirmed Bogle.[15]

Much of this happy sociability Bogle attributed to Tibetan women.
They were treated with greater deference than Bhutanese women, he
maintained. Neither subjected to strenuous labour nor required to
carry heavy loads, they were more delicate of body and refined of
manner. They wore becoming headdresses, studded with gems, that
reflected not only their wealth and class status, but also their
husbands' attention. With their greater leisure, Tibetan women could
indulge in feminine pastimes of self-adornment, gossip 'and other
sociable Amusements' which, Bogle claimed, 'soften the Heart and
Chear the Temper'.[16]

Bogle's mood lightened further as the party entered the Gyantse valley. For the first time in Tibet, they encountered a fertile valley dotted with clusters of whitewashed houses. Dominating the scene, on a sheer outcrop, was the *dzong*. They were lodged a few miles from the town in a house fluttering with prayer flags, surrounded by a willow grove. It belonged to an amiable, elderly Gelugpa monk who some days earlier had greeted them on the road, quizzing Hamilton about a medical complaint. The two Scotsmen were installed in the temple on the upper storey, crowded with 'painted Chests, Matchlocks, Bows, Cushions, and other Lumber', with an altar in one corner, decorated with images and a lamp kept alight to dispel the darkness of ignorance. When everyone else had turned in for the night, Bogle set about the task of writing his journal. With the light failing, he confessed, he had committed a sacrilegious act. To complete the day's entry, he had 'taken the Liberty to steal some Oil' from the altar lamp.[17]

They stayed a day at Gyantse, allowing Hamilton to dispense further medical advice to their host. In the evening they were reunited with Purangir, the *gosain* whose skilful advocacy had brought them this far. He had been sent by the Panchen Lama with three further officials to accompany them on the final leg of the journey. So it was with a substantial train of attendants that the travellers wound their way the next day through the narrow streets of Gyantse, attracting crowds of onlookers. This was the largest town that Bogle and Hamilton had encountered since leaving Bengal. Situated at a junction on the roads between Shigatse and Lhasa (seats of the Panchen and Dalai Lamas respectively), and on caravan routes from Bhutan and Sikkim, Gyantse was a thriving centre of the wool trade. It was famous for its soft, fine cloth, used to make monks' vests. Wool played a major part in the Tibetan economy; exchanged for grain from western Tibet, it was the one product that made life on the high plateaux viable. But yaks, goats and sheep were not only valued for their fleece; they were also beasts of burden. Two days' journey from Gyantse, the travellers overtook a flock of more than a thousand sheep, each carrying a pair of ten-pound loads of grain. Controlled by whistled commands and sheepdogs, the sheep wore bells that allowed them to be found if they strayed. Their packs would not be removed for the duration of the trip, which might last several weeks. At night, the animals would try to find a spot to rest between two small hummocks to take the weight of the loads from their backs.

By 7 November, the embassy had reached the banks of the Tsangpo, one of the highest rivers in the world. To celebrate his arrival, Bogle knelt down to drink and wash in the water, and threw in a rupee for luck. The whole party – twenty-three people, fourteen asses, seven horses and one yak, plus baggage – was ferried across the river in a massive flat-bottomed raft. Exuberant at the prospect of an end to their journey, Bogle and Purangir raced their horses along the sandy tracks to the north. The following day, after almost a month on the road, they made their way up a narrow valley to the monastery of Dechenrubje, the modest residence of the Panchen Lama of Tibet.

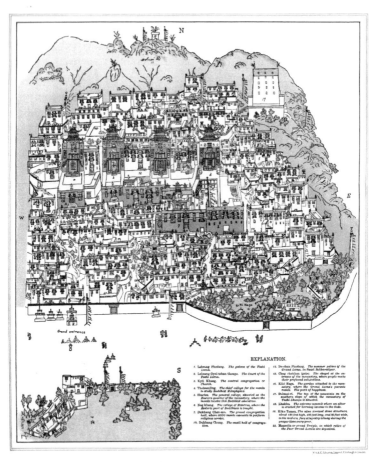

N

E

W

S

EXPLANATION.

1. Labrang Phodang. The palace of the Tashi Lama.
2. Lelzang Gyal-tshan thongo. The Court of the Tashi Lama.
3. Kyil Khang. The central congregation or Church.
4. Tashamiling. The chief college for the monks to study Buddhist Metaphysics.
5. Sharten. The general college, situated in the Eastern quarter of the monastery, where the monks recite thin Buddhist education.
6. Nag Khang. The college of Mantras, where the Esoteric part of Buddhism is taught.
7. Dukhang Chen-mo. The grand congregation hall, where 4000 monks assemble to perform religious service.
8. Dukhang Chung. The small hall of congregation.

14. De-chan Phodang. The summer palace of the Grand Lama, in Royal Selbendigar.
15. Chag chokthan igotar. The chapel at the entrance of the monastery, where people make their profound salutations.
16. Kiki Naga. The garden attached to the monastery, where the Grand Lama's parents reside. The place of happiness.
17. Dolma-ri. The top of the mountain on the southern slope of which the monastery of Tashi Lhunpo is situated.
18. Lhakha. The extreme summit where an altar is erected for burning incense to the Gods.
19. Kiku Taman. The nine storied stone structure, about 150 feet high, 100 feet long, and 60 feet wide, on the western face a tapestry is hung during the prayer time every year.
22. Mausolia or grand Temple, on which relics of the Four Grand Lamas are deposited.

W. & A. K. Johnston, Limited, Edinburgh & London

The Monastery of Tashilhunpo, Tibet

II

Tibet

1774–1775

GOD'S VICEGERENT

The monastery of Dechenrubje was tucked away in a side valley. It made an ideal retreat from the threat of contagion, and for the three years of the smallpox epidemic it had been home to the Panchen Lama and his entourage. Just two storeys high, Dechenrubje stood at the base of a steep hill of exposed rock. Bogle was allotted an upper-floor room, opening on to a wooden gallery that surrounded the central courtyard. Small but brightly painted, the room was 'ornamented with gilded Snakes & fiery Dragons'.[1] The first day of his stay – and every morning thereafter – Bogle was woken before dawn by the chanting of monks and music from the temple. 'After this there is nothing but Timbelline & Cymbelline till the Sun goes down,' he grumbled to his cousin, Mrs Morehead.[2]

Breakfast arrived in the form of a yellow-robed monk bearing bowls of rice and chopped mutton, twisted rolls and tea from the Panchen Lama's own table. There was no shortage of provisions; Bogle had been welcomed with pots of tea and strong spirits, sacks of rice and flour, and whole sides of dried mutton (a staple during the winter months). From the moment that he was installed in his apartment, visitors streamed through his door. For the monks of Dechenrubje, Bogle – with his pale skin and tight-fitting clothes – was an exotic curiosity. 'Being the first European they had ever seen, I had crowds of

Thibetans coming to look at me, as they go to look at the Lions in the Tower,' he wearily observed in his diary.[3]

Bogle and Hamilton's audience with the Panchen Lama was fixed for the first afternoon. From his reading of missionary reports and travel literature, Bogle had gathered that the great incarnate lamas of Tibet were remote figures whose conduct was bound by strict ritual. One of the most popular eighteenth-century accounts of Tibet was contained in Thomas Astley's four-volume *New General Collection of Voyages and Travels* (1747). Astley summarised the findings of Johann Grueber, a Jesuit missionary who, returning overland from China in the 1660s, had spent a month in Lhasa. Grueber gathered that 'the great *Lama* sitteth in a remote Apartment of his Palace, adorned with Gold and Silver, and illuminated with Lamps, in a lofty Place like a Couch, covered with a costly Tapestry. In approaching him, his Votaries fall prostrate with their Heads to the Ground, and kiss him with incredible Veneration . . . he always appears with his Face covered; letting none see it, but those who are in the Secret: that he acts his Part extreamly well, while the *Lamas*, or Priests, who are perpetually about him, attend him with great Assiduity, and expound the Oracles that are taken from his mouth.'[4] In a letter to George, Bogle's sister Mary put the common European view more pithily: 'one thing in Particular was believed, that the Lama of Thibet was not allowed to open his mouth but sat like a statue, and his approbation was only found out by the moving of his Hand or by the Nod of his Head.'[5] Such conduct would make Bogle's task virtually impossible: how to hold negotiations with a mute icon? Could the British envoy be expected to demean himself by kissing 'the Lama's great Toe'?[6]

When finally ushered into the audience chamber, Bogle and Hamilton approached the gilded throne with some trepidation. But Lobsang Palden Yeshé – the Third Panchen Lama, abbot of Tashilhunpo monastery and incarnation of Amitabha, Buddha of Boundless Light – received them with a smile.

In his mid-thirties, short and plump, the Panchen Lama was seated cross-legged on a pile of cushions. He wore monastic robes, a sleeveless yellow jacket and matching satin shawl across his shoulders. On his head was a tall, yellow *pandita* hat, rising to a peak, with long, red lappets falling over the ears. The Panchen Lama was flanked by two of his closest advisers: the chief minister, the Sopon Chumbo, or cup bearer, and his physician, holding sticks of burning incense. Setting the embassy's gifts on the floor, Bogle delivered the customary white scarf, a pearl necklace and the Governor's letter into the Panchen Lama's hands. The two Scotsmen were then conducted to carpet-covered stools and invited to join the Lama for tea, and eat from the array of food spread before them.

Far from remaining mute, the Panchen Lama opened the conver-sation in Hindustani, a North Indian language that he had learnt from his mother, who was probably a princess from Mustang, briefly married to the King of Ladakh. Although the Lama's Hindustani was somewhat rusty, and Bogle's pronunciation hampered by a guttural 'R', they managed to communicate with each other. 'I endeavoured,' Bogle wrote, 'to confine myself within the Compass, and to imitate the Phraseology of his Language; and so we made it out very well.'[7] After courteous enquiries after the Governor's health and Bogle's journey, the Lama proceeded directly to the issue that had first prompted him to write to Hastings. The Bhutanese Desi, Zhidar, he said, had been wrong to invade Cooch Behar and provoke conflict with the East India Company; indeed the Lama had attempted to dissuade him from military action at the time. In responding to his call for peace, the British Governor had pleased the Panchen Lama and performed a pious deed. The Governor had also shown his friendship through his kind treatment of the Lama's envoys, Purangir and Paima, who were 'only little men'.[8]

In reply, Bogle sought to justify the British part in the recent war as a necessary precautionary measure. By invading Cooch Behar, Zhidar had threatened the neighbouring British provinces, he said. It was from motives of self-defence that the Company had sent troops to support the deposed ruler of Cooch Behar. The Governor had been delighted to receive the Panchen Lama's peace proposals and was happy 'to cultivate the Friendship of a Man whose Fame is known throughout the World, and whose Character is held in Veneration among so many Nations'.[9]

The Panchen Lama then returned to the subject of Zhidar, con-cerned that his presence in Tibet might prove an obstacle to amicable relations. Bogle was doubtless aware, he said, that Zhidar had himself been deposed and had claimed refuge with the Lama. The British, Bogle responded, were not concerned with Zhidar's individual fate, only that the Bhutanese should remain peaceably within their country in the future. Drawing the formal discussion to a close, the Panchen Lama diplomatically reconciled both parties' positions: ' "The Governor", said he, "had Reason for going to War; but as I am averse from Blood shed, and the Booteas are my Vassals, I am glad it is brought to a Conclusion." '[10]

With the declarations of amity over, the Panchen Lama could begin to find out more about the ruling power represented by Bogle. Was the Company a king? What was Bogle's position in the Company? What was the name of Bogle's land? Could he repeat that? Again? He'd heard that England was an island. Was it near the land of the cannibals? Or located close to Ceylon? Bogle responded as best he could to this barrage of questions. The Panchen Lama may have been trying to understand Bogle's information in terms of traditional Buddhist cosmology; the only way to conceive of lands beyond the known Asian world of Jamudvipa was as islands in a great encompassing ocean. As in Europe, remote countries were populated with man-eaters. Bogle must have been disconcerted to find Britain so close to cannibal lands.

Just as Bogle carefully noted the Panchen Lama's attire, so too did the Lama. Bogle recorded a little drama over the protocol of dress. 'He desired me to put on my Hat. I declined it in his Presence. He said the Chineze wore their Hats before him, and insisted that I should. I just put it on and took it off again.'[11] Then, after advising Bogle to wrap up warm and to rest after the rigours of his journey, the Lama brought the interview to an end by placing a white satin scarf around his visitor's neck. 'I took leave,' wrote Bogle in his journal, 'much-satisfied with my Reception.'[12]

The first meeting augured well, but Bogle still feared that he and the Company were regarded with suspicion. The Panchen Lama, for his part, wanted to repair the damage done by his initial refusal to admit the British delegation. If, as reported, the Company were a formidable military power, it would be better by far to have them as allies. At their second meeting, two days later, the Panchen Lama set about

explaining his reluctance to grant Bogle entry. With apparent
candour, he went straight to the point.

> 'I will plainly confess', said he, 'that my Reason for at first refusing you
> Admittance was that many People advised me against it; I had heard also
> much of the Power of the Fringies [Europeans]; that the Company was
> like a great King, and fond of War and Conquest, and as my Business and
> that of my People is to pray to God, I was affraid to admit any Fringies
> into the Country. But I have since learnt that the Fringies are a fair and
> just People. I never before saw any Fringies; but am very happy at your
> arrival; and you will not think any thing of my former Refusal.'[13]

Taking this as his cue, Bogle set about proving that the British were
indeed a fair and just people. He launched into a condensed history of
East India Company involvement in Bengal. Capering through a century
and a half, he gave a rosy account of the transformation of the Company
from trading partner to ruling power. Bengal had profited from the
blessings of commerce and the British had exercised the greatest military
restraint. The Company only ever resorted to arms for purposes of self-
defence, and over the past decade the British had not attempted any
expansion of their territory. He ended with a flattering acknowledgement of the Panchen Lama's influence: 'The Governor is above all things
desirous of obtaining your Friendship and favour. As your Opinion is so
generally and so justly regarded in this part of the World, he is sensible
how much the Character of the English is in your Hands; and that their
good or bad name depends greatly upon your Judgement.'[14]

The Panchen Lama, in his turn, was equally keen to demonstrate
the strength of his new-found confidence in the British. To cement his
assurances of friendship, he told Bogle of his desire to revive the
ancient connection between India and Tibet. From around 700 CE
when Buddhism was first introduced into Tibet, many Tibetans had
made the difficult journey to India to acquire religious training and
study Sanskrit, the language of the Buddhist scriptures. In Bengal
alone, there had been a number of monasteries to accommodate them
during their stay. But, with the conquest of North India by Muslims
from Central Asia during the eleventh and twelfth centuries, Buddhist
institutions had come under devastating attack. The final blow had

been dealt in 1192 by the forces of Muhammad Ghuri: monasteries and temples were demolished, monastic lands were confiscated, and the monks were either killed or dispersed. By the end of the twelfth century, Buddhism had ceased to exist as an organised religion in India, and the monastic link between Tibet and India had been violently severed. The Panchen Lama believed however that there were still communities of surviving Buddhists in India. In this, he was following the teachings of Taranatha (1575–1634), an influential scholar of the Jonangpa school of Tibetan Buddhism whose work included a history of Indian Buddhism. For the Panchen Lama, it would be a tremendous religious achievement to reopen regular communication with India. It might even lead to a revival of Buddhism in the land of its birth.[15] In Bogle he saw the means to realise this ambition. ' "I wish", says he, "to have a Place on the Banks of the Ganges, to which I might send my People to pray." '[16]

Delighted by this expression of trust in the British, Bogle eagerly assured the Lama of the Governor's compliance. Hastings, he felt certain, would be only too pleased to gratify this desire. The discussion then turned to the matter of Bogle's own faith. What was the name of his 'great Priest or Gooroo'?[17] For Bogle, this was not a welcome line of questioning. He tried to make excuses about the difficulty of translating religious terms. Above all, he did not want to be identified with the Jesuit and Capuchin missionaries who had preceded him in Tibet. Brought up in a pious Presbyterian household, he was personally unsympathetic to Catholicism. His employers, the East India Company, regarded missionary activity of any kind as potentially disruptive; missionaries might antagonise the local people and so damage trading prospects. In the case of Tibet, the most recent mission would seem to justify the Company's concerns. In 1741, six Capuchin missionaries had arrived at the court of the Tibetan ruler, Pholhanas. Initially welcomed for their medical skills, the Capuchins had quickly made themselves unpopular with the Lhasa monastic establishment. Within months of their arrival, hundreds of monks had descended on the court to protest against the missionary presence. As a result, the Capuchins lost their privileged position at court, their few converts were publicly humiliated or flogged, and the missionaries had no choice but to beat a retreat.

The Panchen Lama clearly had this episode in mind when he pressed Bogle on the matter of religion. 'He enquired if we worshiped the *Criss*, making a Cross with his Fingers, and adding that there were formerly some Fringy [European] Padres at Lahassa who worshiped the *Criss*; but they bred disturbances, and were turned out of the Country.'[18] Hurriedly Bogle explained that it was important to distinguish the various nations that made up Europe or 'Fringistan'. The priests who had been at Lhasa came from another country, spoke another language and practised a different religion from Bogle. The clergy in Britain did not travel overseas, and the Company administration in Bengal allowed complete freedom of worship, as Purangir and Paima could confirm. The British, he claimed, were tolerant and broad-minded: they 'esteemed a good and pious Man of what Religion soever he might be'.[19] To Bogle's considerable relief, this answer seemed to satisfy the Lama. 'He changed the subject,' Bogle wrote, 'and I was not sorry for it.'[20]

The Lama wanted to quiz Bogle on the European curiosities that had already found their way to his court, brought by *gosain*s or as gifts from devotees. Holding up a Chinese porcelain jar decorated with flower-laden shepherdesses, the Lama compared their features to those of his guest. The designs, Bogle explained, were for the export market, copied from European paintings by Chinese craftsmen. Among the Lama's stock of European gadgets was a French pocket compass (sent by the Qianlong Emperor, who had probably acquired it from Jesuit missionaries), a broken-down hand organ from the ruler of Benares and, most surprisingly of all, a *camera obscura* or peep-show with scenes of London. The collection of mechanical objects provided striking proof of the long reach and obscure by-ways of European commerce. For Bogle, it must have been at once reassuring and disconcerting to travel so far, only to discover views of the British metropolis.

Concluding the discussion, the Lama invited Bogle to take a turn about the room, which he understood was the European custom. '"As for me", says he, "here I sit from Morning to Night thus"; at the same time crossing his Hands before him, closing his Eyes, and primming himself up in the Figure of an Image.'[21] By assuming a prim and formal air – 'primming himself up' – the Lama transformed himself from lively conversationalist to religious figurehead.

Bogle was delighted by the Panchen Lama's easy conviviality. From their earliest encounters, he was struck by the Lama's playfulness, his engaging presence and his intellectual agility. In their discussions, the Lama ranged far and wide, displaying an omnivorous curiosity. He wanted to know everything that Bogle had to tell: about world politics and geography, about European science, technology and culture, about stars and watches and crocodiles. 'There is no following the Links by which a Conversation is joined,' sighed a bemused Bogle, as he tried to set down their exchanges.[22] On the page, the twists and turns of their conversations seemed unaccountable. What started as a discussion of European curiosities, for instance, took a most unexpected detour: the Panchen Lama 'understood we had Glasses to look at the Sun and Moon, and enquired about their Appearance. From this the Conversation some how descended to Deeps of the Sea; then got upon Pearl Fishing, and landed us at Ceylon.'[23]

Indulging their mutual hunger for information, the two men quickly grew intimate, and the Lama soon dispensed with ceremony. Attended only by his cup bearer, he would invite Bogle to join him in his apartment. Bareheaded and dressed in simple monastic robes, the Lama would sit on a chair or bench strewn with tiger skins. He might explain the significance of the silk *thangkas* that hung upon the walls, relate an amusing anecdote or comment on the colour of Bogle's eyes. Bogle was evidently flattered by the Lama's attention. Writing in his journal, he noted that 'although venerated as God's Vicegerent through all the Eastern Countries of Asia, endowed with a portion of omniscience, and with many other divine attributes, he throws aside, in conversation, all the awful part of his Character, accommodates himself to the weakness of Mortals, endeavours to make himself loved rather than feared, and behaves with the greatest affability to every body, particularly to Strangers.'[24] To his family, Bogle put the matter more plainly. 'The Lama is a short fat Man, and as merry as a Criquet.'[25] As for the earlier missionary accounts of great lamas, they were 'all a Fib'.[26]

Throughout November, the temperature steadily dropped. With no glass in the windows and only charcoal braziers for heat, Bogle found himself thinking wistfully of the glazed windows and stoves of home.

In his room, basins of water froze during the day, and the ink had to be thawed before he could write (a process which shattered several glass inkstands). Outside it was even bleaker. The only relief from the rocky hills was the odd leafless tree. There was little incentive to stir from the confines of the monastery.

Once, propelled by the spirit of scholarly enquiry and a certain grim fascination, Bogle ventured out to investigate a sky burial site. Funeral ceremonies guided the consciousness of the deceased through the *bardo*, the transitional state between death and a new rebirth, while the body itself was exposed for vultures to consume. First it was dismembered: the internal organs removed, the flesh shredded, and bones crushed and mixed with barley flour. 'I went to visit one of these sepulchral mounts,' wrote Bogle, 'and expected to find it like a Charnel House. Eagles, Ravens, and Hawks hovered over us; but not a vestige of Mortality could I see. At length I was show[n] the Spot where the Body is laid, and could observe some fresh Splinters.'[27] Climbing the mountain, he arrived at the hut of an elderly female recluse, famed for her piety. 'On the Top of this gloomy Hill, an aged Virgin had fixed her solitary abode,' wrote Bogle. 'I wanted much to see the inside of it. At last, after much Rhetoric, I got her to open the only window of her Hovel, and show her wrinkled Face and dismal Habitation.'[28] But, for all the Gothic horror of the scene, Bogle could only report that the woman offered him spirits to drink and prayers for his welfare.

With the weather starting to bite, the Panchen Lama invited the entire delegation to his apartment. After many professions of goodwill, he presented them all with outfits suited to the climate. In the Lama's presence, Bogle was magnificently decked out 'in a purple Sattin Gown lined with Fox Skins, and trimmed at the Neck and Cuffs with a scolloped Gold Lace, which . . . [the Lama] said had come from Russia; a cap of European flowered Silk Brocade, turned up with Sable, and crowned with a red Silk Tassel, and a pair of large red Leather Jack Boots'.[29] Resplendent in blue satin, Hamilton was also transformed. The servants were kitted out with sheepskin-lined tunics and boots.

Bogle loved his Tartar costume. Thoroughly insulated from the cold, he was now spared the constant stares that his European clothes had provoked. Abandoning shirt, breeches and stockings, he went everywhere in furs. 'You have no Idea how comfortably warm they are,' he told his sister Martha. 'If you were to cover yourself with all the Broad Cloth in Sir Samuel Fludyer's ware-house, and make Fires like the Bonfires on the King's Birth Day, you would never, I am convinced, enjoy the same kindly Heat as when clad in Siberian Fox Skins.'[30] Indeed, he continued to Martha, Tibetan clothing was altogether more practical and flattering than that of home. 'The Caps of the Thibetians, faced with Sable, are also much better adapted to a rude Climate than our Hats which are not only uncomfortable but unbecoming, and their Boots in point of Warmth have the same Advantage over our shoes and Stockings.'[31] Taking the inadequacies of European dress as his theme, Bogle inveighed against the 'number of bindings and Ligatures in the Men's Attire', the constraint of women's stays and close-fitting clothes in general.[32] Such garments were 'far colder in cold weather, and hotter in warm weather, than loose and wrapping Cloathes, and as to their being unbecoming, there cannot be a stronger Proof of it than the fondness of Painters, who ought to be the best Judges of this matter, to draw their Figures in flowing Garbs or fancied Habits'.[33]

Bogle's attack on Western clothes as restrictive, ugly and impractical suggests his increasing distance from European customs. As he later explained to Hastings, he planned to 'gain Confidence and conciliate Good will' by respecting local codes of conduct: 'I assumed the Dress of the Country, endeavoured to imitate their Manners, to acquire a little of the Language, drank a Deluge of Tea with Salt and Butter, eat Beetle in Bootan took Snuff and smoked Tobacco in Thibet, & would never allow myself to be out of Humour.'[34] What began as a strategy to win acceptance seems to have developed into a genuine enthusiasm for Tibetan ways.

Nearly two weeks after his arrival at Dechenrubje, Bogle started to talk business. 'My chief Object had hitherto been to remove the Impressions which Teshoo Lama [Panchen Lama] had received to the Prejudice of the English,' Bogle wrote in his journal. 'It was now time I should open to him the purpose of my Mission.'[35] The Governor, Bogle told the Lama, was concerned at the decline in trade between

Bengal and Tibet. He hoped that a free and mutually advantageous trade might be opened between the two countries. As the Lama and the Governor were now united in friendship, 'the Inhabitants of their respective countries might be so in Trade'.[36]

Although the Panchen Lama was primarily interested in establishing a religious house in Bengal, he was quite prepared to discuss commercial matters with Bogle. Long-distance trade supplemented the income that the Gelugpa order derived from its vast landed estates. Most profitable were the trading missions to Peking. In alternate years, the Panchen and Dalai Lamas sent envoys to the Emperor bearing tribute: religious images, relics and rosaries. In return they received presents – gold-plated tea caddies, silver bells and bolts of satin – but, more importantly, the envoys enjoyed the right to trade. At the frontier towns they purchased vast quantities of those twin staples of Tibetan life: tobacco and tea. The fruits of this trade could be seen in the spectacular buildings and gilded images of the great Gelugpa monasteries and, less visibly, in their moneylending activities. For Tibetans, there was nothing incompatible about the pursuit of commerce and religion. Pilgrims, en route for a couple of years, would barter their way round sacred sites, and religious festivals coincided with fairs. As a later traveller put it, 'the monks of Tibet, though cloistered from the vulgar world, have a nice sense of business.'[37]

The Panchen Lama attributed the decline in trade with Bengal to the warmongering of his neighbours. In Bhutan, at least, the situation was now more peaceful. Zhidar's activities were at an end: the former Desi had recently been placed in confinement at Gyantse for fear that he might incite the Bhutanese to rebel. But the Gurkha ruler of Nepal, Prithvi Narayan, was now threatening Sikkim. It had been Prithvi Narayan's appetite for conquest, financed through exorbitant tax demands and fines, that had driven merchants and *gosain*s away from Nepal in the first place. If Nepal were still not a viable route for the Tibet–Bengal trade, then perhaps Bhutan could be explored.

In a few weeks, the Lama planned to leave his retreat at Dechenrubje to return to his main monastery of Tashilhunpo. The threat from the smallpox had subsided and it was time for the Lama to resume his position at the seat of power. At Tashilhunpo, he told Bogle, he would be able to make enquiries about trade and discuss the Company's proposal with his own officers, merchants and representatives from Lhasa. As Bogle 'had come so far a Journey, and had been sent by the Governor', the Lama 'would be ashamed if . . . [he] were to return with a fruitless Errand'.[38] Would Bogle, the Lama asked, care to accompany him on his ceremonial progress home?

TO TASHILHUNPO

The sky was still dark when the cavalcade began to assemble in front of the monastery. Bogle and Hamilton had been woken long before dawn on the day of the Panchen Lama's departure. The date, 7 December, would have been chosen as auspicious for astrological reasons, but as the two Scotsmen waited outside in the early morning the cold was so intense that Bogle feared frostbite. The preparations for the Panchen Lama's journey had been elaborate; it was no simple matter to orchestrate the court's removal. The official train numbered more than 150 men, all mounted on white horses. And then there was the ceremonial paraphernalia: drums, trumpets, banners and bells. A pathway of cloth was laid upon the ground, leading from the Lama's apartment down to the steps where his horse was waiting.

When the Panchen Lama emerged, he was dressed in a yellow sleeveless jacket and monastic robes. On the steps, he exchanged his scholar's hat for a fur-trimmed riding cap. Four men steadied his horse as he climbed into the saddle. A cloak of yellow satin, lined with fur, was draped around his shoulders. Finally the signal was given for the procession to leave.

Heading the cavalcade was the standard bearer, his yellow silk banner playing in the wind; then eight mounted drummers and four trumpeters. Next came fifty horsemen, some in yellow sheepskin caps and crimson coats, others in fur hats and satin gowns, followed by four lamas in monastic robes. In the midst of the procession, shaded by a silk umbrella decorated with strings of coral, rode the Panchen Lama. His closest ministers followed, and, behind them, the two Scotsmen. 'I had the fourth place from the Lama allotted to me,' Bogle boasted to Martha.[1] He was pleased to precede the envoys from the Raja of Benares and the Lama's own nephews. Bringing up the rear were a further hundred horsemen.

Crowds of devotees had gathered to pay their respects to the Lama. Some of them had erected shrines and lit fires by the roadside. The horsemen at the front cleared the way, none too gently. As the Lama passed by, the faithful prostrated themselves three times. The procession had covered half a mile when a great shout rang out from behind them, followed by two more. Wheeling round to face the monastery, the riders acknowledged the farewell cheers of the monks.

The court party advanced at walking pace along the valley, keeping to the banks of the Sang Chu river. Before their departure, the Panchen Lama had enquired if Bogle and Hamilton wished to join the procession or travel separately. He had heard that they liked to ride fast (probably, Bogle imagined, a report of his earlier races with Purangir) and feared that they would find the slow pace trying. By no means, Bogle assured the Lama; he wished to 'attend his Stirrup'.[2] It was his aim to show the Lama every respect; to have a place in the procession was a public sign of favour. Always alert to the fine distinctions of rank and status, Bogle carefully noted down the order of travel in his journal. He laid out the procession as a list, centred on the page, with a separate entry for each participant or group. Stretching down the sheet – just as the cavalcade trailed down the road – the list captured in its very form something of the spectacle of the procession.

At sunrise the Lama's party halted an hour for tea at a small encampment by the road. Tents of white canvas patterned with blue flowers afforded some protection against the cold. The next stage of the journey took them past further crowds to lunch at a hill-top convent which housed two of the Lama's nieces. To honour the Lama, the nuns all filed past. 'Many of them were young and well-looked,'

Bogle couldn't help noticing, 'but their dress, which is the same as the Gylongs [monks], is very unbecoming,' he added, 'and the want of their Hair is a great want.'[3]

From the convent, it was only three miles (and one tea-break) more to Tashitzay, the Panchen Lama's birthplace. A nobleman's residence built high on a hill, the house was large and handsomely proportioned from the outside, but a warren of smoke-blackened rooms within. Tashitzay was home to a remarkable family. At least four great incarnate lamas, belonging to two different orders, had been discovered within its ranks. The Panchen Lama's mother bore three sons to different husbands and all the sons were recognised as incarnate lamas.[4] One of the Panchen Lama's brothers was the Shamar Trulku, the Ninth Red Hat Lama, a high incarnation within the Karma Kagyu school. The Panchen Lama's half-brother, the Drungpa Trulku, was a Gelugpa incarnate and treasurer at the Panchen Lama's court. And one of the Panchen Lama's nieces was the incarnation of Dorje Phagmo, the 'Thunderbolt Sow', one of the few female incarnate lamas in Tibet. This extraordinary cluster of incarnations suggests the concentration of religious authority within particular sections of the Tibetan nobility.

The Panchen Lama himself had been born on the eleventh day of the eleventh month of Earth-Horse year (1738). According to his Tibetan biography, multiple rainbows arched over the sky to proclaim his birth.[5] At eight weeks old, he lisped the sacred syllables, *om mani padme hum*. As an infant, he took delight in the sight of monks and by the age of three was engaged in constant devotions, never joining in the time-wasting games of ordinary boys. News of this paragon reached the monastery of Tashilhunpo and the *dronyer* or chief administrator came to investigate. On the pretext of bathing in a nearby hot spring, the *dronyer* conducted enquiries into the family history and the circumstances attending the birth of the child. He then visited the house equipped with ritual objects that had belonged to the Second Panchen Lama – a rosary, bell and *dorje* (diamond sceptre) – and several decoy sets. With the array of items spread before him, the infant unerringly chose those that had been the Second Panchen Lama's own. 'This excellent manner of acquitting himself established beyond doubt the identity of his soul with that of the late Panchhen,' the biography recorded.[6]

Once an oracle had confirmed the selection process, the Seventh Dalai Lama gave the child the new name of Lobsang Palden Yeshé. The three-year-old was carried in state to Tashilhunpo. Perfume filled the air and a shower of flowers fell from the sky, the biography related. His enthronement was attended by envoys sent by the Manchu Emperor, the Dalai Lama, various Mongol princes and Pholhanas, the ruler of Tibet. To honour the new Panchen Lama, they presented precious ritual items and lavish gifts of gems, silk, satin and silver.

Every stage of the Panchen Lama's upbringing and monastic training was carefully supervised. Twice during his childhood, at the ages of eleven and fourteen, he travelled to Lhasa to stay for six months to receive tuition from the Dalai Lama. It was customary for the Dalai Lama to oversee the education of the Panchen Lama and vice versa, depending on which of the two incarnates was the elder. In ideal circumstances, there would be a considerable age gap between the two Lamas, so that when one was a child, the other could act as his teacher and as the leader of the Gelugpa order. Under this dual system of leadership, power could shift from one incarnation line to the other, but when both attained their majority, the Dalai Lama was always considered the senior partner.

The status of both incarnates was unexpectedly transformed by events which took place during the Panchen Lama's childhood. In 1747, when the Panchen Lama was nine years old, the Tibetan ruler Pholhanas died. Under Pholhanas's nineteen-year rule, Tibet had been closely allied to the Manchu regime in China, but with the accession of his younger son, Gyumey Namgyal, the Manchu alliance was placed under severe strain. Gyumey Namgyal deeply resented the presence of the two Manchu *amban*s or residents, and wanted to see an end to the Chinese garrison in Lhasa. He aimed to train up a Tibetan army of his own and started to correspond with the great Manchu adversary, the Zunghar Mongols. In November 1750 the *amban*s learnt of these plans and decided to take immediate action. They invited Gyumey Namgyal to their residence to receive a letter and gifts from the Emperor. Arriving with only two attendants, the unsuspecting Gyumey Namgyal was easily overpowered and killed. As news of the assassination spread, riots broke out over Lhasa. After a night of violence, the Chinese death toll numbered over a hundred – including the two *amban*s. But this reversal was only temporary. In the aftermath of the uprising, Manchu authority was asserted uncompromisingly. The leaders of the riots were executed and the Chinese garrison reinforced. More importantly, the whole edifice of secular rule was dismantled. In 1751 the Qianlong Emperor issued an edict stating that henceforth the Dalai Lama, assisted by a council of four ministers, should assume full temporal authority over Tibet. He simultaneously proclaimed a Chinese protectorate over Tibet.

Successive Qing emperors had found it expedient to act as patrons of Tibetan Buddhism to reconcile the Tibetans and Mongols to their rule. Through the support that they offered to the Gelugpas, the Manchu conquerors hoped to secure their hold on a remote and potentially unstable border region. This was typical of Qing policy throughout the empire. Originally a nomadic people, engaged in agriculture and hunting, the Manchus depended on the skills and assistance of the peoples whom they had conquered to run their empire. By absorbing the cultural practices of different ethnic groups into a rich eclectic mix, they aimed to maintain control over their vast dominion.

While they honoured the high lamas of Tibetan Buddhism, the Manchu emperors regarded them as political subordinates. The Tibetans, however, considered such patronage to be an acknowledgement of the exalted status of the Dalai and Panchen Lamas. From the Tibetan point of view, the Lama was the spiritual teacher of the patron, and the patron was obliged to offer protection and material support to the Lama. Both parties believed that they could claim the superior position in the relationship; both parties considered themselves the beneficiaries of the arrangement.

Qing involvement in Tibetan Buddhism may have been motivated by political expediency, but the Qianlong Emperor's interest seems to have gone further, nourished by his friendship with Chankya Rolpae Dorje, the chief Lama in Peking. Since childhood, Chankya had been closely associated with the Manchu imperial family and remained the Qianlong Emperor's religious tutor, confidant and adviser on Tibetan matters. He was the only lama to be accorded the title Teacher of the Kingdom by the Emperor.[7] Together they studied Tibetan texts and philosophy. Chankya was even said to have bestowed Tantric initiations on the Emperor.[8] These acts of devotion may – or may not – have been pure statesmanship on Qianlong's part. It is always hard to disentangle the personal from the political in the case of the Emperor. Certainly his public demonstrations of his piety were on a monumental scale: he established monasteries and temples and commissioned works of scriptural commentary and translation. The most important scholar engaged on these projects was Chankya himself, who supervised the translation of Tibetan texts into Manchu and Mongolian.

Chankya also had a more directly political role to play. Whenever there was a crisis in Tibetan affairs, the Qianlong Emperor would consult him. In 1750, following the uprising against the Chinese in Lhasa, Chankya had dissuaded the Emperor from imposing direct rule on Tibet and advocated the appointment of the Seventh Dalai Lama as civil and religious leader.[9] With the death of the Seventh Dalai Lama in 1757, the Emperor decided to install a regent at Lhasa to oversee the government. He dispatched Chankya to Tibet to help search for the Dalai Lama's reincarnation and smooth the transition to rule by regent. In the course of a two-year journey that combined devotion with negotiation, Chankya transmitted imperial edicts, reported back on the situation and met all the prominent figures in Tibet, including the Panchen Lama.

The same year that the Regent was appointed, the nineteen-year-old Panchen Lama took his final monastic vows. It fell to him to supervise the selection and education of the Eighth Dalai Lama. Now that he was fully ordained, the Panchen Lama enjoyed far greater prestige than the Regent. During the childhood of the Eighth Dalai Lama, the Panchen Lama had every opportunity to build up his position and influence in Tibet and beyond.

At Tashitzay, the Panchen Lama had returned to his ancestral home, the seat of his power. The whole valley and surrounding villages – previously part of the Dalai Lama's estate – had been granted as his own. Everyone turned out to greet him. For two days the locals danced out their welcome, the men in colourful costumes, the women hung with amber, coral and pearl. In one dance, some thirty performers moved slowly round in a ring, accompanied by their own singing and clapping. Five men in the middle 'twisted round & cut Capers, with many strange and undescribable motions', noted Bogle.[10] When the dances began to pall, clowns or *atsaras* entertained the crowd with irreverent jokes and ribald comments. Like court jesters or licensed fools, they were allowed to mock everything that was generally held in greatest reverence. 'We had singing, Dancing & Merry Andrews in the Court of the House where the Lama was born,' Bogle wrote to Martha. 'My room looked into it and used to be full of People from Morning till Night.'[11]

Among the visitors crowding into Bogle's room were the Panchen Lama's two nephews, the Pung Cushos, who formed part of the official escort, and their two sisters, the nuns who lived in the convent nearby. Bogle was charmed by the easy-going manners of the two young noblemen. After so long in clerical circles, he found them refreshingly relaxed. The Pung Cushos were about the same age as Bogle and shared similar interests: hunting, smoking, singing, music-making and drinking. The nuns, for all their piety, provided equally lively company. Bogle was particularly taken with the younger sister, who was 'about nineteen, and well-looked', he told Mary, 'having a Complexion as fair and as ruddy as a milkmaid'.[12]

The two days of festivity were brought to a close with a ceremonial benediction. Seated under a canopy, the Panchen Lama dispensed his blessing to hundreds of devotees. The next morning, in the bitter hours before sunrise, the entourage regrouped to continue the journey. Retracing its steps along the valley of Tashitzay, the procession now headed towards the Tsangpo river. After a day's slow journeying through brilliant light and bleak landscape, Bogle was cheered by an invitation to visit the Panchen Lama at the evening encampment.

The Panchen Lama's tent was distinguished from the others by its size, magnificence and warmth. Measuring some sixty feet in circumference, it was crowned with panther skins outside and lined with crimson satin within. Opening the conversation with polite chat about the weather, the road and the construction of his tent, the Panchen Lama turned to matters of more pressing political importance. Gurkha troops from Nepal had recently invaded the border kingdom of Sikkim, he told Bogle. One of Tibet's tributary states, Sikkim had appealed to Lhasa for assistance. The Panchen Lama did not know whether the Regent would authorise military aid, but feared that war with Nepal was brewing.

Nepal's Gurkha ruler, Prithvi Narayan Shah, would be a formidable opponent: he had assumed authority in Nepal through the conquest of neighbouring kingdoms. Bogle already knew something of the rapid expansion of Gurkha power. In recent years the East India Company had offered support to Prithvi Narayan Shah's rivals in an abortive attempt to halt his progress (in 1767 a small British force had succumbed to disease mid-campaign). Ineffectual though it was, British military opposition simply confirmed Prithvi Narayan Shah in his hostility to the East India Company, and when Bhutan was embroiled with the British over Cooch Behar in 1773, Prithvi Narayan Shah willingly sent a force to Zhidar to help fight them.

It was this same Gurkha army that was responsible for the present incursion, the Lama told Bogle. Denied passage across Sikkim, the soldiers had never reached Bhutan. For a year, seven thousand Gurkha troops had remained massed on the Sikkimese frontier. Now they had crossed the border to occupy large parts of the country. By invading Sikkim, the Panchen Lama said, Prithvi Narayan Shah had breached a promise to the Lhasa authorities not to threaten Tibet or its tributary states. 'But,' added the Lama, 'Gorkha is a most faithless and most ambitious man that lives, and it is his way never to have above one enemy at a time, speaking fair to all the world besides, and as soon as he has defeated one power he immediately quarrels with another.'[13] With such an aggressive neighbour, the Panchen Lama may have felt increasingly attracted to the idea of an alliance with the East India Company. How better to ward off an attack from Nepal than by the threat – however remote – of intervention by a European ally?

Leaving the carpeted comfort of the Panchen Lama's tent, Bogle returned to his own. The Lama's readiness to keep him up to date with regional affairs was heartening: to be treated with confidence was certainly an asset in the diplomatic game. But it was also something more, for trust tends to be reciprocal, and from the very start Bogle had been captivated by the Lama's frank and genial manner. He had grown to respect the Lama's opinion and always enjoyed their conversations. Less cheering by far was the prospect of his overnight accommodation. With only a double layer of canvas for insulation, Bogle stoked up a large yak-dung fire and wrapped himself in sheepskin and furs. In the morning, he checked the thermometer, kept safely stowed in the linen basket. The mercury had barely shifted from the bottom of the scale.

That day's ride took them to the Tsangpo. As they neared the river, the riders could make out great crowds gathered on both banks. While the official party repaired to tents for a meal of mutton and tea, the horses were ferried across in large flat-bottomed rafts. After lunch, the Panchen Lama descended to the river on a pathway of cloth, inviting Bogle and three of his closest ministers to join him for the crossing. With the boatmen pulling on their oars, the ferry nosed its way across the broad stream through sheets of floating ice.

In the evening Bogle was summoned once again to the Panchen Lama's tent. It was necessary, the Lama said, to equip Bogle after the fashion of the country. First there was a Tibetan harness for his horse: a thick stuffed saddle with a high peak of gilded iron and a bridle with gilt buckles and bit. Then there was a yellow satin robe with black fur facing for Bogle himself. This was a high honour indeed – although Bogle may not have been aware of the garment's significance. In Tibet, the colour yellow carried religious and political meaning. It was both the colour of the Gelugpa order and a Chinese imperial shade. Under the codes that regulated dress, only top officials were allowed to wear yellow. Through the gift, Bogle had been assigned an elevated place in the court hierarchy. The Scotsman and his mount would now be fittingly attired, 'for', the Lama said, 'you are to go into my Capital Tomorrow'.[14]

The final three miles of the route were lined with crowds in their holiday best, singing and dancing. After so long an absence, the Panchen Lama was coming home. Festivity rather than reverence was the order of the day. To the music of trumpets, drums and bells, the cavalcade wound beneath the towers of Shigatse *dzong*, standing high above on a ridge, dominating the town beneath and the surrounding valley. Then Tashilhunpo opened up to view.

More monastic town than monastery, Tashilhunpo spread across the lower slopes of a steep hill. Whitewashed walls, dark-red façades and elaborate gilded roofs rose in tiers against the bare rock face. Clustering round the Lama's residence were the other monastic buildings; colleges, warehouses and granaries separated by narrow alleyways, temples and mausoleums ornamented with gold, glinting in the sun. To greet the Lama, three thousand monks had assembled outside the palace. Gathered in the palace forecourt, many of them had fixed large pieces of checkered cloth to their clothes, while others played cymbals and drums. When he could ride no further, the Lama dismounted to walk slowly through the complex, stopping now and then to smile at the crowd. The monks bowed low as the Lama passed but, tilting their heads up a little, followed his progress with their eyes. 'There was a look of veneration mixed with sheer Joy in their countenances, which pleased me beyond anything,' wrote Bogle. 'One catches affection by Sympathy, and I could not help, in some measure, feeling the same Emotions.'[15]

THIBET VOCABULARY

A line of shaven heads peered down at Bogle from the skylight. In the ceiling of his apartment was an opening to let in the air and wintry sunshine. The more curious of the monks would climb on to the roof outside to catch a glimpse of the foreigner below. Arranged in the room beneath were Bogle's trunks and travelling chairs, but the luggage only took up a corner of the great, pillared hall. Some fifty feet long by thirty wide, Bogle's room was part of a newly built wing of the Panchen Lama's residence. It would be his home throughout the winter months, until the road down to Bengal was passable once again. Like much of the palace interior, the hall glowed with colour: the walls were plastered green with bands of yellow and blue, the wooden pillars streaked red to appear fluted, and the capitals and ceiling beams 'curiously carved, gilt and ornamented with Festoons of Dragons and Flowers'.[1] The clay floor shone like marble, polished by a young monk who 'every morning gets his Feet upon two woollen Cloths, and exercises himself for three or four hours in Skating about the room'.[2]

For many of the monks the roof-top view was not enough. At all hours visitors came calling. Some wanted to consult the surgeon about their ailments and made their way to Hamilton's room ('much smaller and warmer than mine', Bogle observed).[3] But most came simply to

view the Europeans and their furniture. 'I never forebad anybody,'
wrote Bogle, 'and after giving them a pinch of Snuff and indulging
them with a look at the Chairs &c, which always produced an
Exclamation of "Pah pah pah, tze, tze, tze!", they used to retire
and make way for others.'[4]

A few days after their arrival at Tashilhunpo, the Lama invited
Bogle and Hamilton to attend a grand audience in the main reception
chamber. The Panchen Lama's throne was placed on a dais in an alcove
at the far end of the hall. Elevated still further by a pile of yellow satin
cushions, the Lama presided over the assembly. Ranged beneath him
in order of precedence were the court officials and emissaries sent by
other powers. Bogle advanced respectfully towards the throne, made
three deep bows and presented the customary white cloth to the Lama.
Ever conscious of the significance of gesture and place on ceremonial
occasions, Bogle noted that he was favoured with two minutes of the
Lama's conversation, was served tea from the Lama's own golden
teapot (a privilege accorded to few), and was seated on a cushion level
with one occupied by the envoy sent by the Dalai Lama. Hamilton had
a less exalted position near the door.

The two Scotsmen watched as hundreds of people came to pay their
respects. There were crowds of ordinary men, women and children;
streams of monks and nuns; local castle governors, Mongol pilgrims,
and devotees from the eastern province of Kham. Tashilhunpo was a
great centre of pilgrimage; people travelled for months to circumam-
bulate the monastery (the particularly devout prostrating themselves
repeatedly to measure out the route with their bodies). The most
fortunate would receive the Panchen Lama's personal benediction.
They came equipped with presents according to their status: purses
filled with silver and gold, religious images, bundles of incense, whole
sides of dried mutton, packages of tea, bags of rice and flour, simple
white cloths. In turn they filed up to the throne for the Lama's
blessing. Monks and high-ranking laymen received the Lama's hand
directly on their heads, nuns and people of the lower orders had a cloth
interposed, while the heads of the most humble (including babies
strapped to their parents' backs) were brushed with a tassel on a stick.

Between benedictions, the Lama and assembled dignitaries took tea.
Entertainment was provided by a troupe of young boys, clothed in

colourful chintzes and brocade, who leapt and twirled to the music of pipes, bells and drums, beating time with small axes. Pairs of monks conducted theological debates in various parts of the hall. Debating formed an important element of Gelugpa training, and over their years of study monks would memorise scores of arguments and refutations. Traditionally, disputation was accompanied by a set of stylised gestures. The proposer would stand and emphasise his question by shouting, clapping his hands or stamping his feet. The respondent would sit to hear the question, then jump to his feet to answer. 'Religion was the Subject of their debates, perhaps the Immortality of the Soul, or the unchangeable Nature of Right and Wrong; but my Ignorance of the Language rendered them quite unintelligible to me,' wrote Bogle. 'They were carried on with much vociferation and feigned warmth, and embellished with great Powers of action, such as clapping Hands, shaking the Head, &c.' With characteristic irony, Bogle added, 'These Gestures are no doubt very improper and ridiculous, because they are quite different from those used by European Orators, who are the true Standards of what is just and what is graceful.'[5]

The festivities concluded with dinner. Six low tables were covered with painted wooden platters heaped with mutton (dried, hashed, boiled and roasted), pounded rice, biscuits, sweets, treacle cakes and dried fruit from China and Kashmir. 'The meat was tough and sinewy,' Bogle complained, 'but the Lama presently sent me a Leg of most excellent boiled Mutton off his own Plate, and smilingly beckoned to me to eat of it.'[6]

The day of ceremonial was the first of many at Tashilhunpo. During his stay Bogle calculated that he must have spent at least a fortnight attending festivals and services. When the Panchen Lama was to officiate at one of the many temples, a small tent would be erected for Bogle on the temple's flat roof where he could retire from the ritual for a couple of hours. The rest of the time was spent seated cross-legged, looking down on proceedings from an upper-floor gallery. Although he never declined an invitation, Bogle found little diversion in temple visits and festivals. To amuse himself, he watched the faces of the participants, struck afresh by the looks of rapt devotion fixed on the

Lama. But before long his attention would wander. 'I have not yet reconciled myself to the sitting cross legged on a Cushion, which it is necessary to do on those publick Occasions,' he grumbled to Mary, 'and am much subject to sleepy feet.'[7]

Matters theological held scant appeal. For Bogle, the religion practised in Tibet was in some way connected to Hinduism, 'though', he confessed in his journal, 'I will not pretend to say how'.[8] To his mind, the two faiths were not distinct but shared many of the same deities, texts and sacred sites. But the issue was too complex and confusing to be explored in any depth. 'In short,' Bogle concluded, 'if the religion of Thibet is not the offspring of the Gentoo [Hindu], it is at least educated by them.'[9]

More to Bogle's taste were speculations on the possible influence of Tibetan religion on Christian culture. Like the missionary writers before him, Bogle saw many parallels between the institutions of Tibetan Buddhism and Roman Catholicism. Both popes and high incarnates were considered infallible and held in great veneration; both exercised spiritual authority over vast tracts of land. But – Bogle could never resist an anti-Catholic jibe – only lamas led exemplary lives and exerted a benign and pacific influence. The list of resemblances between the two faiths seemed unending: 'Celibacy of the Clergy, the Foundation of Monasteries and Nuneries, the vows taken in their religious Houses, the merit of Pilgrimages, the Shaving of the Heads, the Counting of Beads, the Burning of Lamps and Incence, the Mattins Vespers &c., the manner of chanting the offices, together with the Form of the Censors, Cap and other parts of the Dress'.[10] While missionary writers saw such parallels as evidence of ancient Christian influence in the region and considered Tibetan Buddhism a debased version of Christianity, Bogle suggested that the influence might work in the opposite direction. 'In endeavouring to account for this amazing uniformity,' he wrote, 'I am sometimes led to think, that as many of the Barbarous Natives who conquered the Roman Empire came from Russia and Siberia and were consequently Votaries of the Lamas, they imported their Rites and Ceremonies, into Europe, which were afterwards either adopted or allowed by their Pastors in order to reconcile them more eagerly to Christianity.'[11] With this conjecture, Bogle casually undermined the origins and pedigree of the whole Christian tradition.

The longer that he stayed in Tibet, the more Bogle started to question European values. Much of his spare time was spent playing chess. He found a worthy opponent in Depon Patza, a Tibetan general who, having campaigned hard on the chessboard, was ordered to Lhasa the following day to receive his command of 18,000 men bound for Sikkim and the occupying Gurkha force. The general's place was taken by a succession of Tartar pilgrims. 'They have no Idea of our unsociable Method of playing,' Bogle wrote to his cousin William Scott. 'When a Siberian sits down to Chess he gets surrounded with three or four of his Countrymen who lay their Heads together and consult with him about the Propriety of every move. I had nothing for it but to engage an equal Number of Tartars on my Side and to combat them with their own Weapons.'[12] From his experience of communal matches, Bogle concluded that chess might have had a Tartar origin. 'Let no man say they are too rude and too stupid a People to find out so ingenious a Game,' he cautioned Scott.[13] For English-speakers, Tartars were associated with uncouth violence: to call a man a Tartar was to suggest that he was rough and irritable, to call a woman one, that she was shrewish. But Bogle began to challenge these notions. 'If I may judge by those I have seen and by what I have learnt, they merit a very different Character. They are merry, acute, good humoured and possess that plainness and honesty of manners which I prize before all others.'[14] The Tartar stereotype, Bogle argued, was born out of European cultural arrogance: 'But they are to be reckoned Barbarians by us Upstart sons of three Hundred Years because they know nothing of Greek and Latin, of Painting or Sculpture, and are ignorant of all those frivolous Arts which "occupy and distinguish polished Nations".'[15]

Bogle ended his defence of Tartar values with a dig at one of the great figures of the Scottish Enlightenment, the historian William Robertson. The reference to 'polished Nations' was a quotation from Robertson's discussion of the benefits of commerce.[16] Like many of his contemporaries, Robertson maintained that trade had a civilising effect on societies. Commerce between nations, he argued, nurtured peace and wore away prejudice, encouraged law and order, softened and refined manners. But Bogle had little time for social polish. Championing bluff Tartar honesty over refinement, he implicitly questioned the value of commerce. At the same time he managed to ignore his own role as trade envoy and the implications of Robertson's argument: that over time his commercial activities might inculcate the social graces even among the Tartars.

That Bogle dared to challenge a renowned figure such as Robertson – historian, Principal of Edinburgh University and leader of the Church of Scotland – was a measure of his confidence. He wrote with the authority of experience, while Robertson had never ventured outside Britain. During his stay, Bogle gradually amassed a great store of information on Tibetan life. Unlike his companion, Hamilton, he had all the makings of a gentleman scholar. Endowed with the patience, application and intellectual curiosity that Hamilton lacked, he embarked on a wide-ranging study of Tibetan culture. The breadth of his enquiries can be gauged from the categories of his 'Thibet Vocabulary', a book of nearly forty pages, filled with transliterated Tibetan entries and their English equivalents. The subjects covered included Dress, Arms, Parts of a House, Furniture, Utensils, Manufactures, Of Books and Writing, Of Government & Professions, Pastimes, Customs & Religion.[17] It was the product of many hours spent closeted with monks, learning Tibetan.

No subject was too humble to escape Bogle's attention. Admiring the construction of Tibetan butter churns, he sent his sister Annie a detailed description so that one might be made for the Daldowie dairy. The Tibetan design, he imagined, might ease the labours of the dairymaid: 'I have often observed with Concern the pains which Doll is forced to take in making Butter, how she is obliged to call in the Assistance of the Lads – and after all if a witch upon her broom has happened to fly over the Dairy in the Night time or there be but an evil Eye in the whole Country Side it is all labour in vain. Now if my journeyings can any way help to release Dolly from all her wayward Toils, how happy would it make me.'[18] It was five years since Bogle had been at Daldowie, but his vivid reminiscence demonstrated that he still shared his sister's house-keeping concerns. Written from such a distance, descriptions of domestic life served to connect George with home. A solution for Doll's supernatural problems, he suggested, might also be found in Tibet: 'I am sensible that still the Kirn may be planet struck or elf shot, but as the people in this Country are well skilled in Charms and Incantations, I will make it my business to find out some proper Spells – and will afterwards communicate them.'[19]

If he did not fulfil his promise to send spells, Bogle did write to Annie about Tibetan ghosts:

Like ours they show themselves only in the Night time. They come not however clad in a winding sheet and a white Face, but in bare Bones as Death appears to the Man with the Bundle of Sticks in Esop's Fables. They have blood red Eyes which shine in the Dark. But the period of their Appearance is not unlimited like Captain Weer's Spirit or the one at Mrs Corbet's Bleachfield who are allowed for Generations to visit the Glimpses of the Moon, and frighten us Sons of Men. They are permitted to walk the Earth only during the Interval of their Transmigration, that is between the Time that the Soul leaves one Body till it enters into and animates another which is a Space of forty nine Days.[20]

Playful as it is, this exploration of popular belief reveals Bogle's interest in comparing the two cultures. From his Tibetan informants, he must have learnt something of the intermediate state of *bardo*, the forty-nine-day period between death and rebirth, when the mind can travel wherever it wishes attached to a kind of ghost body (visible only to clairvoyants). To communicate this concept to his sister, Bogle invoked the supernatural in more familiar guise: the ghost of Major Thomas Weir, executed for witchcraft, riding through Edinburgh streets on a headless black horse. Through the parallel, the Tibetan belief appears neither more nor less fanciful than the Scottish one. Above all the comparison reveals Bogle's desire to investigate every aspect of Tibetan life – and death.

With the winter months before him, Bogle had ample opportunity to fulfil Hastings's instruction to observe and gather information. He broadened the scope of his enquiry by quizzing the many different types who gathered at Tashilhunpo on commercial, diplomatic or spiritual business: Kashmiri merchants, envoys, *gosain*s and wandering holy men. From the emissary sent by the Raja of Benares, for instance, he learnt about the Marathas and the region bordering Nepal, and from Kashmiri traders based in Lhasa about Kashmir, eastern Tibet and China. In his idiosyncratic and haphazard way, Bogle amassed anthropological notes on the customs of peoples right across Asia.

Bogle was less successful in his attempt to further negotiations about trade. The Panchen Lama had promised that when he reached Tashilhunpo he would discuss Bogle's proposals with representatives from Lhasa. Both the Dalai Lama and the Regent had sent envoys to Tashilhunpo to greet the Panchen Lama on his return. A few days after their arrival, they paid Bogle a visit, bearing gifts from Jampel Delek, the Regent: barrels and boxes of Chinese delicacies. Inside, Bogle discovered, were strong spirits, small cakes, fish ('less than a Minnow dried') and mushrooms. 'The Fish we could never find out how to dress,' complained Bogle, 'but the Mushrooms served greatly to improve the simple and unsavoury Economy of our Table.'[21] Despite this gesture of amity, the envoys did little but repeat the old arguments against opening Tibet up to East India Company trade: it was contrary to ancient custom and, although the Regent would do all he could, the country was subject to the Manchu Emperor. 'This is a stumbling Block which crosses me in all my Paths,' wrote Bogle in exasperation.[22]

Why was the disapproval of the Emperor invoked so frequently? Suspecting that it was just a pretext masking the Regent's distrust of the Company, Bogle quizzed the Lama on the Regent's disposition. Jampel Delek had indeed 'received such Accounts of them [the British] as raised his Suspicions', the Panchen Lama said, ' "and", added he, "his Heart is confined, and he does not see things in the same view as I do" '.[23] But surely the Panchen Lama was the chief of the country during the Dalai Lama's minority? Wouldn't the Regent follow his advice? Bogle received no direct answer from the Panchen Lama on the nature of his authority; his questions touched on the fraught relations between Tashilhunpo and Lhasa. The relationship between the two competing seats of power could not be reduced to a simple hierarchy. The Lama, however, assured Bogle that he did not doubt that he would succeed in reviving trade between Bengal and Tibet once the current conflict with Nepal was settled, 'but that it might require a year or two to do it effectually'.[24] Two years was too long for Bogle. Thanking the Panchen Lama, he pointedly explained his situation: 'being sent by the Governor upon this Business I could not help being zealous for its Success; that it depended on him whether I should return to Bengal happy and crowned with Reputation, or covered with Shame.'[25]

At the end of December, the Lhasa envoys came to take their leave of Bogle. Since their initial encounter, there had been no further meetings between them, despite Bogle's requests for one. Would they be so good as to carry a letter to the Regent? No, came the unexpected response, not if it concerned trade. They would be happy to carry a mere letter of form, thanking Jampel Delek for his gifts, but any mention of business, and it would go undelivered. Bogle was shocked. No conversation in Tibet had caused him such concern. He had worked so hard to establish trust, apparently to no avail. He was still suspected of being a spy, a plotter, a troublemaker. Even his letters were dangerous. He applied for an immediate audience with the Panchen Lama. But the Lama's assurances that the envoys were only 'little Men and knew no better' did not pacify Bogle.[26] He retorted that the envoys' behaviour pointed to the Regent's continuing suspicions. 'God was my Witness,' swore Bogle, 'that I wished him [the Regent] well, the Lama well, and the Country well, and that a suspicion of Treachery and Falsehood was what I could not bear.'[27] It was a most undiplomatic outburst.

THE BUSINESS OF A TRAVELLER

A negotiator should above all avoid losing his temper: so advised the diplomatic manuals of the time. Patience was a highly desirable quality in an envoy, the Dutch diplomat and historian Abraham de Wicquefort reflected, and if it did not come naturally, then it should be cultivated.[1] By venting his exasperation, Bogle had broken a cardinal diplomatic rule, but in refusing to take his letter the envoys had also infringed European diplomatic codes. One of the jobs of an ambassador, according to Wicquefort, was to maintain a good correspondence between heads of state: to deliver letters and solicit answers.[2] Of course, earlier in the mission Bogle had himself refused to receive delivery of the letter from the Panchen Lama to Hastings denying his party entry to Tibet. But if he recognised the tactic, it would only have added to his sense of frustration. If he could not correspond with Lhasa, how could he possibly perform his role? The finer points of the Tibetan political system also eluded him. Who exactly was in charge of matters of trade and foreign policy?

To soothe Bogle, the Panchen Lama said that the Regent's rule would be over within a couple of years. The Dalai Lama would then be of age, and the government should revert to him. But for now, persisted Bogle, how should be approach the Regent? Could he read the Panchen Lama a draft of the letter that he wanted to send? Most certainly, came the response. But, once again, Bogle had not entirely mastered the Tibetan idiom. ' "Every Country", quoth the Lama, "has its particular Manner of writing. If you please I'll write a Letter for you." '[3] Bogle accepted the offer eagerly. The Lama dictated a short letter of formal compliment and thanks, slipping in a brief mention of trade:

> I have received the Chineze Wine, Fish, Mushrooms, Biscuit &c. that you were so good as to send me, in great Abundance, and all very good of their kinds. May your Country enjoy Tranquility and yourself Happiness. I request in the name of the Governor my Master, that you will allow Merchants to trade between this Country and Bengal. I have sent you a Gun, a piece of Broad Cloth, and a Handkerchief, which you will please accept of.[4]

When Bogle applied to the Lhasa envoys the next day, he found them willing to carry the letter. The Lama had evidently exerted some pressure.

Bogle's hope was that the Lama's good offices would win the Regent round. He felt increasingly certain that he had gained the Lama's confidence. Here at least he had succeeded in establishing those relations of trust so essential to negotiation.[5] For, despite their very different cultures, beliefs and stations in life, the two men had much in common. Both were intellectually curious, good-humoured and astute. From the long conversations recorded in Bogle's journal, they evidently relished each other's company.

But, in the light of the friction between the Panchen Lama and the Regent, it might be worth pursuing other contacts with Lhasa. Shortly after he had arrived at Tashilhunpo, Bogle was approached by a man who said that he had been sent by the Regent. He was known as the Chauduri, an official from one of the small hill kingdoms near Nepal. He had been at Lhasa, he said, where the Regent had shown him great favour and had deputed him to visit Bogle. According to the Chauduri, the Regent was far from suspicious of Bogle. Indeed so delighted was he at the prospect of friendship with the Company that he proposed to send the Chauduri as his envoy to accompany Bogle on his return trip to Calcutta. At a subsequent meeting, the Chauduri

went so far as to promise the Regent's ready consent to the establishment of a Company trading base at Lhasa and, if the Governor so
wished, the introduction of the Bengal rupee into Tibet.

More than encouraging, the Chauduri's remarks were completely at
odds with everything that Bogle had learnt of the Regent from other
sources. His claims were supiciously extravagant. Should he be
believed? The Lhasa envoys said not, but gave no reason for their
warning. Bogle decided to be enthusiastic in return, but make it clear
that he would mention the matter to the Panchen Lama. 'I was
perhaps wrong in this,' wrote Bogle, 'and a Man more artful than
myself, knowing too the little Cordiality that there was between
Gesub [the Regent] and the Lama, might perhaps have carried on his
Negotiations with Chowdry, without communicating them to the
Lama. But I must own, in my small Experience through life, I have
always found Candour and plain Dealing to be the best Policy.'[6] But
Bogle's openness was not without calculation: 'I had no notion of
running the Risque of forfeiting the Confidence of one, who, I had
every Reason to think, was well disposed towards me and my
Constituents, in order to take the chance of opening, through an
uncertain Channel, a Connection with a Man who I believed entertained no very favourable Sentiments of me.'[7] Despite his doubts
about the Chauduri and his own assertions of integrity, Bogle
admitted that he held out certain inducements to promote Company
interests: he gave 'some personal Promises' to the Chauduri and at
least considered 'making him some Presents' – what we would now
call bribes.[8]

When informed of the Chauduri's activities, the Panchen Lama
decided to write to the Regent for clarification of the Chauduri's
status. In his reply, the Regent denied any connection with the
Chauduri. He had never given him a commission to Bogle, he wrote,
indeed he knew the man only by sight. Could the Lama send the
imposter back to Lhasa immediately? But the Regent's disclaimer did
not clear the matter up for Bogle, who had been following his own line
of enquiry. 'I confess I was equally at a loss to reconcile this Letter with
the Intelligence I had received,' he puzzled. 'For although I gave little
Credit to the Chowdry's vaunting Discourses; I had been informed by
all the World that Gesub [the Regent] had made him a present of

between four and five thousand Rupees, and could hardly think he would be so generous to a Man he had only seen once, merely for his Beaux yeux.'[9] It seemed probable that the Chauduri was indeed the Regent's agent, sent to sound Bogle out, to discover the extent of the Company's ambitions in the region. In that case, it would have been impossible for the Regent to acknowledge him publicly. On his return to Lhasa, Bogle imagined, the Chauduri would have been debriefed rather than punished.

Surprisingly, the Chauduri returned to Tashilhunpo some months later. 'I was on the Reserve; so was he,' recalled Bogle.[10] In their conversation, the Chauduri aimed 'to let himself down softly, and to do away every thing he had before said'.[11] The Regent was well disposed towards the Company, the Chauduri reported, but concerned not to offend the *ambans*. There was still some talk of sending the Chauduri to Calcutta, but only after the rains. However, the Regent had still not replied to the letter about trade that the Lama had written on Bogle's behalf. 'I had full Opportunity to have reproached him for his fruitless Promises about procuring me an Answer from Gesub [the Regent], of his confident Assurances of being sent with me to Calcutta, and so taken some Revenge upon him for deceiving me. But what good Purpose would it have served?' asked Bogle.[12] 'I therefore took leave of him with fair, but guarded Words.'[13] The affair was never satisfactorily resolved for Bogle, but remained a potent reminder of the need to watch his diplomatic step: to appear trusting and trustworthy, but never to trust too far.

Even in his dealings with the Panchen Lama, intimate and convivial though they were, Bogle felt that he should tread carefully. He was always aware that he was under scrutiny. On one occasion, the Lama offered him a highly desirable map of Tibet, full of the detail missing from European atlases. 'This was a splendid Object,' declared Bogle, 'and to obtain it I was sensible would reflect much Lustre on my Commission.'[14] But, much as he longed for the cartographic prize, diplomatic thoughts came crowding in.

I considered that the Company could have no Interest in this Country but that of Commerce; and that to know a number of outlandish Names, or to correct the Geography of Thibet, although a matter of

great Curiosity, and extremely interesting to Geographers and Map-
sellers, was of no use to my Constituents, or indeed to mankind in
general, and that to this I might be sacrificing Objects of far greater
Importance, by encreasing that Jealousy which had hitherto so cruelly
thwarted me in all my Negotiations.[15]

So, affecting indifference, Bogle thanked the Lama for the kind offer,
but declined the map. Since the British were not interested in Tibet
from a military point of view, he elaborated, the lie of the land was no
concern of theirs. Were he to accept the chart, he said, he would give
the Regent grounds for suspicion. But the Regent would never find
out, urged the Lama. He could not answer for that, came the reply. Of
far greater interest, continued Bogle, were the laws and customs of
Tibet, 'as every Country excelled others in some of these Particulars, it
was the Business of a Traveller to inform himself of those, and to adopt
such as were good.'[16] Pleased by this response, the Lama promised to
supply Bogle with all the information that he desired. Bogle, in his
turn, offered to write the Lama an account of Europe. And so, the two
men – equally eager to increase their stock of knowledge – entered
into a remarkable pledge of cultural exchange.

The process of writing and translating the account of Europe was far
harder than Bogle had anticipated. He started with an initial draft in
English which was then translated into Tibetan. He had to contend
with the interpreter, 'a kind of Being who is generally more apt to
follow out roundly his own Ideas, than to keep strictly to yours'.[17]
Indeed at every stage, Bogle had to write with Tibetan notions in
mind. 'I had to fancy myself a Thibetian,' he remarked, 'and then put
down the things which I imagined would strike him.'[18] How could he
describe the institutions and customs of Europe in comprehensible
terms? What would appear familiar and what curious to a Tibetan
readership? Would they approve of European ways?

Like Gulliver in Jonathan Swift's great satire *Gulliver's Travels* (1726),
Bogle found himself having to account for European ways to a ruler from
an entirely different society. Turning first to Britain, Bogle spent time
trying to explain the hereditary monarchy, the role of parliament, trial by

jury and the navy (a novelty to a people living at such a distance from the sea). London he described as a city of stone and brick with paved streets and houses supplied with water from lead pipes. Transport for the upper classes was by four-wheeled carriage; a method which allowed one to travel at speed and in comfort over considerable distances. 'These carriages are generally well painted and gilded,' Bogle wrote, 'they have glass windows, and are hung upon springs to make them easy, so a Person can eat sleep read or play at Chess.'[19]

Education in Britain was not restricted to the clerical class and even some of the peasants could read. For printing, the British used movable type (rather than wooden blocks). Every day a paper of news was printed and distributed. To study works on government, philosophy and law, the upper classes learnt Latin and Greek – the language of Alexander the Great. The physicians of Britain were renowned, wrote Bogle. Every large town had houses where the sick were tended at the public expense. Surgeons acquired their skills at the sick houses and through the dissection of dead bodies. Some seventy years earlier, inoculation against smallpox – that great scourge of Tibet – had been introduced from Turkey and epidemics no longer swept the land.

To amuse themselves the British played at cards, danced at assemblies and visited the theatre. 'There is a large Hall where everybody sits one above another for the advantage of seeing, at the End of this there is a Stage with Cloths painted so as to represent Rooms woods Mountains Rivers &c. Upon the Stage is represented some Story; those that are intended to make people laugh are called Comedies, those that are intended to make people cry are called Tragedies.'[20] To illustrate a tragic plot, Bogle appended a summary of Thomas Otway's play, *Venice Preserv'd*.

Bogle's act of imaginative identification led him to criticise his own country. 'Having mentioned many of the good Customs of England, I shall now write on some of the bad ones,' he declared.[21] Although the legal system was fair, many offences carried the death penalty (as opposed to the Tibetan system of levying fines). The manners of the people could in certain respects be improved: drunkenness was widespread, both among country gentlemen and among the lower classes, and gaming was a particular vice of the wealthy. 'And there is a Custom which although I am ashamed to mention I must not conceal.

It is called duelling.'[22] The idea of spilling blood in the defence of honour was rendered ridiculous in the attempt to explain it: 'There is no Reproach to an Englishman so great as to say you lye. If a Man is detected in a Lye no body will keep Company with him, everybody shuns him as an infected Person. If any Man says to another you Lye, he challenges him to fight him in single Combat. They settle the Time and Place where they are to meet, each Man goes with a Sword, attended with one friend to look on and see that every thing is fair, the two Persons fight untill one of them is disarmed is wounded or is killed.'[23]

In viewing his own country from a Tibetan perspective Bogle was adopting a device more commonly found in fiction. In *Gulliver's Travels*, British society appears increasingly absurd in the accounts delivered by Gulliver to a range of overseas monarchs, little and large. By the time of his final voyage to the noble Houyhnhnms, Gulliver has disowned his own society entirely, in favour of Houyhnhnm ways. While Bogle did not aim at satire, his descriptions of British institutions certainly made the familiar appear strange. Given that he was writing as the Company's official envoy, it is extraordinary that he allowed himself the licence to criticise Britain at all. Generally he was concerned to promote the country. Britain, he claimed, never waged war but by necessity and never plundered its enemies. The people were allowed to follow whatever religion they pleased. The country abounded in crops and livestock and was famed for the excellence of its manufactures.

Bogle's national bias was particularly evident when he crossed the Channel. The French, he observed, enjoyed none of the freedoms of the British; they were subject to absolute rule, oppressive taxation, a corrupt legal system and religious persecution. They professed the same faith as the missionaries who had formerly been at Lhasa. 'The People of France,' he commented, 'are very merry and more polite than the English but are much given to Flattery and not so sincere. They dance better than the English but their Musick is not so good. They are more fond of Dress and Show – the Men all powdering their Hair, and many of the women painting their Cheeks red.'[24]

Holland fared much better in his account. The Dutch were free, industrious and sober. The country had grown wealthy through trade.

Its towns and houses were so clean that 'one might eat off the Streets'.[25] But, after a fleeting mention of Flanders, the grand project that Bogle had envisaged faltered. With no reference books to hand, he had to rely on his own (and Hamilton's) experience and memory. Writing about Britain was easy enough, but when he reached Continental Europe, Bogle had to draw on his youthful travels in France and his father's reports of studying at the University of Leiden in Holland. Beyond that, his knowledge grew distinctly hazy and when he reached the borders of the German principalities, the account abruptly gave out.

After weeks of work, Bogle decided to present the Tibetan version of the account to the Lama. Unfinished as it was, the account 'afforded a great feast' to the Lama's 'insatiable Curiosity'.[26] Much of the friendship between the two men was based on the exchange of information, on the intellectual excitement of mutual discovery. The Lama read the first part of the account in Bogle's presence. The Lama – like Bogle – would have been faced with the difficulty of comprehending the material presented to him. Both men would have relied heavily on intermediaries like Purangir to act as cultural go-betweens, to explain one society to the other. The process of cultural translation would involve drawing parallels between the societies that might sometimes illuminate, sometimes distort. When presented with new information, both the Lama and Bogle searched for points of correspondence between the two cultures. The Lama's initial response to Bogle's account was to compare British and Chinese forms of government. Although 'the former Emperors of China, like the Kings of England, used to do nothing without the Advice of their Councils', the Lama commented, 'the present Emperor was extremely tyranical and put every one to Death who opposed his Will.'[27]

Much as the Lama was interested in the politics of the contemporary world, his primary concerns were spiritual. Some of the information presented by Bogle was put to a use that the Scotsman would never have imagined, let alone have understood. Later that year, the Lama would write a book about the land of Shambhala, a text that would become an authoritative guide to this mythical realm. In the Kala-chakra tradition, the land of Shambhala is both an ideal and an actual place. As an ideal, it is the intermediate place between *samsara* (that is, the cycle of rebirth and suffering) and *nirvana* (liberation from rebirth and suffering), and it may be attained in a state of meditation. As an actual location, it is situated somewhere north of the Himalayan range. It is extremely difficult to reach, and the journey is fraught with dangers, both natural and supernatural: the traveller must cross vast deserts, forests full of wild beasts, mountains inhabited by beautiful goddesses, demons, flesh eaters and hungry ghosts. Only those who are neither tempted nor terrified may reach the perfect land of Shambhala. Ringed by high snowy mountains, the lotus-shaped kingdom is filled with sandalwood forests and lakes. At its heart is the capital with palaces made of gold, silver and jewels. The ruler is benign, and the people beautiful, healthy, virtuous and wise.

In his guidebook, the *Explanation of Shambhala together with a Narrative of the Holy Land*, the Panchen Lama drew on traditional texts to describe the magical hazards and symbolic trials encountered en route to the hidden land. But at least half the book was devoted to the geography of India, the holy land of the title. The Panchen Lama made use of material provided by his various informants, Bogle included. Bengal, he wrote, is ruled by the British, who arrived first as merchants and then extended their territory. Under the secular rule of British law, he observed, every man is allowed to follow his own religion. The British king is hereditary and lives on an island in the sea.[28] In this small way, the Panchen Lama incorporated Bogle's narrative into the Kalachakra tradition. He also asked the Scotsman to assist him further in his spiritual studies. In his journal Bogle bemusedly noted the Panchen Lama's request that, on his return to India, he should 'enquire particularly about the Situation of a Town called Shambul [Shambhala], about which he said the Pundits of Bengal would be able to inform me'.[29]

For his part, Bogle was given lessons in the rudiments of Tibetan law, history and cosmography. The Lama sent him papers on various subjects and dispatched monks to explain them. Bogle was an assiduous student. Learning about the penalties for murder, for instance, he carefully recorded nine social categories – from high lamas to landless craftsmen – and a sliding scale of fines payable as compensation to the victim's family, ranging from the weight of the corpse in gold to varying quantities of flax, barley and butter. Tibetan common law was based on ten moral precepts laid down in the seventh century by Songtsen Gampo, the first Tibetan king. Bogle listed the precepts in transliterated Tibetan, before offering a translation. Like the Lama, he was quick to draw parallels between cultures. Noting the precepts' similarity to the Judaeo-Christian code, Bogle gave them the title 'The Ten Commandments', and followed Biblical phraseology in his translation. To a European reader they appeared instantly familiar; the first precept, for example, stated 'Thou shalt not kill.'[30]

Although he found common ethical ground between the two traditions, Bogle was most struck by the ways that the Tibetan legal code differed from the British. 'The Right of Primogeniture unknown, the frequency of Fines, the Scarcity of Capital Punishments bears no Ressemblance to the Laws of England,' he wrote.[31] The more that Bogle found out about Tibetan law, the more he was led to reflect on British codes. Considering the Tibetan maxim that if 'a Man kills his Slave it is a great Crime if another Man kills him it is a small one', he commented that it was based on 'more generous Principles than what are to be found either in the Law of England or its West India Plantations'.[32] In the process of learning about another culture, Bogle began to question his own. 'We are so much used to admire the Laws and Customs of England and they have been the Subjects of so many Panagiricks,' he observed, 'that they are esteemed among Englishmen as the Standard of Excellence by which the Laws of other Nations are to be judged.'[33] By this stage in his travels, Bogle could no longer hold unwaveringly to this article of British faith.

LIVING LIKE A THIBETIAN

Throughout the monastery the preparations were under way for Losar, the Tibetan New Year. Everywhere monks scrubbed and swept, whitewashed and oiled. The festival, determined by the lunar calendar, fell in mid-January that year. By New Year's Eve, the night of the dark moon, the monastery had to be purged, purified and decorated. For the lay people, too, it was a period of ritual and cleansing, of patching up quarrels and paying debts, of stitching new clothes and making special Losar delicacies. The New Year was a time for the family to gather, to join in the rituals, celebration and feasting that banished the evils of the old year and welcomed in the new.

From their various homes across the country, the Panchen Lama's relatives converged on Tashilhunpo. They were lodged just outside the Lama's residence in a guesthouse surrounded by trees. A Tartar tent was pitched in the grove to accommodate the overflow. From the Lama's birthplace came his cousin, the Governor of Tashitzay, together with his wife and family. The Governor's wife had two further husbands in the Lama's young nephews, the Pung Cushos. In this largely ecclesiastical family, the Pung Cushos lived a life of leisured ease with few onerous responsibilities. Like young European aristocrats, they diverted themselves with sport and feasting, with company and song. Bogle felt that relations between the Pung Cushos and the Tashitzay Governor were somewhat strained, and the two brothers were lodged slightly apart from the other members of the family – and their wife – in the tent.

Staying in the main house were the Pung Cushos' two sisters, the charming nuns whom Bogle had met at Tashitzay. Their widowed mother, the Chum Cusho, also had an apartment there. She too had been a nun in her youth, but was required to leave the order after she had formed a liaison with the Panchen Lama's brother, then himself a monk. For years the Panchen Lama had not acknowledged the couple, but since his brother's death he had taken more of an interest in the family. Included in the family circle was another of his brother's daughters, by a different wife. Now twenty-seven, this niece was the only abbess in the country to head a male monastic institution. She embodied the deity Dorje Phagmo, the 'Thunderbolt Sow', and presided over Samding monastery near the sacred Yamdrok Lake, some weeks' journey to the east. The various members of this remarkable family were to stay at Tashilhunpo for the rest of the winter. In the months before the spring thaw, Bogle would have ample opportunity to get to know them.

The seasonal ritual began with dances. The guests joined hundreds of spectators crammed into galleries overlooking a large flagged court-yard. First came the clowns or *atsara*s chasing and tumbling round the court, mocking the solemnity of the proceedings. Then lines of monks dressed in glorious brocades processed to the music of trumpets, pipes, cymbals and drums. From a seat in the uppermost gallery, Bogle looked down without enthusiasm. Some twenty monks in animal masks danced beneath him. But the performance was hard for an outsider to follow, harder still to describe. The 'ludicrous Tricks of a merry Andrew, or the solemn dances and Ceremonies of Priests, dressed in Masquerade Habits of many Collours . . . make but a sorry Appearance on Paper', Bogle told his sister Mary.[1]

But there was one ritual that attracted his notice. Laid upon the ground was an image of a man, painted in white. After various rites, the figure was carried to a large bonfire where it exploded noisily in clouds of smoke. The significance of this ceremony remained obscure to Bogle. 'I was told it was a Figure of the Devil,' he wrote, 'but am not sufficiently skilled in the Thibetian Mythology to enter into particulars.'[2] The image did not look anything like the devil of Christian tradition, but seemed strangely familiar. 'One thing is certain,' Bogle observed with wry detachment, 'it was painted white with regular Features; and . . . I could not help sometimes fancying that it much resembled an European.'[3]

In fact the figure represented the old year's evil, and, with its ritual combustion, the New Year festivities could begin. The Losar celebrations extended over a fortnight with much feasting, visiting and drinking for the laity. Among those who came to visit the Scotsmen were groups of Mongol pilgrims. Hamilton was used to being consulted on matters medical, but was surprised to learn that his reputation now extended to other fields: 'having heard of his great skill in the occult sciences, they were come to have their fortunes told, and at the same time stretched out their hands for that purpose,' related Bogle. 'While he was hesitating whether to carry on the Joke a little further; they desired him first to tell what had happened to them last year, and then proceed to unfold their future destiny.'[4] Finding his soothsaying skills unequal to the test, Hamilton had to admit defeat.

During this period Bogle and Hamilton became better acquainted with the Pung Cushos. They often whiled away two or three hours in each other's company, either in Bogle's apartment or at the Tartar tent. Together they drank *chang* (rice beer) and smoked, listened to the elder brother play upon his flute, or sang songs to the accompaniment of the *danyen* or Tibetan guitar. To honour the Scotsmen, the Pung Cushos invited Bogle and Hamilton to a picnic on a hillside some miles outside Tashilhunpo. There were archery contests and races, displays of song and dance. 'Our friends had prepared a great Feast for us,' wrote Bogle, 'not knowing what we would like, took care to have every kind of Flesh and Fowl, they could think of. After dinner, Tables covered with Fruits were brought in, and they insisted on presenting us with dresses and Horses.' Much *chang* was consumed, and it was no easy matter for Bogle to ride his new mount home. 'I had enough ado to keep it from running away with me,' he confessed.[5]

A couple of months later, the brothers again extended their hospitality to Bogle and Hamilton, proposing a short trip to their country estate. Bogle and Hamilton readily agreed, and the Panchen Lama's consent was easily obtained. The two Scotsmen were delighted at the prospect of escaping the monastery; for too long now, their lives had been regulated by religious routine. Thankfully, the Pung Cushos' interests were decidedly secular. Hunting was their preferred pastime, but out of respect for the Panchen Lama, they refrained from the sport near Tashilhunpo. Away from their uncle's seat, though, matters stood rather differently. 'As to the Pung Cooshos,' Bogle wrote, 'they are little scrupulous about this [the taking of animal life] or any venial Sin, and so but it comes not to the knowledge of the Lama, will do anything you like.'[6]

The expedition would be relatively modest: a dozen attendants formed the Pung Cushos' train. Bogle decided that he would live 'like a Thibetian' and take only one Indian servant on the trip.[7] But it was hardly an impromptu affair; as with the Panchen Lama's progress, tents were erected at frequent intervals along the route for refreshment breaks. The first day's journey took them north towards the Tsangpo. They lodged at a headman's house in a village in the broad river valley. Arriving in the late afternoon, they were served first with tea, then with dinner. Bogle detailed the menu: 'A Cup of Hashed Mutton, not unlike a greazy Curry; another of boiled Rice; a third of raw Beef beat into a Jelly, and highly seasoned with Loll Merrick [red chillies] and other Spices. It is far from unsavoury, when one can get the better of European Prejudices. A joint of mutton well boiled, and another just scorched on the outside but quite raw within.'[8] To his brother John, Bogle explained the eating arrangements. 'There is no such thing as Spoons and Forks. Everybody carries, hung at their Side, a Chineze Case containing a Knife, two Ivory Sticks, a tooth Pick and an Ear Pick; that as the Thibetians are not like the Chineze, skilled in the management of these Sticks, their Fingers serve the purpose of Spoons & Forks.'[9] The meal was washed down with 'a dram of Brandy' and 'many quaffs' of *chang*.[10] Fruit, sweetmeats and pipe-smoking followed.

With the meal over, the evening entertainment began. Catching the last of the light, they went out to the garden for an archery contest.

The target – a black cloth painted with a small white circle – was set up at a fair distance. Those who hit the mark were awarded ceremonial scarves. 'I also received one though unmeritedly,' admitted Bogle.[11] As darkness fell, they retired indoors to sit around a fire, drink *chang* and sing, play chess or listen to the music of the *danyen*. Finally, as they headed for bed, the Scotsmen discovered yet another meal laid out for them. The Pung Cushos, concerned that Tibetan food might not be to their guests' taste, had ordered them a supper of European fare – eggs, fish and roast chicken; 'as if', groaned Bogle, 'we had not tasted meat that day'.[12]

The sun was not yet up when they were eating again. On waking, Bogle and Hamilton discovered the Pung Cushos breakfasting on tea and mutton. 'As I can always eat at any Hour of the day or night, I did not fail to partake with them,' commented Bogle.[13] Before departing, they exchanged gifts of fruit, sweets and dried mutton with their village host, who presented them with silk handkerchiefs with a small quantity of gold dust knotted in one corner. An hour's ride brought them to the first tea-stop, a tent erected on the bank of the half-frozen Tsangpo. While the party waited for the ferries that were moored on the opposite side, Bogle diverted himself by sliding on the ice of a nearby pond. This was the nearest he could come to skating – one of his favourite amusements. 'I wish I had Skates,' he had written to Bess months before, in anticipation of the winter.[14]

On the far side of the river, the sandy banks made for easy riding. With spirits buoyed by the exercise and sustained by butter tea, the young men headed on, 'now and then interchanging a Pinch of Snuff or a whiff of Tobacco'.[15] In the afternoon, the Pung Cushos halted to make offerings to a sacred mountain, leaving Bogle and Hamilton to contemplate the view. With the clear skies and sharp light, they could see for miles, up and down the valley. The wide river looped between bare, red mountains. The exposed rocks and dusty soil offered little sustenance to plant life. The area was notorious for its sandstorms; whirlwinds would rage along the valley, sucking up vast quantities of grit and, when their force was spent, would dump the sand in great mounds on the valley floor. When the deity of this inhospitable place had been placated, the party remounted their horses and turned up a side valley to the north. With one more stop for 'excellent mutton

Puffs', they completed the final leg of the journey to the Pung Cushos' seat.[16]

Darkness had already fallen when they arrived at the castle of Rinjaitzay, situated on the lower slopes of a hill, surrounded by scattered houses and a monastery. They passed through the central court, guarded by mastiffs, and ascended several ladders. The room allocated to Bogle may have been the grandest, but was certainly not the homeliest in the fort: multiple pillars supported the gilded roof, and muskets, swords, bows and arrows decorated its walls. It adjoined the prayer room, gleaming with butter lamps. The Scotsmen were greeted with heaped platters of fruit. This was just the prelude to supper, 'the Sixth Time I had seen Meat that day', reckoned Bogle.[17] It was with some reason that he warned his brother John to choose the moment when he sat down to read his account: 'if you read this Letter before dinner it may probably set your Mouth a-water'.[18]

But the exercise was as hearty as the meals. Each day of their stay brought Bogle and Hamilton a new diversion: hunting parties with dogs, or nets, or guns or bows. The quarry was equally diverse: hares, partridges and musk deer. Sometimes the prey eluded the cooking pot. The cook allowed three partridges, shot by Hamilton, 'to fly away some Hours after they were dead', Bogle whimsically noted.[19] And Bogle himself took pity on others that seemed so tame, 'it would have been a Sin to kill them'.[20] In setting the birds free, Bogle claimed that he had performed an act of great piety in the eyes of his Tashilhunpo servants. But the musk deer had a sadder fate. Taken alive as a curiosity and shut up in a closet, it died the first night in captivity.

The fort itself was something of a menagerie. In addition to packs of hunting dogs, the Pung Cushos kept a wolf chained to the foot of the entrance steps and a tiger cat on the roof. One night the whole household was roused by a terrible uproar, a great yelping and howling. Fearing intruders or worse, everyone stumbled from their beds, Bogle and Hamilton in their shirts, the Tibetans huddled naked under blankets. A bloody scene met their bleary eyes. From the light of a single lamp, they could make out that the wolf had broken free and attacked the dogs. Now the big cat was bearing down on the wolf, clawing at its face. The beasts were pulled apart and the wolf tied up.

'Each of our motley Group,' Bogle recalled, 'after looking a little at one another, returned laughing to Bed.'[21]

With its varied diversions, the week of sport passed all too quickly. It was with regret that Bogle and Hamilton took leave of their hosts. The return journey was far less relaxed than the outward one. The two Scotsmen pushed on without tea breaks through a sandstorm – to reach Tashilhunpo, after dark and exhausted, the same evening.

The Pung Cushos were not the only members of the Panchen Lama's family to strike up friendships with Bogle and Hamilton. The Chum Cusho, their mother, received Bogle at her apartment. He found her 'a cheerful widow of about five and forty, with a ruddy Complexion, and the remains of having once been handsome'.[22] She plied Bogle with tea, mutton, broth and fruit. After her husband's death, Bogle learnt, the Chum Cusho had decided to devote herself to acts of piety. Laying aside her silks and jewellery, she assumed a simple dress and went on pilgrimages to the holy sites of Tibet and Nepal. 'She is not however a Prey to Grief,' Bogle told Mary, 'but on the Contrary is one of the most jocose and facetious women I have met with.'[23] Throughout the visit, she was 'as merry as a Cricket' (the phrase echoing Bogle's description of Panchen Lama in a letter home).[24]

Seated beside the Chum Cusho were her two daughters, the nuns. Bogle noted their appearance with care. 'They were dressed in a Jacket of worseted woollen Frize, their Heads Shaven, their Arms bare from the Shoulders, a short red serge Petticoat, and woollen Hose of the same Collour, gartered under the Knee.'[25] The elder sister was about twenty-seven or eight, around Bogle's age. Her personal attractions, according to Bogle, were few. She was 'dark complexioned and hard featured', he wrote in his journal.[26] But the younger sister caught his attention. At nineteen, with her fair skin and ruddy cheeks, she conformed more closely to European standards of beauty. 'She as well as her elder sister, are very merry in common,' Bogle told Mary, 'but were on their Good Behaviour in the Presence of their Mother.'[27]

In preparation for his visit, Bogle had purchased quantities of coral beads, highly valued in Tibet. He intended them as a gift to the Lama's extended family, as an emblem of friendship, both personal

and political. He had observed that rosaries strung with coral beads
were the only form of ornamentation permitted to nuns, and hoped
that such a present would be acceptable both to the Lama's nieces and
to their devout mother. But this unexpected gift seemed somehow to
have infringed the rules of hospitality. Only after much persuasion did
the Chum Cusho and her daughters accept the coral. As for the Pung
Cushos, they were even more reluctant. 'I believe I spent an hour in
their tent before I could get them to agree to take my beads,' wrote
Bogle. '"You", said they, "are come from a far Country; it is our
business to render your Stay agreeable; why should you make us
Presents?"' [28]

Having finally accepted the coral, the Chum Cusho conducted
Bogle to meet her stepdaughter. Dorje Phagmo, one of the few female
incarnations in Tibet, was seated cross-legged on a cushion. Although
dressed in the habit of an ordinary nun, she wore her hair long, falling
loosely over her shoulders. Once he had paid his formal respects, Bogle
knelt to receive her blessing. Stretching out her hand, she touched his
head, after the manner of the Panchen Lama. But the rest of the visit
passed awkwardly. The conversation was halting, with the Chum
Cusho filling in the frequent silences. Dorje Phagmo had none of the
liveliness of her half-sisters or the intellectual curiosity of her uncle.
She spoke seldom and seemed to be suffering from some unidentified
malaise. Despite her fine features and expressive eyes, she looked 'wan
and sickly', and there was 'an expression of Languor and Melancholy in
her Countenance'. [29] Bogle attributed her listless air to her 'Sedentary
and joyless Life . . . sitting cross Legged from morning to night on a
Cushion', and only saw her the once. [30] But when Hamilton learnt of
her indisposition, he offered his medical services. Dorje Phagmo
remained his patient, receiving daily house visits for the duration
of her stay.

Bogle's relations with the two nuns were far more relaxed. Sometimes they came calling with their brothers. They were curious to see
what Bogle looked like in his European clothes and asked him to dress
up for them. Bogle modelled his coat, shirt, waistcoat and breeches.
'We prevailed on the youngest Sister to put on my Coat,' he recalled,
and 'had a great deal of Laughing and merriment'. [31] In his journal
Bogle allows us only glimpses of these high-spirited occasions: 'who

can repeat the little unimportant trifles which gladden Conversation and serve to while away the Time?'[32]

Was it possible that Bogle's relationship with the nuns went beyond teasing and flirtation? He evidently did not consider the nuns' vows of chastity as absolutely binding. Writing to Mary, he observed that Tibetan nuns enjoyed a considerable degree of freedom. 'The nuns are allowed to go abroad, where they sometimes form such Connections as puts an End to their Monastick Character, and to their Life of Celibacy.'[33] Bogle was not merely fantasising here. For some Tibetan women, particularly those of noble birth, taking orders was entirely a matter of convention (much as was the case in medieval Europe). Not all nuns strictly adhered to their vows, as the history of the Chum Cusho herself demonstrated. If a liaison were discovered, the nun would have to leave the order, but she was not heaped with disgrace. If there were no children, according to Bogle, the affair was 'seldom taken notice of'.[34]

The garden house may have held other desirable female occupants – companions or servants – who went unrecorded in Bogle's journals and letters. Tibetan society was notably tolerant of relationships between unmarried men and women. It is not clear whether Bogle was writing from experience or hearsay when he asserted that 'Tibetan women are kind, tender-hearted and easily won.'[35] All that we know is that by the following spring Bogle would be suffering from a sexually transmitted disease – probably gonorrhoea – contracted either in Tibet or in Bhutan. Following medical practice of the time, Hamilton would advise doses of salts, frequent bathing of the affected parts in warm milk and water, 'an abstemious diet . . . cooling purgatives and the application of poultices in which a small quantity of mercurial Ointment is dissolv'd'.[36]

A tradition current among members of Bogle's family suggests that he may have established an enduring relationship with a Tibetan woman. His descendants believe that he had a Tibetan wife. She is recorded in a family tree as 'Tichan sister of the Teshoo Lama' – a name that may be related to the Tibetan name of Dechen.[37] From what we know of the Panchen Lama's family, it is unlikely that Tichan was the Panchen Lama's sister, but it is possible that Bogle began a liaison with a woman while in Tibet. There is no trace of a Tibetan female companion in his journals or correspondence, but women of such ill-defined status as concubines or *bibi*s often went unrecorded, so the absence of any written evidence is not in itself conclusive. The family, knowing of Bogle's association with Tibet, may have retrospectively endowed him with a Tibetan wife, but the authentic-sounding Tibetan name makes it hard to dismiss the story simply as a romantic fabrication.

13

A LAST FAREWELL

Almost imperceptibly, the deep chill of the Tibetan winter began to lift. Throughout Bogle's stay, the skies had remained clear, but now the sun began to impart a little warmth. With the spring thaw, the route to Bengal would reopen, and Purangir and the two Scotsmen would be able to set out on their return journey. Before their departure, the Panchen Lama would have to give Bogle a final decision on the matter of trade.

The Panchen Lama wanted to demonstrate his commitment to friendship with the Company and restore former trading relations with Bengal. But he was not keen to introduce any innovations in the conduct of the trade. From all that he had gathered, the British were a rising power in India, and it made sense to cultivate the connection. Above all, he wished to reinvigorate religious links with India, the land of Buddhism's birth. But the Regent – whom he could not afford to antagonise – was steadfast in his opposition to the Company. It was a difficult, if not impossible, balancing act.

But how much longer would the Regent remain in power? In a couple of years, the Dalai Lama would come of age and, all being well, the government should revert to him. The Regent himself was neither young nor healthy. In February news arrived that he was seriously ill; some said that he was on his deathbed, if not already dead. For days he

remained sunk in a state of semi-consciousness, before slowly regain-
ing his strength. Even before this collapse, the Regent had apparently
been finding it hard to cope with the demands of office. There were
rumours that he had written to the Qianlong Emperor, requesting
permission to resign. More worrying, from the Panchen Lama's point
of view, was the suggestion that the Regent had recommended his
own nephew to succeed him. Any dynastic ambitions on the Regent's
part could only undermine the position of the Panchen and Dalai
Lamas. The Panchen Lama swiftly dispatched a spy to Lhasa to find
out if there was any truth in the story.

News also arrived of the declining health of Prithvi Narayan Shah, the
Gurkha ruler of Nepal. According to the Panchen Lama's informants, the
King's body was covered with blotches and sores. Even so, his messengers
continued to deliver threatening letters. While he did not seek a quarrel
with Tibet, the Gurkha King wrote, he was prepared for war. Invoking
his Rajput warrior ancestry and string of conquests, he desired the
Tibetans to cut all links with the Company. Bogle should be sent back
and no further Europeans admitted. Nepal would henceforth be the
channel through which Bengali goods would be conveyed to Tibet.
European curiosities would in future be banned from the region.

It was typical of the Gurkha ruler to speak with such bluster. His
troops were already courting confrontation with Tibet by occupying
Sikkim (although the Tibetan army sent to Sikkim had been forced to
turn back, finding its way blocked by snow). But then rumours began
to spread that Prithvi Narayan Shah had in fact died. It was reported
that the Newar people of Nepal had shaved off their eyebrows and
beards. This mourning rite could only mean that either the King or
his heir was dead. Confirmation of the Gurkha ruler's death followed
from a variety of sources: the Panchen Lama's informants at Lhasa, the
*gosain*s and Kashmiri traders. At Prithvi Narayan Shah's funeral, they
said, three of the King's wives and six of his concubines had performed
the rite of *sati*, throwing themselves on the burning pyre.

The Nepalese throne now passed to his eldest son, Pratap Singh
Shah. By all accounts, Pratap Singh did not share his father's
expansionist drive. The Panchen Lama hoped that, under his rule,
relations between Nepal and Tibet might improve. He would write to
the new king immediately, he told Bogle, to encourage the free

passage of merchants and goods through Nepal. Indeed signs of reconciliation were already emerging. Following the death of Prithvi Narayan Shah, the commander of Gurkha forces in Sikkim had announced a suspension of hostilities and proposed a three-year truce.

If peace prevailed and the new Gurkha king were to prove better disposed towards the Company than his father, then the south-westerly route through Nepal might once again provide a conduit for trade with Bengal. But the route running south through Bhutan looked more likely. Following their recent defeat by Company troops, the Bhutanese might be more amenable to British demands. The Panchen Lama was prepared to exert what influence he could. He had already written to the Desi to request the free passage of Company goods through Bhutan. He would send a member of his staff to accompany Bogle and Hamilton on their return journey to help with negotiations at Tashichodzong. In the meantime, as a gesture of goodwill, he would invite some of the leading merchants, both Kashmiri and Tibetan, to visit Tashilhunpo. Bogle could then explain his proposals in person to the principal traders of the region.

Given the Regent's continuing distrust of British intentions and the likely disapproval of the *amban*s, the Lama decided that there should be as little change in the conduct of trade as possible. As far as actual commodities were concerned, the earlier pattern of commerce should be followed. The caravans from Bengal should be restricted to the traditional goods: broadcloth, cottons and silks, tobacco, sugar, diamonds, pearls and coral. European mechanical devices – those curiosities that so intrigued the Lama himself – should be reserved for dignitaries alone. New-fangled gadgets such as watches and telescopes should not fall into the hands of the common people. The Manchu Emperor would be certain to disapprove and the Chinese merchants in Lhasa would complain that they no longer had a market for their goods. The Lama's conservative approach extended to personnel: no Europeans should enter Tibet to trade. In the present climate, the Lama could not think of admitting Company servants; he would have to tell Bogle that the trade could be conducted only by Asian intermediaries.

Bogle was understandably disappointed by the decision to exclude the British from direct involvement in the trade. Although Hastings had not explicitly instructed him to seek admission for Company servants, to have gained this point would have added greatly to the lustre of his achievement. Much of his future – not to mention his finances and those of his family – depended on the outcome of the mission. He had, he felt sure, managed to persuade the Panchen Lama that the British presented no threat to the region. Why, then, this obstruction? Presumably the Lama was anxious to avoid confrontation with Lhasa. But reflecting on the problems that he had encountered in both Bhutan and Tibet, Bogle had to concede that the Panchen Lama had good reason. If every Company servant were to meet with similar opposition, the trading scheme would, quite simply, be unworkable.

The Lama also requested that any envoys sent in the future should not be European. 'I will be plain with you,' he told Bogle. 'I wish the governor would not at present send an Englishman. You know what Difficulties I had about your coming into the Country, and how I had to struggle with the Jealousy of Gesub Rimbochay [the Regent] and the People at Lahassa. Even now they are uneasy at my having kept you with me so long. I could wish therefore that the Governor would rather send a Hindoo.'[1] In a couple of years, the situation might be different. If the Regent's rule were at an end and the Dalai Lama had assumed full authority, then perhaps Bogle could return.

The restrictions placed on Europeans entering Tibet did not mean that the Panchen Lama wanted to cut contact with the British. Far from it, he was eager to pursue his original proposal of founding a monastery on the banks of the Ganges, a river that he venerated after the fashion of the Hindus.[2] India was not only sacred as the source of Buddhism but especially dear to the Panchen Lama as the land where – in previous incarnations – he had lived.[3] A monastery in Bengal would be able to provide shelter to Tibetan pilgrims visiting the holy sites in India. It might also be able to make contact with those Indian Buddhists whom the Panchen Lama believed had somehow survived the twelfth-century attack on Buddhist institutions by the Central Asian forces of Muhammad Ghuri.

As the time for Bogle's departure approached, the Lama issued more detailed instructions. He had in mind a modest establishment that would accommodate monks on pilgrimage. The monastery should be built in the Bengali style, and located close enough to Calcutta for the monks to visit the Governor. The exact situation he left to the British authorities and Bengali *pandit*s. He would give Bogle a hundred pieces of gold to cover the building costs, and request him to transport the necessary images, carpets and vestments for devotional use. The Gelugpa outpost would, he envisaged, function as both a religious and diplomatic base. To supervise its construction and management he chose Purangir, his original envoy to the Governor and Bogle's valued guide.

Why would the Lama place a Shivaite *gosain* in charge of a Tibetan Buddhist monastery? Since the Panchen Lama seems to have believed that *gosain*s were the inheritors of Buddhist Tantric tradition, there would not have been an unbridgeable religious divide between the two faiths. Unlike the Tashilhunpo officials, Purangir had the necessary local knowledge to operate in Bengal. Not only did he speak the language, but he also had a sound grasp of business through the banking and trading activities of his sect. He was used to the heat of the plains (a climate considered dangerous, if not fatal, for Tibetans). More importantly, over the past year he had proved his skill and trustworthiness as a negotiator, intermediary and informant. The same could not be said of all the wandering holy men supported by the Panchen Lama at Tashilhunpo. Purangir, the Lama told Bogle, 'has served me very well, and I have not found him guilty of so many Lies as most other Faquirs, and I hope the Governor will show him favour.'[4] With Purangir installed near Calcutta, the Panchen Lama could expect regular dispatches on the political situation in Bengal. Some lingering doubts about the *gosain* may, however, have remained. The Lama requested Bogle to keep an eye on Purangir and inform him if he behaved improperly. In the event of the *gosain*'s death, Bogle was entrusted with the task of selecting his replacement.

Once established, the Panchen Lama imagined, the Calcutta monastery might attract monks from other regions. He had written to Chankya Rolpae Dorje, the chief Lama in Peking, about his connection with the British, recommending that Chankya should also send monks on pilgrimage to the holy sites in India. Once again, the Panchen Lama's rationale was partly spiritual, partly diplomatic.

Such a religious deputation, the Panchen Lama supposed, might prove the initial step towards establishing diplomatic relations between Bengal and Peking.

The Panchen Lama had first made the acquaintance of Chankya nearly two decades previously. The Peking Lama had travelled to Tibet after the death of the Seventh Dalai Lama to oversee the transfer of power to the Regent, by the order of Qianlong. He was entertained at Tashilhunpo for some three weeks. The Panchen Lama regarded him as one of his most influential contacts. 'I . . . am but a little Man in comparison of the Changay Lama [Chankya],' he told Bogle, 'for he is always in the Emperor's Presence, and has a great Influence over him. The favour which the Emperor shows to me and the Delay [Dalai] Lama, is in a Measure owing to Changay Lama's good Offices at Court.'[5] Chankya did indeed have the Emperor's ear. Over the course of a long reign, Qianlong had come to rely on his interpretation of Tibetan and Mongolian affairs. As cultural mediator and political fixer, Chankya was unsurpassed.

If a monastic deputation from Peking were kindly received by the Governor in Bengal, the Panchen Lama reasoned, then Chankya might speak well of the British at the imperial court. The Lama held out to Bogle the tantalising prospect of a route – albeit circuitous – to the Qianlong Emperor. This would be a grand diplomatic prize: no official British delegation had yet gained access to the imperial court. Bogle was at once sceptical and excited. 'I own I encouraged all this,' Bogle wrote to Hastings, 'in the view of strengthening the Intercourse and Connection with Thibet, and thinking it would be of Advantage to the Company to open any Channel of Communication with the Court of China; and although I am not so sanguine as the Lama, about the success of his Endeavours, however sincere, to obtain leave for you to send a Person to the Emperor, I do not altogether despair, by your Favour, of one day or other getting a sight of Pekin.'[6]

By the end of March, the midday temperature was pleasant enough and 'the ice melted faster than it froze'.[7] Although the earth and trees remained bare, spring was undoubtedly on its way. But the thin air meant that none of the daytime heat was retained, and the thermometer still plummeted at night.

With the change in the weather, Bogle began to contemplate his return to Bengal. Would his mission be hailed as a success? He had built a strong relationship with the Panchen Lama, of that he was certain. And he had negotiated a revival of old patterns of trade. If he had failed to gain admission for Europeans into Tibet, then that could be attributed to the opposition of the Regent. He had surely achieved everything possible, in the circumstances. But should he trust his own judgement? He knew his optimistic nature only too well: 'I am apt to be pleased, when I see others desirous of pleasing me; to think a thing is very good, when it is the best I can get, and to turn up the white side of everything. A Man more sagacious and distinguishing than myself might probably give a very different Account of his Reception in Thibet,' he confided to his journal.[8] But there was nothing for it; he would have to wait until his return to hear the Governor's views on the matter.

There had been no word from Calcutta for almost six months. Either Bogle's letters had gone astray or, as he suspected, they had been intercepted, perhaps by the Chinese. All that had arrived was a brief note, torn open, from Lieutenant Williams in Cooch Behar, and a letter from his friend David Anderson, Persian translator to the Murshidabad Council. From Anderson he had learnt of the 'late Revolution in Politicks' in Calcutta.[9] During Bogle's absence, the three new Councillors, Clavering, Monson and Francis, had arrived from Britain to form the new Governing Council, designed to act as a check on the Governor General's authority. From the very start, the new Councillors had made their opposition to Hastings clear. But Bogle comforted himself with the thought that the changes in the upper echelons could hardly touch him. 'As to myself,' he told Anderson, 'I consider my Credit as depending so much on the Fate of my present Commission, and my Rank in the Service as so subordinate, that I never dream of being affected by it.'[10]

But Anderson's letter rekindled Bogle's interest in Calcutta politics. 'I begin to be tired of the listless Life I have so long led,' he wrote to Robert, 'and wish for Society and Business again.'[11] While he presented himself as an impatient man of affairs to his brother, he showed quite another face to his sister Elizabeth. 'When I look on the time I have spent among the Hills it appears like a fairy dream,' he told Bess. 'The novelty of the Scenes, and the People I have met with, and the novelty of the life I have led, seems a perfect Illusion.' His stay in Tibet, Bess learnt, was an enchanted interlude, far removed from worldly matters. 'I may set this down as the most peaceful period of my Life. It is now almost over, and I am about to return to the Hurry and Bustle of Calcutta.'[12] As often in his correspondence with his sisters, Bogle emptied his account of all political and commercial reference. He concluded with a grand valediction that transformed Tibet into one of the mountain idylls so beloved by Rousseau (but completely ignored his own role as trade envoy):

> Farewell ye honest and simple People. May ye long enjoy that Happiness which is denied to more polished Nations; and while they are engaged in the endless pursuits of avarice and ambition, defended by your barren mountains, may ye continue to live in Peace and Contentment, and know no wants but those of nature.[13]

The last week was occupied by endless leave-takings. A constant stream of monks came to Bogle's apartment to wish him well 'with Pots of Tea, little Presents, kind Looks, and kind Expressions'.[14] The members of the Panchen Lama's family were also packing up and returning to their various homes. Dorje Phagmo had already left for her monastery near Yamdrok Lake, and the Pung Cushos were to escort their mother and two sisters back to Tashitzay. 'I this day took Leave of Chum Coosho and the two Nuns,' wrote Bogle in his journal, 'not without many Blessings and advices from the old woman, and many promises to the Nuns of writing them and sending them Lories [parrots with bright plumage] and Looking glasses.'[15] The final meeting with the Pung Cushos was more affecting. 'My parting with the Pung Cooshos was a harder Task. I never could reconcile myself to the thoughts of a last farewell, and however anxious I was to return to Bengal and to the world, I could not take leave of my Thibetian Friends with Indifference, and would now find little Satisfaction in repeating the Circumstances of it.'[16]

Bogle's farewells to the Panchen Lama lasted the entire week. A

ceremonial leave-taking was followed by daily meetings in private
where the two men discussed the details of their plans and agreements.
Last-minute requests for curiosities were made on both sides. Could
Bogle send the Lama a telescope, the skins of two lions and a crocodile?
Would the Lama procure Bogle a list of all the comets recorded by the
Chinese? Could some musk deer and shawl goats be reared in captivity
and then dispatched to Calcutta during the cold season? (Most of the
animals sent in a previous convoy to Hastings's menagerie had died en
route.) The Lama had never heard English spoken, would Bogle oblige?
Bogle recited some verses of Thomas Gray's *Elegy Written in a Country
Churchyard*. For the Lama, the choice of poem was immaterial, but it may
have held some significance for Bogle. A lament for lost rural simplicity,
Gray's *Elegy* memorialised life led 'Far from the madding crowd's
ignoble strife'. The pastoral innocence of the poem, although offered
as an emblem of Englishness, was a world away from the commercial
realities of the East India Company; indeed, it was much closer to
Bogle's idealised vision of Tibet.

'As the time of my Departure draws near,' Bogle wrote to
Elizabeth, 'I find that I shall not be able to bid adieu to the Lama
without a heavy Heart. The kind and hospitable Reception he has
given me and the amiable Dispositions which he possesses, I must
confess, have attached me to him, and I shall feel a hearty Regret at
parting.'[17] Bogle detailed the Lama's many 'amiable Dispositions' in
a letter to Hastings:

> Of a cheerful and affable Temper, of great Curiosity, and very
> intelligent. He is entirely Master of his own Affairs; his Views are
> liberal and enlarged; and he wishes, as every great Man wishes, to
> extend his Consequence. From his pacifick Character, and from the
> Turn of his Mind, naturally gentle and humane, he is averse to War
> and Bloodshed, and in all Quarrels endeavours by his Mediation to
> bring about a Reconciliation. In Conversation he is plain and candid,
> using no Compliments or Flattery himself, and receiving them but
> badly if made to him. He is generous and charitable, and is universally
> beloved and venerated by the Thibetians, by the Calmacks [Mongols],
> and by a great Part of the Chineze.[18]

Bogle concluded with a frank declaration of affection: 'I never knew a Man whose Manners pleased me so much or for whom, upon so short an Acquaintance, I had half the Heart's liking.'[19]

It is impossible to know how far Bogle's feelings were reciprocated. The Lama certainly seems to have singled Bogle out for special treatment. A monk, sent to explain matters of Tibetan law, once tried to convey to Bogle a sense of the particular favours conferred on him. ' "How propitious is your Destiny!",' the monk exclaimed, ' "among so many of your Countrymen you alone have had the good Fortune to arrive into the Presence of the Lama, and what superior advantages have you had over other Travellers who are only allowed to see him at a Distance while you are admitted into Long Conversations and he has laid open to you the Treasures of Religion and the Principles of Justice, which are hid from the rest of Mankind." '[20]

On the morning of 7 April, Bogle made his way for the last time to the Panchen Lama's apartment. Receiving the Scotsman with his customary grace, the Lama expressed his regret at Bogle's departure. Great had been his satisfaction, he declared, at learning about the customs of Europe. He wished Bogle a safe journey and promised to remember him in his prayers. His parting words were delivered with such sincerity that Bogle 'could not help being particularly affected'.[21] Observing his distress, the Lama tried to cheer Bogle with the prospect of a future visit. Then he bestowed his final blessing. 'He threw a handkerchief about my neck,' wrote Bogle, 'put his hand upon my head, and I retired.'[22]

The Qianlong Emperor

III

Bengal, Tibet & China

1775–1793

14

MELANCHOLY HALL

The post-monsoon breeze ruffled the trees surrounding the garden house. Built outside Calcutta, garden houses offered a welcome retreat from the urban heat. The richest Company servants favoured lavish mansions fronting the river, but this modest house was far from fashionably located. The trees shielded the garden house from a view of Calcutta's burial ground. The British dead had already filled one cemetery and were fast colonising a second. In death, as in life, Calcutta residents flaunted their wealth and status; magnificent mausoleums, monuments and obelisks crowded the cemetery. So frequent were the funerals that the chaplain had a special allowance to cover the cost of palanquin rides to the burial ground.[1]

The low rent and secluded situation of the house appealed to Bogle. With its encircling trees, it reminded him of the hermitages he had seen on his travels. Hamilton, by contrast, noticed only the neighbourhood, and named it 'Melancholy Hall'.[2] But, just three months after his return to Calcutta, quiet and obscurity were precisely what Bogle wanted. 'I hug myself in unimportance,' he wrote to his friend David Anderson in October 1775, 'and can without Reluctance give up Consequence, Influence, and even Advantage, rather than be engaged in Business which might draw upon me Censures or which I do not like.'[3]

Bogle's homecoming was far from the diplomatic triumph that he had fondly imagined. His three-month journey down to Calcutta through Bhutan had been uneventful. Hamilton had preceded him down to the plains and Bogle had spent a fortnight in negotiations at Tashichodzong. Compared to his easy friendship with the Panchen Lama, with whom he could converse freely in Hindustani, Bogle had found relations with the Desi distinctly strained. With Purangir as his adviser and the Tibetan Padma as his interpreter, it had been hard to talk informally. To Bogle's mind, the Desi had been 'difficult of access, stiff and Ceremonious in his Manners, and indecisive in Business'.[4] To his annoyance, the Desi had seemed more interested in the Bhutanese claim to some disputed border villages than in fostering trade links with Bengal. In the end, the Desi had agreed to send representatives to Calcutta to deal directly with the Governor General on these matters. For a long time, the trade talks had remained stalled. 'I found all my Arguments, Proposals, Promises, and even oblique Threats ineffectual,' Bogle told Hastings. 'In short I despaired of being able to carry my Point.'[5] Bogle's frustration had been compounded by his desire to conclude business as quickly as possible. Purangir was anxious to return to Calcutta, and the rains were expected shortly. Bogle had struggled through the monsoon once on his travels and was not keen to repeat the experience. In addition, his health was not of the best; he urgently required the attention of a physician well versed in venereal complaints.

The turning point in the negotiations had come when Bogle proposed that the trade should be conducted exclusively by Hindu and Muslim merchants. No British Company servant would enter Bhutan. To Bogle's mind, this concession, although regrettable from the Company's point of view, was absolutely necessary to reach any kind of agreement. On this assurance, the Desi had grown much more receptive to Bogle's plan. Other incentives had followed: Bhutanese goods would enter India at Rangpur duty-free; Bhutanese state officials would retain their traditional monopoly on the import of certain goods like indigo and sandalwood. To seal the talks, a 5,000-rupee gift had been made to the Desi, 'in consideration of his allowing merchants to Trade through his Country to and from Thibet'.[6]

But Bogle's relief at concluding his negotiations had been tempered by the arrival of a letter from the Governor General. Far from welcoming his protégé back, Hastings had suggested that he need not hurry home. 'I am not anxious to see you now in Bengal,' Hastings wrote ominously in May 1775, 'my Power is suspended, and my Friends involved in the Effects of my own situation.'[7] During Bogle's absence, the Calcutta political scene had been utterly transformed. When Bogle had left the city the previous year, Warren Hastings had presided easily over policy-making, appointments and the social scene. Now, with the arrival of the three new Councillors from Britain, Hastings's authority and prestige had been completely eclipsed.

The 1773 Regulating Act had made provision for a governing Council based in Calcutta. It was made up of the Governor General and four Councillors. Only two of the five members represented the Company interest: the Governor General himself and Richard Barwell, a high-ranking official of immense fortune. Representing the government were the three new Councillors, who had been appointed by the King and the Prime Minister. Two were military men: Colonel George Monson had seen active service in south India, but owed his present position more to his connections than any aptitude; General John Clavering was the Commander-in-Chief, and had been privately assured that he was governor general in waiting. The third, Philip Francis, formerly First Clerk in the War Office, was the only one to possess any real talent, but all his energy, intelligence and vitriol were directed against the Governor General.

In their debates, all Council members had a vote of the same weight. The Governor General's casting vote came into play only if an issue divided the Councillors equally. From the start, the three new Councillors acted in concert and voted together. Hastings could no longer simply assume control of Company business and official appointments; all proposals now had to come before the Council. To the Governor General's intense frustration, many of his initiatives were blocked. For a decisive man, accustomed to command, this was an intolerable situation. Hastings could no longer direct Company policy or reward his favourites. It was difficult for him to see a way around the inbuilt government majority. His only option seemed to be to wait for the majority ranks to be depleted, either through sickness or through that ultimate leveller (and frequent visitor), death.

The Court of Directors in London had supplied the new Council with a list of sixty-one 'Instructions' on policy and procedures. The first, which recommended 'the most perfect harmony' between the Councillors, was flouted almost immediately. Instruction no. 35 ordered that an inquiry be held 'into all oppressions which may have been committed either against the natives or Europeans, and into all abuses . . . in collection of revenue or any part of civil government'.[8] On this authority, the new Councillors launched an investigation into the conduct of the Governor General himself. In the process of their research, they discovered a Bengali administrator, Raja Nandakumar, who had been closely involved with the Company, but had recently been dismissed by Hastings. To the new Councillors, Nandakumar alleged that Hastings had accepted bribes in exchange for government appointments. In response, Hastings brought a prosecution for con-spiracy against Nandakumar. And the following month apparently unrelated charges of forgery were pressed against the Raja. On the basis of these charges, the Raja was arrested. What made the timing of the arrest even more suspicious was that the forgery allegations related to events dating back some six years.

The trial of Nandakumar opened on 8 June 1775, just over a month before Bogle returned to Calcutta. It was to become one of the most notorious episodes of Hastings's career. The trial was conducted at the Supreme Court, another institution newly established under the Regulating Act. The presiding judge was the Chief Justice, Sir Elijah Impey, an old schoolfriend of Hastings. The court interpreter was Alexander Elliot, a Hastings protégé and one of Bogle's closest companions. Under the British law administered by the Supreme Court, forgery was a capital offence; under the Hindu and Muslim laws of Bengal, it carried no such penalty. At the start of the trial, Impey rejected the argument that it was inappropriate to transplant the death penalty for forgery to Bengal. Once set in motion, the wheels of British justice ground remorselessly on. On 17 June Nandakumar was found guilty, and Impey pronounced the death sentence.

The Raja's execution took place on 5 August, outraging Bengali public opinion. Nandakumar was a man of rank, popularly believed to be upright. There were demonstrations of protest in Calcutta (although Bogle, recently arrived in the city, is silent on the matter).

To contemporaries and later commentators, both Indian and British, it seemed that Hastings had interfered in the course of the law, that he and Impey had been guilty of judicial murder. While the circumstances of the case remain suspicious, some historians have cleared Hastings of direct interference. At the very least, however, Nandakumar must be numbered among the early casualties of the conflict that broke out between Hastings and the new Councillors. The Raja, as one historian has noted, was the unfortunate victim of 'the internecine war among those who were ruling Bengal'.[9]

Bogle was also caught in the crossfire. 'The late Change in the Government of this Country is particularly severe upon me,' he wrote to his father. 'I had sacrificed a great deal to get myself some Credit, and it was now I expected to have reaped the Fruits of it.'[10] Rather than the anticipated garlands and rewards, Bogle discovered on his return that he was without an official job. The Select Committee, which he had served as secretary, had been disbanded under the reforms of the Regulating Act. Within a few months, the Diwani Adalat, or Court of Appeals, where he had been registrar, was also abolished. The only post that remained was that of private secretary to Hastings, which provided Bogle with a modest income of sixty-three rupees a month. Nor was there any prospect of a new appointment, Bogle reported to his brother Robin: 'T'other day Mr Hastings proposed me for a very high Office. He was seconded by Mr Barwell, but it was carried against me by the other three Members.'[11] Bogle did not suspect the Councillors of any personal animosity; they were simply voting along party lines, as he explained to Robin: 'my Attachment, to Mr Hastings, against whom they have taken a direct Line of Opposition naturally renders me obnoxious to them. They received me with politeness: but they have imported strongly the Violence of your European Politics, and no Man can be a favourite of both Parties, without a Duplicity of which I am incapable.'[12] Despite Bogle's frustration and disappointment, he had little option but to remain loyal to his patron: 'The particular favours with which Mr Hastings has honoured me, leave me however, in these times in no Suspence as to the Line I am to take – there is only one honourable one.'[13]

The divisions within the Council spread out into the wider British community. 'The Factions in Calcutta render Society, beyond the Circle of one's intimate Friends, very unpleasant,' Bogle complained to his father. 'I intend therefore to lead a quiet Life, untill I see what turn Things will take.'[14] But within a few months even the circle of Bogle's intimate friends was severely diminished. With so few opportunities open to Hastings's favourites in Calcutta, the Governor General thought them better employed as his representatives in London. One by one, Bogle's friends embarked on the long voyage to put Hastings's case to the government and to lobby the Directors and Proprietors of the East India Company on his behalf. By October 1775, Bogle was moaning, 'there is hardly anybody I can say more to than talk about the weather or the Roads.'[15] Colonel Macleane had departed at the start of the year, Alexander Elliot and John Stewart soon followed. Elliot carried with him authorisation to publish an 'authentic' account of Nandakumar's trial; Macleane and Stewart were empowered to act as agents for Hastings in London. Bogle regretted Elliot's absence in particular, as he lamented to Anderson: 'Elliot's Departure for Europe was a severe Stroke upon me, and tore to pieces the little Web of Happiness which my fond Fancy had wove. Amidst all these storms, I promised myself great Satisfaction & Solace in his Conversation. Now he is as far as Point Palmiras.'[16]

By the time that Bogle's friends arrived in London, Lord North's government was reeling from even worse news. In April 1775 American protests against British taxation had erupted into violence and within months the conflict had escalated into full-scale war. Writing to his son, the elderly George Bogle voiced the outrage felt by many conservative Scots at this 'most unnatural, unprovoked Rebellion against us their Mother Country'.[17] The immediate problems posed to North's government by 'this Rebellious Parricide' would have overshadowed the battles on the Calcutta Council, but in their origins the troubles in America were not unrelated to the East India Company.[18]

For some years colonists in America had objected to the British parliament's assumption of the right to impose taxation on tea sold in the colonies. Company sales in America had slumped as a result. In 1773 the government passed the Tea Act as part of the measures aimed at averting Company bankruptcy. The Act allowed the Company to export tea directly to the American colonies to specific agents, thereby cutting the cost to American consumers and establishing monopolies in the trade. Angered even further by this legislation, activists in Boston staged a dramatic protest. When a cargo of tea docked in the harbour, a group of colonists, disguised as Mohawk Indians, boarded the ship and heaved £10,000 worth of tea overboard. As the first act of resistance to British rule, the 'Boston Tea Party' has long occupied pride of place in the narrative of American Independence, but its connection with the financial plight of the East India Company is perhaps less well known.

With no official job, few friends and little money, Bogle experienced a slump in spirits. Just months before, he had been negotiating treaties and forging alliances; now he was forced to remain on the sidelines, watching the ugly antics of a local power struggle. His decline in status – from diplomacy to redundancy – was both swift and shocking. He could take some satisfaction from the knowledge that Hastings had been pleased by his conduct. But what, in the present circumstances, did the Governor General's favour amount to?

If he could not reward Bogle as he would have wished, Hastings could at least encourage Bogle's literary efforts. The journal that Bogle had already forwarded convinced Hastings that a fuller version should be published. It would be a rich addition both to the literature of travel and to the stock of knowledge of humankind. And there might be more tangible gains too. Bogle would make his name and his patron might improve his. How better to win gentlemen round than with an account of endeavour and enterprise in an unfamiliar land? The journal could play its part in the campaign for the hearts and minds of the government, the Directorate and holders of East India Company stock.

Strewn about Bogle's desk were his Tibet notes, reams of paper covered in elegant, cursive script – journals, memoranda, notebooks, routes, reports, observations; a mass of material that Bogle feared would never be reduced to order. But such was the task before him: Hastings was keen to see an account of his travels in publishable form. Little more than a week after Bogle's return to Calcutta, and only two days after Nandakumar's execution, the Governor General had forwarded a copy of Bogle's journal to the renowned Dr Johnson. The hope was that the grand old man of literary London would give his advice and perhaps even exert his influence to secure publication.

Hastings's acquaintance with Samuel Johnson dated back to his four-year stay in England in the 1760s. Johnson's encouragement may have been a factor in Hastings's patronage of research into India and the surrounding region. Johnson enjoined Hastings to 'examine nicely the Traditions and Histories of the East . . . survey the remains of its ancient Edifices, and trace the vestiges of its ruined cities' and to patronise 'experimental knowledge and natural history'.[19] Hastings claimed that the pressures of office prevented him from personally conducting research, but drew Johnson's attention to his protégés' studies. The two men maintained a friendly correspondence, writing in particular whenever one had a favour to ask the other. Johnson recommended friends entering East India Company service to the Governor General, and forwarded new books, including his own as yet unpublished *Journey to the Western Islands of Scotland*. Hastings responded with requests and suggestions of reading matter for Johnson, including 'the journal of a friend of mine into the country of Tibbet, which, though bordering on this, has till very lately been as little known to the inhabitants of it as if it was at the distance of many degrees'. He whetted Johnson's appetite with the promise of novelty: 'The people, their form of government, their manners, and even their climate differ as much from Bengal as Bengal does from England.' Hastings worked in a reference to the *Journey to the Western Islands* to compliment Johnson. 'When I read the account of your visit to the Hebrides,' the Governor General wrote, 'I could not help wishing that a portion of that spirit which could draw so much entertainment and instruction from a region so little befriended by nature, or improved by society, could have animated Mr. Bogle.' Although less than flattering to Bogle, the parallel with Scotland may have been suggested by Bogle's own descriptions of Bhutan as a Highland idyll. If Bogle's account lacked the sophistication of Johnson's, then Hastings still hoped that the great Doctor would find it 'not unworthy of . . . perusal . . . [and] at least be pleased with the amiable character of the Lama'.[20]

No record of Johnson's reply exists. Perhaps Hastings's letter never arrived, or Johnson's answer got lost. Maybe Johnson simply received too many manuscripts soliciting his attention to find the time to respond. Whatever the case, it may have been for want of encouragement that Bogle's literary efforts foundered. All that we know is that a year and a half later, the project remained unfinished. In a letter to his brother Robin, in February 1777, Bogle found all kinds of excuses and justifications for the delay. He had been preoccupied with the state of affairs in Calcutta, he said, and in any case the journal might not be his last word on Tibet: 'I don't despair of again visiting that part of the World, I am solicitous to avoid saying any thing where I am not well founded or where I might be contradicted by others who may at some time or other come after me.' Beset by fears of inaccuracy, he was at the same time anxious that making his findings public might not serve the national interest: 'I have doubts of the propriety of publishing to the whole world an Account of a Country hitherto little known. It is putting other Nations in possession of Knowledge which may be of use to them, and I am not certain of the World enough to be of that Mind. It is sacrificing real advantages perhaps to idle Curiosity or Vanity.' But, as he finally admitted, the possible opportunism of rival European powers was less daunting than the scale of the task: 'if I had more leisure on my hands I would very probably get the better of these Scruples'.[21]

There may have been other reasons for Bogle's failure to write up his notes. In the months following his return, it seems likely that he slipped into some form of depression. By the end of 1775, Hamilton suggested – albeit playfully – that life at Melancholy Hall had infected Bogle's spirits. In a letter dated December of that year, he imagined Bogle as a recluse, working glumly on his notes in his house by the graveyard. Shunning society, surrounded by the literature of mortality, Bogle sinks into melancholia. 'I figure you to myself,' wrote Hamilton, 'sitting at a table in a large almost empty hall wrapt up in a Thibet Gown with a fur cap on, here Harvey's meditations amongst the tombs – there Young's night thoughts and our countryman Bunyan's works open before you. Sometimes I see you in the Varanda repeating – Beneath those Aged thorns that yew trees shade &c &c –.'[22] Hamilton has Bogle misquoting Thomas Gray's *Elegy Written in a Country Churchyard*, the poem recited in happier times to the Panchen Lama.

Hamilton's teasing hyperbole hardly provides definitive evidence of Bogle's mental state. In furnishing Bogle with volumes associated with the fashionable genre of graveyard poetry, Hamilton may be suggesting that Bogle's despondency was just a modish pose. But it does seem that Bogle was profoundly affected by the political situation in Calcutta. In March 1776, he explained to his family that he could not write at any length because of 'Anxiety and Vexation . . . from the uncertainty' that he was in.[23] He was preoccupied, he tells Martha, with thoughts of his future: 'I have a very deep Stake depending on the Issue of the present Disputes, and 'till that is determined I cannot be free from Disquietude. I have laboured many years in expectation of a future Reward, and that now hinges upon Mr Hastings being restored to authority.'[24]

Financially, at any rate, the situation was now a little less precarious. At the end of December 1775, Bogle had officially presented his mission report and accounts. The Council, in a rare display of unanimity, had agreed to the Governor General's proposal that Bogle should be allowed a backdated monthly salary of 1,200 rupees to cover the period of his mission. Much of this allowance was sent back to Daldowie to service the family debts. But there still seemed scant prospect of Bogle ever being in a position to provide for the family as he had wished.

The embattled situation in Calcutta may have distracted Bogle from work on his journal, but in London John Stewart pursued the aim of making the mission more generally known. In 1776 he secured his election to the Royal Society, the most prestigious intellectual institution in Britain. Acting both as Hastings's agent and Bogle's friend, Stewart submitted an account of Bogle's travels in a letter to Sir John Pringle, the Royal Society's President. Papers read out to the Royal Society reached a wider public through the *Philosophical Transactions*, a journal to be found on many an educated gentleman's library shelves.

On the evening of 17 April 1777, the fellows of the Royal Society gathered in Crane Court, a town house off Fleet Street that served as the Society's premises. As usual, a lamp was lit above the entrance to indicate that a meeting was to take place. As the fellows settled in their seats in the Council Chamber, Sir John began to read from

1 Warren Hastings, by an anonymous Mughal artist. As Governor of Bengal, Hastings was faced with the daunting task of reviving East India Company finances. Keen to expand the Company's trade, in 1774 he appointed George Bogle to head the first British expedition to Tibet.

2 The East India Company was brought to the verge of bankruptcy by the insatiable British demand for tea. The Chinese were the only suppliers of this valuable commodity. In this painting of a Canton tea warehouse, Europeans (their hair protected from tea dust with handkerchiefs) supervise Chinese workers emptying straw baskets of tea into a large pile for checking.

3 To reach Tibet, Bogle travelled through Bhutan. The route followed to the Bhutanese capital of Tashichodzong was often precipitous. Cut into steps in the rock face, the path skirted deep gorges.

4 The great fort of Tashichodzong, the seat of the ruler or *Desi* of Bhutan.

5 Bogle's party was detained for more than three months in Tashichodzong, first by the Panchen Lama's reluctance to admit the mission, then by the outbreak of rebellion. They stayed in the house pictured here, close to the fort, overlooking the Thinchu river with its covered bridge.

6 The Third Panchen Lama, Lobsang Palden Yeshé. During the
Dalai Lama's childhood, the Panchen Lama ('Great Scholar') was
the most important Incarnate in Tibet.

7 The Panchen Lama greets George Bogle. This painting represents the start of the friendship between the two men. The Panchen Lama receives a ceremonial white scarf, presented on behalf of Bogle, who is wearing Bhutanese dress and posed dramatically against a window.

8 Of the many different kinds of wandering monks in India, *gosain*s (pictured second from the left) specialised in trade. Some, like Purangir, also served as messengers and informants. Travelling tirelessly between Bengal, Tibet and China, Purangir acted as diplomatic agent for both the Panchen Lama and the British.

9 The Qianlong Emperor presided over the largest, richest empire in the eighteenth-century world. In this formal portrait, he wears court dress of imperial yellow and is seated on a golden dragon throne.

10 Master of his image, Qianlong was depicted in many different guises throughout his long reign. In this painting, he is represented simultaneously as Tibetan Buddhist monk, living Buddha, and universal monarch.

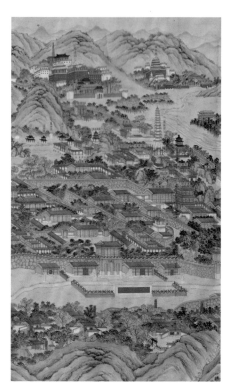

11 In 1779 the Qianlong Emperor invited the Panchen Lama to visit him at Chengde, his favourite mountain resort. He went to extraordinary lengths to honour the Panchen Lama, building him a copy of his own home monastery (pictured here, behind the Chengde palace complex, on the left).

12 When the Panchen Lama fell seriously ill in Peking, the Qianlong Emperor produced this picture of a sacred Sal tree as a get-well gift and public expression of concern. The inscription above is in four languages – Chinese, Tibetan, Manchu and Mongolian – to reach the many different peoples of the Qing empire.

Stewart's letter: 'The kingdom of Thibet, although known by name ever since the days of MARCO POLO and other travellers of the twelfth and thirteenth centuries, had never been properly explored by any European till the period of which I am now to speak.' As Sir John read on, the audience learnt that Hasting's enthusiasm for a mission stemmed from his eagerness 'to seize every opportunity which could promote the interest and glory of this nation and tend to the advancement of natural knowledge'. Bogle was introduced as a man 'whose abilities and temper rendered him every way qualified for so hazardous and uncommon a mission'.[25] For the most part, the letter summarised Bogle's findings on Tibet: geographical, ethnographical and commercial. The Panchen Lama was presented as amiable and intelligent, mild of manner and 'without starchness or affectation'. Indeed, everything within the Lama's palace 'breathed peace, order and dignified elegance'.[26] The gracious Lama presided over a country replete with valuable products: yak tails, shawl wool, musk and gold (tantalising lumps of solid ore 'about the size of a bullock's kidney').[27] What fellow of the Royal Society or reader of the *Philosophical Transactions* could remain in doubt of the possible profits of the mission – in terms both of knowledge and of bullion?

Bogle's exploits were celebrated not only in the pages of the *Philosophical Transactions*, but also on canvas. Some time after his return to Calcutta, Bogle posed in Bhutanese robes for the artist Tilly Kettle. The first British portrait painter to find employment in India, Kettle had previously painted Indian nawabs and East India Company servants in Madras. Moving to Calcutta, he painted many of the Company grandees, including a portrait of Hastings – a relaxed image of the beleaguered Governor General, comfortably seated. The painting of Bogle was something of a departure for him. More an imagined scene than a portrait, it depicts Bogle's first meeting with the Panchen Lama. It does not attempt to recreate the exact circumstances of the meeting (for a start, Bogle wore European clothes), but rather offers a theatrical staging of the event (see plate 7).

The painting focuses on the presentation of the ceremonial white scarf (*khatag*) to the Panchen Lama. Seated cross-legged on a dais, the Panchen Lama holds out one hand receptively and fingers prayer beads with the other. The scarf is proffered, not by Bogle, but by a Tibetan figure, possibly Paima – an acknowledgement of the role that was played by intermediaries throughout the mission. Perhaps the stooping posture of presentation was considered inappropriate for Bogle, who stands to the left, looking on. The upright Bogle retains his dignity; the drapery of his robe somehow recalls the fall of a Roman toga. Behind him, billowing green curtains frame a view of a temple backed by jagged mountains – a sign of the distance that Bogle has travelled and the rigours that he has undergone. But, for all the heroic associations of his pose, Bogle is identified with his surroundings through his dress. The painting commemorates a moment of cultural accommodation.

To what extent did Bogle prompt Kettle in his staging of the scene? Presumably he provided most of the props: items of clothing and painted silk *thangka*s to decorate the walls, maybe even a view of Tashilhunpo to provide the model for the temple outside. But many of the details are muddled. No one would have worn hats or smoked in the presence of the Lama, and the Panchen Lama himself would never have worn a fur-trimmed riding hat indoors.[28] Some of these inaccuracies, however, seem to relate to Bogle's wider understanding of Tibet. The seated pair cheerily puffing on pipes, for instance, manage to convey that jovial bonhomie which Bogle associated with Tibetans in general.

Little is known about the history of the painting. Given Bogle's impecunious state, it seems likely that it was Hastings who commissioned Kettle to produce the work. As a memorial of the alliance forged between the East India Company and the Panchen Lama, the painting had an obvious political value for the Governor General. Indeed it appears to have played its part in Hastings's campaign to win support at the highest level in Britain. At some stage, the painting must have been presented to King George III. It is still to be found in the royal collection, but throughout the nineteenth and for most of the twentieth century the subject of the painting was forgotten. The scene was placed in an amorphously defined orient, variously described as 'An Indian subject, an Asiatic Merchant exhibiting silk and other valuable merchandise to a Chinese Grandee' and 'The introduction of Linen to the Great Mogul'.[29] In these palace inventories, the *khatag* has been transformed from a symbol of respect into a commodity –

perhaps a significant mistake, given the commercial aims of the mission.

But the view of posterity was not uppermost in the thoughts of Hastings and Bogle. The battle with the Council consumed much of their energy and frustrated many of their plans. So entrenched was the situation that it took a death to break the deadlock. In the summer of 1776, Colonel Monson took to his bed and, some ten weeks later, died. Hastings had little reason to regret Monson's passing. Now at last he could exercise his casting vote – at least until London nominated a replacement councillor. For Hastings, the delay in communication between London and Calcutta came as a welcome restoration of authority. In the months that followed Monson's death, Hastings quickly made a number of appointments. In November 1776, Bogle was once more in an official post. Together with his friend David Anderson, he was to superintend the valuation of all the lands held by the Company in Bengal. This was the groundwork for a new revenue settlement. It may have provided a guaranteed income, but the work was far from exciting. It required painstaking attention to detail. 'We remain in Calcutta,' Bogle complained to his brother Robin. 'It is a laborious Job.' For the time being, Bogle was relegated to the ranks of the penpushers.[30]

TIBET GARDEN

The river slapped noisily against the side of the ghat. The Hugli at Ghusari, just across the river from the northern boundary of Calcutta, was notorious among boatmen for its troubled waters. The monsoon storms had swollen the river and the boatmen would have to negotiate the hazards of the Ghusari whirlpool. Purangir waited as porters loaded trunks into the budgerow. Although the monsoon was in full spate, the *gosain* was setting out on a journey. By Hastings's order, Purangir was to carry a letter and gifts for the Panchen Lama. The party that embarked at the ghat in August 1776 was much smaller than Bogle's deputation. A guard of five sepoys was to accompany Purangir as far as Cooch Behar. The trunks and packages stowed in the budgerow contained the presents for the Panchen Lama. There was a splendid crimson and gold saddle, but the consignment consisted mostly of items of scientific and optical equipment: carefully packaged magnifying glasses, spectacles, sundials and surgical instruments. But Purangir was not just a courier. Recognising the *gosain*'s diplomatic talents, the Governor General had given him the duties of an envoy. He was instructed to relay particularly sensitive matters in person. As a draft of a letter from Hastings to the Lama records, the Governor General had 'the greatest confidence in Purangiri and has therefore entrusted to him some important matters which he will represent to him [the Lama]'.[1]

The steps of the ghat ran up to the imposing gateway of the new monastery, built according to the Panchen Lama's instructions. In December 1775 the East India Company had granted a thirty-acre plot on the banks of the Hugli to Purangir, first on a lease, and then, once the Directors' consent had been gained, as a freehold.[2] The riverside doorway led under a gallery of thick, square pillars into a central courtyard. Built without arches, and with small openings in the blank outer wall, the main building was set in the extensive gardens that gave the monastery its name: Bhot Bagan or Tibet Garden.[3]

Consecrated in June 1776, a year after the mission's return to Calcutta, Bhot Bagan was placed in Purangir's charge. The prayer-rooms off the central courtyard housed the images and shrines donated by the Lama, but Purangir's quarters would have contained the objects of his devotion: Hindu deities and *Shiva-linga*s. In its union of different faiths, Bhot Bagan was certainly remarkable, but religious traditions did not always remain distinct in eighteenth-century India. Across the sub-continent, rulers saw the political advantages of patronising faiths other than their own. At Ajmer in Rajasthan, for instance, the Hindu Marathas supported an important Muslim sufi shrine which was also revered by the local Hindu population.[4] In the case of Bhot Bagan, the British provided the land for the monastery in the hope of cementing the alliance with Tibet. The Panchen Lama placed a *gosain* in charge partly because of the supposed affinity between Tibetan Buddhist and *gosain* beliefs, and partly because Purangir enjoyed a privileged relationship with the British and extensive trading connections.

Having supervised the building work, Purangir was responsible for providing accommodation and assistance to any visiting Tibetan monks and traders. The monastery was in effect a guest house and trading base. Purangir was well qualified to administer the complex. He could give advice to traders on how best to dispose of goods and buy Bengali wares. He himself had returned to Bengal with some 10,000 rupees' worth of gold dust (which Bogle had offered to sell on his behalf to Hastings).[5] From his time at Tashilhunpo, Purangir would have known something of Tibetan Buddhist monasteries. But in any case, as a member of the Giri, he would have been familiar with the operation of Dasnami monastic establishments (*math*s). Purangir had been initiated as a Giri at Joshi Math near the source of the Ganges in the Himalayas. The Giris were permitted either to reside in monasteries or to follow the life of a wandering ascetic. On their travels, they could seek food and shelter at any Dasnami monastery. Providing hospitality was therefore an established part of Giri monastic life, so Purangir would have well understood this part of his post. Uniquely accommodating, the Dasnami order combined a centralised monastic structure with the autonomy of itinerant life. A Dasnami ascetic might adhere to the routine of monastic ritual or be subject to the irregularities of life on the road.[6] It was perhaps this flexibility within the system that made it possible for Purangir to adopt his very individual role.

Purangir was certainly not the first member of his order to be associated with the Panchen Lama. It must have been his guru, Sukhdeogiri, who first introduced him to the Lama. Sukhdeogiri was an elderly and wealthy *gosain* who had long traded to Tibet from his monastery at Patna. He was well known to the Panchen Lama, who recommended him by letter to Hastings.[7] Among the Giri, the most significant relationship was that between a guru and his disciple or *chela*. The *chela* was first admitted to the order by his guru, and at his death the *chela* could expect to inherit from him. When a guru had many disciples, they were ranked according to seniority and duties. At the guru's death, his wealth was distributed among his disciples, according to their rank.[8]

Purangir appears to have had a troubled relationship with his guru Sukhdeogiri. At the time of Bogle's mission they seem to have been close. Sukhdeogiri and two other *gosain*s accompanied Purangir on the return trip to Bengal. It was safer to travel in convoy, and Sukhdeogiri was returning with the proceeds of many years' trading. He was even in the position to supply a loan when Bogle ran short of ready cash. Soon after the mission arrived in Calcutta, he and one of the other *gosain*s continued to Benares, a particular *gosain* stronghold.[9] There he was pursued by a charge relating to his time at Tashilhunpo. The Panchen Lama wrote to inform Hastings that Sukhdeogiri was accused of stealing a conch shell (a ritual item). The case was investigated by a *gosain* council which found Sukhdeogiri innocent.[10] Whether or not there was any substance to the charge, it is clear that Sukhdeogiri did not enjoy the unblemished reputation of Purangir. In later years, guru and disciple appear to have fallen out. 'They were not latterly on very good terms,' Bogle wrote to his friend David Anderson, 'as the old Man was a perfect Devil.'[11]

For Purangir, Bhot Bagan was his Calcutta base, just across the river from the seat of power. The proximity allowed the British to call on his services whenever necessary. Purangir's disciple Daljitgir reported that Bhot Bagan regularly supplied the Bengal government with translators to work on correspondence with Tibet.[12] But Purangir did not live there permanently. In addition to his duties at the monastery, he continued to cultivate the links between the Panchen Lama and the Company. Following the Panchen Lama's stipulation that no European should enter Tibet, Purangir became more indispensable than ever. Quite literally a go-between, Purangir went where Bogle could not. For a number of years, he would continue to travel back and forth to Tibet. Originally the agent of Tashilhunpo, Purangir now also became the envoy of Calcutta. But he seems to have retained his allegiance to the Panchen Lama. Over the following years, Purangir appears to have been employed by both regimes. He possessed the commercial and diplomatic intelligence desired by both sides. His mobility, cultural knowledge and reputation for trustworthiness served him well. The trade in information was truly as valuable as gold dust.

With Purangir taking on the role of envoy, there was little active diplomacy to engage Bogle. He could only cultivate his connection with Tibet through gifts, minor commissions and letters. The Lama was equally keen to keep up the dialogue, writing directly to Bogle, in addition to his official correspondence with Hastings. The Lama's letters to Bogle were less formal than those to the Governor General. He kept Bogle informed of his own activities and Purangir's movements and reassured him that he had Company interests at heart.

Down in Calcutta, Bogle made himself useful, arranging for the repair of three of the Panchen Lama's collection of broken-down watches. He was a thoughtful present-purchaser, recalling particular requests and evidently bearing the recipients in mind. In November 1775, he dispatched two sets of chess-men to Tibet (perhaps the curious design would be a talking point in the communal matches). He sent the

Lama's nephews a royal hunting saddle for their favourite pastime. The following year, a messenger was entrusted with the care of some dogs for delivery in Tibet (seven months' wages to cover the trip). For the Lama's nieces, he purchased two small lockets and two *lories*, the brightly coloured parrots he had promised the nuns on parting. By presenting the nuns with such gifts – which would have been equally suitable for European gentlewomen – Bogle was behaving with polite gallantry. He honoured his word to send the Panchen Lama a lion skin and a telescope, adding all kinds of optical instruments: perspective glasses, opera glasses and spectacles.[13] These gifts were not mere trinkets. They implied that the Lama possessed that scientific curiosity which was normally associated with the educated European elite. Indeed the concentration on optical instruments suggests that Bogle was also disseminating technological means to view the world, bringing it, so to speak, into European focus. The Panchen Lama acknowledged the receipt of the 'Telescope for Stars' and marvelled at the lion skin: 'Before your arrival in this Country even a Hair of a Lion had never been seen, and People were even astonished at the mention of it.'[14]

The exercise in diplomatic courtesy extended into other areas too. Bogle looked to the needs of pilgrims sent by the Panchen Lama to visit sites in India associated with Tantric deities.[15] In January 1776, he was responsible for organising a trip to Orissa, to the famous Jagannath temple in Puri, for a pilgrim from Tibet. He employed two brahmans and a wandering ascetic to act as the pilgrim's guides. Sadly, by June 1776 he was obliged to pay for the expenses incurred 'in burning the Body of a Bootea, who died on the return from his Pilgrimage'.[16] By dispatching pilgrims to worship at sacred Indian sites, the Panchen Lama was himself accruing spiritual merit. In this system of pilgrimage by proxy, it was acceptable for others to offer worship on the Panchen Lama's behalf. Using funds sent by the Lama, Bogle added to the Panchen Lama's spiritual stock by organising the performance of rites at the more remote sacred sites.[17]

As far as Bhutan was concerned, Bogle fostered relations with the Desi through attention to the Bhutanese deputation sent to Calcutta. The Desi's representatives had accompanied Bogle to Bengal to put the Bhutanese case in the border dispute with Cooch Behar to the Governor General. Bogle saw to it that their reception in Calcutta equalled his own in Tashichodzong. A house was hired for their accommodation, and they were equipped with clothing and bed linen appropriate to the climate. Just as Bogle had received blankets and padded gowns in Bhutan, so the Bhutanese were presented with sheets and robes of flowered muslin and taffeta.

As for entertainment, the Company could not offer anything to match the weeks of sacred dancing that had so bored Bogle, but there was the annual, amateur Christmas play. Every winter season, the Company servants would stage all-male performances of popular plays, funded by general subscription. 'The Scenes are brought from London, and we have a man to paint them, and another to shift and manage them,' Bogle had told his sister Mary, on first arriving in Calcutta. 'As to our Performers, we are Performers ourselves, and no Gentlemen whatsoever thinks it below them to contribute his Assistance, some have a Turn for acting, others sing, others dance and, those that can play upon the violin or any other Instrument fill the Orchestra.'[18] The 1770 season included Thomas Otway's tragedy *Venice Preserv'd* (the plot of which Bogle would summarise for the Panchen Lama) and Susannah Centlivre's comedy *The Wonder*. The performances were admirable, according to Bogle. 'The Gentlemen in general played their Parts vastly well, but particularly one who in his younger days was upon the Stage in London. The greatest Curiosity however is a young Lad that plays a womans Part amazingly well, and is to be sure the most effeminate Creature in the world.' But the junior writers who arrived with Bogle were less promising. 'We are rather deficient in Actresses, owing to the young Gentlemen that came out this year being in general not very handsome or too tall, or strong voices.'[19] Too old to play the ingénue, Bogle distinguished himself as the Third Witch in *Macbeth* a few years later. For the Company servants, in the distant setting of Calcutta, the productions recalled the traditions of home.[20] But it is difficult to imagine what the Bhutanese envoys would have made of the spectacle. The play was probably as incomprehensible and tedious for them as the religious festivals had been for Bogle.

For all his efforts, it was not Bogle but Hamilton who was deputed to return to Bhutan to investigate the boundary dispute. Perhaps the matter was considered too minor for Bogle; maybe Hastings wanted to keep his favourite close at hand; or perhaps Bogle had not fully recovered his health by November 1775 when the party set out. Whatever the case, the choice of Hamilton did not seem altogether wise. The forthright Hamilton, Bogle suspected, might be ill-suited to the delicate art of diplomacy. 'I would advise you by all means to avoid Disputes, Controversies and Quarrels with anybody, or if you think a Man a Rogue, to tell him so, or even to give him Reason to suspect your thoughts; it will only serve to throw Difficulties in your Way, whatever you have to do,' he counselled Hamilton. 'The warmth of your Temper, and your natural aversion from Deceit and Artifice may render this Advice not unnecessary,' he added pointedly. 'But in dealing with the Booteas you must follow the Rule of the Apostle Paul, of being all things to all men.'[21]

Bogle's concerns proved well founded. Within months, Hamilton was quivering with frustration. No matter what he said, Hamilton asserted, the Bhutanese persisted in the mistaken belief that he was empowered to settle the border dispute, rather than just investigate it. 'I have protested, I have swore, I have stormed, I have cursed,' he ranted to Bogle. And, despite his best efforts, he seemed also to have given offence to the Company servants on the other side of the contested border. It would have 'required the wisdom of Solomon and the patience of Job to have satisfied both parties', he exclaimed. 'How then can you possibly suppose that I who am endowed with a very moderate share of either, should accomplish so arduous an undertaking?'[22]

Hamilton was no more successful as a scholar than as a negotiator. Bogle had hoped that Hamilton, with his medical training, would compile a report on the state of medicine in Tibet, but Hamilton was not convinced that such a study would have any scientific value, 'as the inhabitants of that country seem to be much further behind Europeans in the progress they have made towards the advancement of medical knowledge than in most other Arts or Sciences'.[23] However, he conceded, the Tibetans were more successful than Europeans in treating certain eye disorders. This was not, he argued, because they had a better understanding of the complaint or structure of the eye ('in reality they are entirely ignorant of both'), but because they had better surgical tools.[24] Indeed the lancets and instruments used in cataract operations were so well designed that Hamilton sent examples down to Calcutta to be copied. As for the report that Bogle had requested, he had gathered the information, but was still attempting to compose it. 'I have already committed to the flames a quire or two of Paper sullied with these impotent efforts,' he confessed to Bogle, 'and believe I shall at last be under the necessity of supplying you with materials and you may work them up the best way you can.'[25] It is unclear whether Hamilton ever sent Bogle his notes; no trace of them remains today.

Hamilton was better at forwarding political intelligence. He sent word of the fate of Zhidar, the former Desi of Bhutan, who had first sought refuge with the Panchen Lama, and then been imprisoned at Gyantse. Zhidar, he wrote, 'was invited by the present Deb Rajah [Desi] to reassume the reins of Government in Boutan, and he like an old fool believing him in earnest made his escape out of prison, upon crossing the frontier was met by some of the present Debs people who soon made him shorter by the head which they have fixed upon a pole at Punica [Punakha] as a memorial of the late Rajahs folly and of the presents perfidy.'[26] With the assassination of Zhidar, potential insurgents were deprived of a figurehead, and the Bhutanese regime hoped to secure itself from the threat of future rebellion.

Other news, less momentous politically, was more important personally. At the end of May 1776, Hamilton wrote: 'I was very much concern'd to learn by a formall note accompanying the Lama's letter and by the return of one of mine that the Ping Cooshos were both dead, it seems they died within a few days of each other.'[27] As abrupt as it was shocking, the news would have been hard for Bogle to take in. The lack of explanation and uncanny timing could only have increased the impact. Did both the Lama's nephews succumb to a disease? Was there an accident? Could it have been foul play? Bogle simply did not know.

But sudden loss was a familiar sensation to the British in Bengal. Death stalked the young and vigorous. The following year, Hamilton was again dispatched to Bhutan in a final attempt to settle the border dispute and conclude the agreement on trade. The journey through the monsoon was worse than ever. In Cooch Behar, bridges were washed away, and Hamilton had to abandon his horse to swim across rivers and wade waist-deep along flooded roads. He learnt en route that the final Company ruling on the border had gone against the Bhutanese. By the time that he reached Buxaduar, he was deeply disillusioned and despaired of ever reaching a trade agreement. He wrote to Hastings requesting a new posting. He explained his decision to Bogle in a bravura passage of xenophobic self-pity:

> rather than remain in my present situation, in a country where the performance of a few superstitious rites and ceremonies is consider'd as more meritorious than the exercise of those virtues useful to society, where human nature has arriv'd at a greater pitch of depravity than I have elsewhere experienc'd it; where I am secluded from all social communication with the rational part of mankind, where there is no imolument whatever to be derived and where my allowances are barely equal to my expence, I will troop after a Brigade, do the duty of a regimental hospital for life, or what is equally bad return to Scotland and have it inscribed in large characters over my door – A.H. Late Surgeon in the East India Companies Service, bleeds for sixpence, draws teeth for a shilling.[28]

In a brief postscript, he accounted for his frame of mind. An epidemic was raging at Buxaduar: 'What with the Reliques of my journey, anxiety of mind on many accounts, & stench of the dead & dying, I myself am far from being well.'[29] Less than two weeks later, Hamilton was sufficiently concerned about his health to draw up his will. No more than a brief note, it stated that after the sale of his property and effects, his debts in Bengal and Europe should be settled. Any sum that remained should be sent to his father in Scotland, 'as a small acknowledgement of his paternal care'.[30] Hamilton never left Buxaduar, the village that he had grown to hate. He died three months later, in October 1777.

In his final pessimistic months, Hamilton had seen no possibility of concluding an agreement with Bhutan, but by the end of the following year the Company managed at last to ratify a trade treaty. The Desi agreed that he would 'in no way hinder the passage and trade of Hindu and Mussulman merchants'. There were certain conditions: trade in some items, including sandalwood and indigo, remained a Bhutanese monopoly and Bhutanese goods would enter Bengal duty-free. Most importantly for the Bhutanese, 'no English or European merchants shall be allowed to enter the hills'.[31] Despite these concessions, the protracted efforts of Bogle and Hamilton had finally paid off. With the trade route northwards at last open, Company servants in Bengal could turn their attention to the more distant – and possibly illusory – goal of using the Panchen Lama as the means to reach the Qianlong Emperor himself.

16

TO ADVENTURE FOR POSSIBILITIES

Dull as Bogle found his work on revenue valuation, it offered the perfect humdrum antidote to the high drama of Calcutta political life. As one who 'held the first Place in Mr Hastings' Confidence', Bogle was swept along in the storms that assailed the Governor General.[1] When news of the scandal surrounding Nandakumar's trial and execution arrived in London in April 1776, the Company's Directors were sufficiently alarmed to vote for the recall of the Governor General. Hastings had lost the confidence of the Court of Directors, but he still maintained support among the investors of the Company. When the motion for his recall came before the Court of Proprietors, it was defeated. The factionalism that had so paralysed the Bengal Council seemed to have spread to London. Seeing that there could be no compromise between the parties, Lord North, the Prime Minister, made it clear that one of the two contending factions must stand down.

It fell to Hastings's chief agent in London, Lauchlin Macleane, to respond to Lord North. Because of the delay in communication between India and Britain, Macleane was not yet aware that the death of Monson had reinstated Hastings in a measure of his former authority on the Calcutta Council. Assuming that the situation in Bengal was as embattled as ever, Macleane judged it best by the end of the summer for the Governor General to resign. Macleane had in his possession a letter that he understood authorised him to tender Hastings's resignation. Paying only the most cursory attention to the question of Macleane's authority, the Company Directors accepted the resignation, and appointed Edward Wheler, a former Chairman of the Court of Directors, as the next governor general. Before he left, Wheler learnt of Monson's death, and renounced the post of governor general for Monson's vacated seat on the Council.

The impact of this news, when it reached Calcutta in June 1777, was startling. Far from dousing the flames of factionalism, it served only to fan them. Hastings was unsurprisingly shocked to hear that he had resigned. On the opposing side, General Clavering decided to seize the moment. As senior Councillor and Commander-in-Chief, Clavering had long considered himself Hastings's successor. He had been instructed to act as interim governor general, but did not wait to observe due form. On 20 June, with the backing of Francis, Clavering declared that he was the new governor general. Summoning a Council meeting, he first swore himself in, then demanded from Hastings the symbols of his office: the keys to the Treasury and the Fort. Hastings placed Company forces directly under his own command. Rumours and panic spread through the British inhabitants of Calcutta. At Hastings's insistence, the Justices of the Supreme Court met in emergency session to pass judgement on the contending claims.

Overnight, the judges came to a unanimous decision. They ruled that the Governor General had neither tendered a formal letter of resignation nor authorised his London agent to do so. Clavering was forced to stand down, and the four-day coup was over. 'During the contest,' the diarist William Hickey observed, 'the partisans of each party were excessively violent, putting the Settlement into a state of the greatest anarchy. For several successive days a general insurrection was hourly expected, so much so that the competitors themselves were extremely alarmed for the consequences.'[2] The stress and subsequent disappointment seem to have been too much for Clavering: two months later, his resistance weakened, he died of dysentery.

Recounting the extraordinary sequence of events to his father in November of the same year, Bogle reflected that Clavering's death had 'releived Mr Hastings from a great Part of the Opposition to which he had been so long exposed'. But Hastings's long-term prospects remained uncertain: 'How far it will give stability to his Government, must depend on the Pleasure of the Supreme Power in England.' For his own part, Bogle wished 'for the Service of the Company, and of the British Nation, that Mr Hastings will be confirmed and his Hands strengthened, being possessed of Talents and Experience which it may be difficult to equal, of a Mind more just and disinterested than commonly is to be found in a Man who has passed so many years in public Business, and of a moderation of Temper which is the best Security against these dangerous Commotions to which a country so distant from the Seat of Government is exposed'.[3] Such a glowing tribute – though scarcely 'independent of partiality', as Bogle claimed – testified to the devotion that Hastings could inspire.[4] The years of political adversity seem to have strengthened the bond between protégé and patron.

The loyalty that Bogle consistently demonstrated was finally rewarded by Hastings a year and a half later. In April 1779 the issue of Tibet once again came to the Governor General's attention. The time was right, Hastings judged, to attempt a second mission to the Panchen Lama. Circumstances had changed in Lhasa, he declared to the Bengal Council. From correspondence with Tibet, he had learnt of the death of Jampel Delek, the Regent who had been so obstructive in the matter of trade. The Dalai Lama, he told the Council, 'having attained to full Age has been confirmed by Teshoo Lâma [the Panchen Lama], recognized by the Emperor of China, and has taken upon himself the exercise of his Office, and that this event, as was foreseen, has added much to the influence of Teshoo Lâma, both in the Administration of Thibet, and at the Court of Pekin'.[5]

This gloss on recent events in Lhasa was at best optimistic, at worst misguided. It appears that Hastings's Tibetan correspondent – presumably Purangir or the Panchen Lama himself – had omitted to report that the twenty-year-old Dalai Lama had in fact declined governmental responsibility. At Jampel Delek's death in March 1777, the young Dalai Lama had informed the ruling council in Lhasa that he would continue with his studies. A second regent,

Ngawang Tsultrim, had been appointed by Peking to succeed Jampel Delek. Ngawang Tsultrim had for many years been the Qianlong Emperor's personal tutor and confidant. With the installation of the new regent in August 1777, the Panchen Lama – far from enjoying the enhanced position that Hastings imagined – was learning how to negotiate with the new Lhasa regime.

Hastings, however, assumed that the moment was propitious to reopen trade negotiations. With the conclusion of the Bhutanese border dispute some months previously, the passage of merchants to and from Bengal would be eased. He was hopeful, he told the Bengal Council, that the Company's commercial expectations of Tibet would 'in great measure be fulfilled', and that friendship with the Panchen Lama might 'eventually produce advantages of a far more extensive nature'.[6] For Hastings the long-term goals were all orientated towards China; the Panchen Lama's connection with Chankya, chief Lama in Peking, might offer the means of opening communication with the imperial court. It had been the Panchen Lama himself who had first proposed the scheme to cultivate support for the Company at Peking. Entranced by the plan, Bogle had managed to convey his enthusiasm to Hastings.

The Panchen Lama had sketched out the lines of obligation and influence, of religious patronage and prestige in a letter to Bogle. Chankya, he told Bogle, 'is my Preceptor, and also a Lama, by the Blessing Of God, my Application will be well received by him, and he will never act contrary to it. He will attend to my wish [with] his Heart and Soul and as he is the priest of the Emperor of China, the Emperor will consent to whatever he represents without opposition, and may God grant that a mutual freindship may be established by a free Intercourse of Letters.' This was a most optimistic reading of the relation between the Panchen Lama and Chankya. The chief Lama of Peking was one of the most astute political operators of his day. He was closely identified with the Emperor and would only act in accordance with his own and the imperial court's interests. The Panchen Lama once more affirmed his sincere wish to promote British interests, expressing his 'hearty Desire': 'that your Name may be known in the Countries of China, in those of Calmacks (Tartary) and the adjoining Kingdoms – & that Merchants, Diwans [officials] with their Commodities may arrive

& be exalted in the Govrs Presence. And that Vakeels [envoys] from your Quarter accompanied by Merchants may proceed & be honoured in the Presence of the Emperor of China. This will be for Advantage of the Inhabitants & of the whole world.'[7]

The Panchen Lama's professed desire was well calculated to appeal to British commercial instincts. He seemed to share a European sense of the mutual benefits that could arise from commercial and diplomatic exchange. But, apparently fearful of obstruction, he enjoined Bogle to secrecy: 'I am very intent on accomplishing these objects, but it will be proper to keep them concealed, that the Chiefs of this Country, may not be able to counteract or defeat it, so as to occasion Delays.'[8] It seems that the Panchen Lama was set on pursuing a foreign policy in defiance of Lhasa. He may also have wished to keep the scheme secret because it flouted the rules of Qing trading practice.

The cultivation of trade links with other countries was never a major concern of Qing foreign relations. From other states the Qing principally sought acknowledgement of China's central place in the world order – of its political, cultural and military supremacy. To display an overt interest in foreign goods or technology would be to admit that China was not self-sufficient and might compromise the Qing's claims to supremacy. Embassies sent by foreign princes were regarded as a means of establishing the overlordship of the Qing Emperor. In theory, merchants occupied a lowly position in Chinese society; farmers, rather than traders, were credited as the main creators of the country's wealth (although in practice the Qing court relied heavily on the taxes gathered from trade). In Confucian social hierarchy, scholars, peasants and craftsmen all took precedence over merchants. Contact between Chinese merchants and European traders was stringently regulated; European traders were only allowed to do business at Canton during a specified trading season and were prohibited from learning Chinese. By restricting European movement and linguistic knowledge, the Qing hoped to protect their empire from any social unrest caused by the presence of foreigners.

Since the early eighteenth century, all transactions with Europeans had been handled at Canton by a designated guild, the Co-Hong. *Hong* merchants were responsible for the organisation of the trade and the conduct of foreign traders, both servants of the European trading companies and private merchants. The *hong* merchants fixed prices, controlled the quantity of trade and collected custom dues; they provided linguists and functionaries to attend European ships; they even managed the behaviour of Europeans while in port. In effect, the Co-Hong acted as a kind of intermediary between European traders and the Qing state. To the European traders at Canton, the Emperor appeared utterly remote and inaccessible.

The East India Company had long resented the power of the Co-Hong. In 1771, with the help of a well-placed bribe, the Company managed to break the guild's monopoly. Unable to deal with outside competition, many *hong* merchants went bankrupt. For years *hong* merchants had been borrowing money from private British traders, in defiance of an Imperial Prohibition. Attracted by the towering interest rates (typically 20 per cent), British individuals had lent immense sums to these merchants, but increasingly found that they were unable to reclaim them. Under the Canton system, British merchants had no means of legal redress on defaulting debtors. By the late 1770s, the issue of the Chinese merchants' debts had become a major grievance, particularly in Madras, where many of the British creditors were based.

In 1778 Hastings had tried to circumvent the restrictions at Canton by sending an envoy to Annam in Cochin China (southern Vietnam). The aim of the mission was to find a suitable port where ships from China and India could meet to trade at a safe distance away from the official Chinese gaze (and to pre-empt French moves in the region). There was nothing new about the idea of an alternative venue for the China trade. In 1763 a young Company servant from Madras named Alexander Dalrymple had located the island of Balambangan off the northern coast of Borneo (now the Malaysian state of Sabah) as a site for a British settlement. But the project had met with local and European opposition and never really prospered; it was abandoned in 1775. Hastings however remained keen to repeat the experiment. What prompted the 1778 mission was the chance arrival in Calcutta of two officials from Annam. They had taken passage on a privately owned British ship that had been blown off course, and had been compelled to return to Calcutta. Much as he had launched Bogle's mission in response to the Panchen Lama's letter, so Hastings leapt at the opportunity presented by the officials' fortuitous presence in Calcutta. He appointed a Company servant, Charles Chapman, to escort them back to Annam. Chapman's brief was to conclude a commercial treaty, establish a trading base, and compile a report on all aspects of the region. But political circumstances did not favour the mission. Annam was in the grip of a rebellion, and Chapman's negotiations at the capital of Hué degenerated into open hostility. Within less than a year, Chapman was back in Calcutta with little concrete to show for the venture.[9]

A month after Chapman's return, Hastings was eager to pursue the Company's Tibetan contacts as a means of opening negotiations with Peking. 'It is impossible to point to the precise advantages which either in opening new Channels of Trade, or in obtaining redress of Grievances, or extending the privileges of the Company may result from such an Intercourse,' he told the Council in April 1779.[10] But, given the significance of the China trade, the potential was immense:

> Like the navigation of unknown Seas, which are explored not for the attainment of any certain and prescribed Object, but for the discovery of what they may contain, in so new and remote a search, we can only propose to adventure for possibilities. The attempt may be crowned with the most splendid and substantial Success, or it may terminate in the mere Gratification of useless Curiosity; but the hazard is small, the design is worthy of the pursuit of a rising State, the Company have both approved and recommended it, and the means are too promising to be neglected.[11]

By comparing commerce to exploration, Hastings added a dash of heroic glamour to the enterprise. Who better to head this voyage of discovery, the Governor General suggested, than the resourceful Mr Bogle?

In a rare display of unanimity, the members of the Council gave their approval to the scheme. Only Philip Francis, the most inveterate of Hastings's opponents, added a sceptical caveat to his signature: 'Although my Expectations of Commercial Advantages to be derived from a Communication with Thibet are by no means so sanguine as those expressed by the Governor General, I have no objection to our making the Experiment proposed.'[12] On 19 April 1779, it was resolved that 'Mr. George Bogle be deputed to Bootan and Thibet for the purpose of cultivateing and improving the good understanding subsisting between the Chiefs of those Countries and this Government, and to endeavour to establish a free and lasting intercourse of Trade with the Kingdom of Thibet, and the other states to the Northward of Bengal.'[13]

The prospect of leaving Calcutta appealed deeply to Bogle. The previous year had been an unhappy one. Two of Bogle's closest friends, John Stewart and Alexander Elliot, who had been in London representing Hastings's interests, had found new appointments in Bengal. But neither survived their return long. The newly married Stewart did not even make it to Bengal, dying on board ship. 'What a melancholy and mournfull Situation must the poor Wife have been in!' Bogle's father wrote in commiseration to his son.[14] Elliot had more of a chance to re-establish his friendship with Bogle. But, a year into his return, he was appointed envoy to the court of Nagpur, and died en route. 'This is a Stroke which I cannot support,' Bogle wrote in distress to David Anderson.

> It dashes at once every prospect of Happiness I had formed to myself and leaves me nothing but Dregs. I loved him above all the world and well he deserved it. He was so much of everything that is good and great that he was an Angel rather than a Man – and now Anderson he is gone forever.[15]

As far as his career was concerned, the year had also gone badly. With the work on the revenue settlement completed, Bogle was appointed to the newly created office of commissioner of law suits. His role was to conduct the Company's defence in cases brought against it in the Supreme Court. As he explained to his brother Robin, the post brought only frustration: 'the Causes were always given against us'.[16] 'I never was engaged in any Business that gave me so much trouble,' he complained to his father.[17] Fearing that the job would subject him to the 'Risque of Censure and Discredit', he tendered his resignation, and the post was as a result abolished.[18] In Calcutta there was no immediate likelihood of high office or substantial remuneration.

The family finances were still in a precarious position. His sister Annie was a prudent housekeeper, and had cut back on the purchase of luxury goods in recent years. But the London business was suffering from the interruption in trade caused by the war in America, and Daldowie was still under threat. His father had suggested a scheme to keep the estate in the family that required George to make enough money to cancel its debts. Daldowie would then be assigned to him until such time as Robin, the eldest son and heir, could redeem it. George agreed to the proposal, but expressed his fears to Robin. 'I am afraid my friends may be disappointed,' he wrote to his brother. 'The Accounts of my Thibet Embassy – my Offices of Secretary &c. and my Situation about Mr Hastings may have led them to consider me in the light of a Nabob – But these are all airy built Castles.'[19]

He was unlikely to make a fortune on his new expedition to Tibet, but the pay and allowances were handsome enough: his salary was fixed at the same level as a lieutenant colonel, and he was granted double full *batta*, an allowance to cover his travel and living expenses. He was in hopes of winning favour with the Company Directors in London by locating a Tibetan source for the regular supply of luxurious *pashima* wool for export to Europe. He had already dispatched a messenger to obtain samples to send to London, he reported to the Calcutta Council in April 1779. The item would be mentioned in the next General Letter from Bengal, Bogle was assured, with a request for instructions on the extent of investment and best manner of packing the delicate wool to survive the homeward voyage.

But the grander prize lay in the possibility of opening diplomatic relations with Peking. In Madras, the concern of the British private traders over the Chinese merchants' debts was growing. Two years earlier, the Madras merchants had grouped together to petition the British government to send an official mission to Peking. But the government would only act through the Company, and the Company representative in Madras, the Governor Thomas Rumbold, was reluctant to take on the responsibility. The total now owing to British private merchants amounted to some £2 million, by Bogle's calculation. In addition, the Company had many complaints about the conduct of business at Canton, but no means to make representations to Peking. If only Bogle could find some channel to communicate these grievances to the imperial court, then who knows what rewards a grateful Company – or indeed government – might not lay at his feet?

Dreams of diplomatic glory aside, there was the anticipation of a return trip to Tashilhunpo. Retracing his steps, he would certainly regret the loss of his companion, Alexander Hamilton, and of his genial hosts, the Pung Cushos. But, against this, Bogle could set the prospect of seeing the Panchen Lama once more. Writing to his brother, he represented the mission as a chance to renew the relationship. 'I was again appointed,' he told Robin, 'to pay a Visit to my friend the Teshoo Lama in Thibet.'[20]

THE EMPEROR'S INVITATION

The plans for the Qianlong Emperor's seventieth birthday were under way when Chankya suggested inviting the Panchen Lama. Would it not be a demonstration of true imperial piety, the chief Lama proposed, to invite the Panchen Lama to the *wanshou*, the celebrations for the long life of the Emperor? Chankya recalled that, at their meeting some twenty years previously, the Panchen Lama had expressed the desire to visit him in Peking. But it would be no small matter to persuade the Lama to undertake the gruelling journey from Tashilhunpo, a distance of some two thousand miles.[1] Were he to accept, there would be the complex preparations along the route to receive the entourage, and the Panchen Lama's arrival would have to be commemorated in truly splendid style. But, as Chankya well knew, the very scale of the undertaking would appeal to the Emperor.

The Qianlong Emperor's reign was not only the longest in Chinese history but also the most ostentatious.[2] Extravagant displays of imperial power were themselves an expression of the Emperor's claims to universal monarchy. An aggressive expansionist, he presided over the vast westward growth of the Chinese empire, effectively doubling its extent. Intervening in Tibet in 1751, Qianlong had declared a Chinese protectorate over the country. Later the same decade, a series of ruthless wars against Muslims and the Zunghar Mongols led to the annexation of immense Central Asian territories, some six million square miles, and the destruction of the entire Zunghar people. Under the Qianlong Emperor, China extended its dominion over the largest unified empire in the world.

Such a vast domain required a ruler of proportionate stature. The Manchus adopted the Confucian ideal of the emperor as the father of all peoples, the supreme human and the intermediary between Heaven and Earth. To this was added the Buddhist ideal of the *cakravartin*, or 'wheel-turning king'. The *cakravartin* was a ruler whose conquests in the name of Buddha advanced the world a stage closer to universal salvation.[3] In Buddhist teaching, the *cakravartin* was also associated with the Bodhisattva Manjusri or Wisdom. Promoted to the status of a bodhisattva, a living enlightened being, the Emperor touched divinity. Through the annual cycle of court ritual, the grand sacrifices to Heaven and Earth and the Imperial Ancestors, he acted out his exalted role. His status was woven into the cosmic symbols of his glorious silk dragon robes, and his many attributes were celebrated in endless portraits depicting him in a variety of guises from Taoist priest to living Buddha. By fusing the different traditions of the peoples of the empire, the Emperor offered an awe-inspiring spectacle of universal majesty.

Superabundance and excess defined the Qianlong Emperor. A voracious collector of paintings, he was also a most prolific poet – even if he did not write all of the 40,000 poems attributed to him. He lavished patronage on the arts and scholarship. The more ambitious the scheme – be it architectural, historical, theological or linguistic – the greater the Emperor's enthusiasm. He particularly favoured projects that attempted to encompass the many cultural traditions of his empire. At Chengde, just north of the Great Wall, Qianlong poured funds into an immense landscaped park contrived to represent scenes from all around the empire.[4] Here he built his Xanadu, an extravagant pleasure ground. Indeed the ruins of Shangdu, the Yuan dynasty's summer resort and original of Coleridge's Xanadu, were not very distant.[5] In addition to the lakes, islands, prairies and hills, Chengde was studded with replica palaces and temples, uniting the iconic monuments of China, Central Asia and Tibet. The park was used to host delegations from Inner Asia and Russia, to hold imperial audiences, ceremonies, banquets and special gatherings. It was a great stage for the display of all-embracing imperial bounty.

Between 1767 and 1771 the Qianlong Emperor built at Chengde a version of the Dalai Lama's residence. The Chengde Potala, the Putuozongcheng miao, was erected to commemorate the visit of Mongol tribes on the occasion of Qianlong's sixtieth and his mother's eightieth birthdays. A third of the length of the Lhasa original, the red building dominated the temple area. But, grand as it was, the façade was no more than a blind wall. Like many of the Tibetan-style constructions, it was a great theatrical illusion.[6] The buildings were intended as a mark of respect to the visiting Mongols, a demonstration of the accommodating and all-inclusive nature of the Qing empire. The nomadic Mongols had always constituted the greatest threat to Qing supremacy, and, through such monumental gestures, the Emperor aimed to conciliate them to Qing rule.

The building's completion happened to coincide with the mass return of the Torghut Mongols. For nearly two centuries the Torghut Mongols – or Kalmuks – had occupied an area north of the Caspian Sea. But, after escalating conflict with Russian and Ukrainian settlers and increased Russian demands for tax and military service, a group of some 170,000 Torghuts had set out on the long trek east to seek the Qianlong Emperor's protection. Only half survived the rigours of the journey, but, arriving at the Chinese border, they met with a warm welcome. The Panchen Lama may have acted as an intermediary in the negotiations between the Torghut leaders and Qianlong.[7] The Emperor granted them the depopulated lands formerly inhabited by the Zunghars, and fêted their leaders at Chengde. With the addition of some inscriptions composed by the Emperor, the Putuozongcheng miao was turned into a monument to their return. In the voluntary Torghut submission, the Qianlong Emperor saw the fruits of his patronage of Tibetan Buddhism and evidence of the beneficence of his rule.[8]

The Mongols also played their part in the invitation to the Panchen Lama. Many of their leaders would be invited to Chengde for the imperial birthday celebrations. They would no doubt be impressed if the Panchen Lama were to undertake the arduous journey to Chengde himself. The ability to attract such a revered figure as the Panchen

Lama would demonstrate the extent of imperial virtue. At a single stroke, the Emperor would acquire religious merit, endear himself to the Mongols and enhance his own prestige. As usual, Chankya's advice was most astute. He knew exactly how to appeal to Qianlong's political and religious ambitions. With his knowledge of both the imperial court and the Tibetan Buddhist hierarchy, he made himself indispensable. A cultural mediator and diplomatic negotiator, Chankya brought together different worlds for political and religious ends (functioning, in these respects, rather like Purangir). All possible efforts should be made to induce the Panchen Lama to visit first Chengde, then Peking, the Emperor decreed, in time for the seventieth-birthday celebrations the following year.

But would he accept? The Panchen Lama had previously declined several invitations from the Qianlong Emperor on the grounds that the journey to Peking would expose him to the risk of smallpox infection. This was the customary explanation given by Mongol leaders and high lamas for refusing to undertake the lengthy expedition. Whether it masked a deeper political reluctance, the excuse was readily accepted. It was acknowledged that travellers crossing the northern border of China were particularly susceptible to smallpox, and imperial edicts exempted non-immune dignitaries from making the journey to Peking.

Smallpox was one of the great killers in China. Epidemics might be expected to rage once every three years. The disease was known as the 'gate of life or death': children could not escape infection; but, if they survived, they might make it through to adulthood. As newcomers to China, the Manchus – the imperial family included – had been very vulnerable to the disease. Smallpox even determined the matter of succession. Qianlong's grandfather, the Kangxi Emperor, had been selected precisely because he had survived the disease in childhood. Although the technique of inoculation had been known since the eleventh century, it was not in widespread use in northern China – although the Kangxi Emperor made a point of having his own children inoculated. Peking was notoriously smallpox ridden. In 1763 an epidemic had claimed the lives of 17,000 citizens. Unsurprisingly, hosts of smallpox deities existed to protect sufferers and ward off death.[9]

Great as the threat of smallpox was, so too were the potential religious and political gains for the Panchen Lama. There was the precedent of the Fifth Dalai Lama who, in 1653, had accepted an invitation to the court of the Shunzhi Emperor. To follow in the footsteps of such a celebrated figure – the first monk ruler of Tibet – could not fail to add a certain lustre to the Panchen Lama's reputation. By establishing a direct connection with Peking, he would also strengthen his own position with regard to Lhasa. No more munificent patron of the Gelugpas existed than the Qianlong Emperor. He had already demonstrated his commitment to the faith by commissioning vast works of Tibetan Buddhist scholarship, building temples and endowing monasteries. If the Panchen Lama were to accept an invitation to Peking, he would secure the Emperor's continuing support. The long journey east, a grand progress through his spiritual domain, would give the Mongol people a chance to pay their respects. On arrival, the Panchen Lama would approach the Emperor as his religious teacher. According to the Tibetan understanding of the traditional relationship between lama and patron, the lama was clearly the spiritual superior of the patron. His duty was to impart Buddhist instruction, bestow Tantric initiations and receive offerings from the patron on behalf of his sect. The patron would, in return, extend his protection to the lama and undertake to promote the cause of Buddhism in his realm.[10] Here was an unparalleled opportunity to expand Gelugpa influence throughout the empire.

Towards the end of January 1779, Chankya learnt that the Panchen Lama would be willing to make the journey to Peking. He informed the Emperor, who immediately issued a decree to the *amban* in Lhasa, instructing him to visit Tashilhunpo with a formal invitation and the gift of a precious pearl rosary. By April the Emperor was impatient for a reply, concerned that the decree and rosary had gone astray, suspicious that a messenger might have pocketed the pearls. With his obsessive eye for detail, he ordered that all the courier posts along the way be searched for evidence of the rosary's wooden carrying case. But the following month, news arrived from Lhasa. The Panchen Lama, the *amban* reported, would set out from Tashilhunpo on 29 July 1779; he would over-winter at the great monastery of Kumbum in Amdo, before proceeding to

Chengde to arrive in time for the Emperor's birthday celebrations the following autumn.[11]

As soon as the date for the Panchen Lama's departure was fixed, orders were sent to all the officials stationed along the route from Tashilhunpo to Chengde. They should confirm arrangements for the daily supply of food and provisions to the Lama's entourage, inspect the condition of pasture for pack animals, check the state of yurts and lodgings, examine boats for river crossings.[12] To prepare for the visit, the Emperor himself began to learn Tibetan, so that he would be able to converse directly with the Panchen Lama. In Peking, restoration work started on the Yellow Temple, where the Fifth Dalai Lama had stayed more than a century before. Architects and craftsmen were dispatched to Chengde. No expense would be spared. In less than a year, a new temple must be added to the park's collection: a second Tashilhunpo, the Panchen Lama's home from home.

In Calcutta, Bogle was also preoccupied with the preparations for a journey. Before he could set out for Tibet, there were presents to be purchased, contacts to be informed, servants to be engaged. Then a messenger from the Panchen Lama arrived. The elderly Emperor, Bogle learnt, had been seized by a great desire to see the Panchen Lama before his death. After repeated invitations to Peking, the Panchen Lama had finally accepted. In two months' time, he would set out from Tashilhunpo. But Bogle would not be forgotten. The Panchen Lama would do his best to obtain a passport for Bogle to travel to Peking, either by the overland route, or by way of Canton.

All at once, Bogle's long-cherished dream seemed within grasp. With the Panchen Lama's help, he might be the first Company servant to reach the Forbidden City. But he must proceed with great caution. If the authorities at Canton were to hear of his plans, they would do their best to obstruct them. Bogle set about organising presents 'to pave the way' to the imperial court: pearls and coral, Arab thoroughbred horses, muslins and 'best Birds' Nests'.[13] He also had to carry out commissions for the Panchen Lama. It was necessary, the Panchen Lama had written to Hastings, to present rare gifts on the occasion of the Emperor's birthday, and he enclosed a lump of raw gold to cover the cost. It fell to Bogle to purchase quantities of coral and pearls, 'fair, round, without Blemish, bright', and made into strings of '108 Beads as is the Custom of China'.[14] Although he managed to locate eight strings of pearls, Bogle found only two of the coral. The difficulties of trade between India and Tibet had forced most of the coral merchants out of business. In an amicable gesture, Hastings declined to receive the Panchen Lama's gold, doubtless hoping that the Panchen Lama would prove an even better friend to the Company as a result.

While he waited to hear about his own passport, Bogle thought it wise to send Purangir on ahead to Tashilhunpo. The 'Gosseine', he wrote in a memorandum, 'is in great favour with the Lama' and 'much attached to me'.[15] Purangir was also in debt to Bogle, to the tune of nearly 7,000 rupees. Bogle expected reimbursement from the Panchen Lama, anticipating that he would send valuable 'presents' in return.[16] Purangir would carry the pearls and coral, arriving at Tashilhunpo in time to join the Panchen Lama's entourage on its journey. Purangir was briefed on the Company's concerns about China and instructed to deliver letters from the Governor General. 'I pray to God,' Hastings wrote to the Panchen Lama, 'that your Journey towards China and your Interview with the Emperor may be prosper[ous] and auspicious, that your Steps may be marked with Blessings and Happiness to the Nations of Tartary and China.' It was important to keep lines of communication open during the Panchen Lama's expedition. 'While you are removed at so great a Distance,' Hastings added, 'I shall be anxious to receive frequent Accounts of your Welfare, and earnestly wish that during that Interval there may be some effectual mode established for preserving and extending the Friendship which is happily established between us.' But if letters were to fail, or go astray, Purangir was entrusted to represent the Company's interests. 'For the Rest I beg leave to refer you to Poorungeree who is fully acquainted with all Particulars and will explain them in your presence.'[17]

If the Panchen Lama could not obtain authorisation for Bogle to follow the overland route, then he might gain access from Canton. From there, Purangir could conduct him to Peking to meet up with the Panchen Lama. Through the Lama's good offices, Bogle hoped that he might gain an audience with the Emperor's adviser, Chankya. He could converse with him in the Tibetan that he had picked up on his earlier mission 'so as not to be at the Mercy of Interpreters'.[18] Buoyed up with enthusiasm, Bogle regarded the prospects as distinctly promising. 'If I succeed in procuring Passports,' he wrote, 'I shall then be in a Situation to urge any points at the Court of Pekin with the greatest Advantage. But even if I should be disappointed, I don't think it is possible for me to fail in procuring a Channel of Communication with the Court of Pekin, and get some Person stationed at Canton through whom Representations can be made.'[19]

Purangir set out for Tashilhunpo in mid-August. But at some point in the exchange and interpretation of messages between Tashilhunpo and Calcutta a misunderstanding about dates arose – whether through linguistic error, change of plan or deliberate attempt to mislead is not clear. Hastings was under the impression that the Panchen Lama was due to leave in September. In fact the date of departure had been set for the preceding July. Finding himself months behind the Panchen Lama when he arrived at Tashilhunpo, Purangir set off in arduous pursuit.

More worrying for Bogle was the absence of any news about passports. As the weeks wore on, the silence continued. How long would he have to wait for an answer from the Panchen Lama? It was difficult to remain in a state of arrested readiness. In the past few months, Bogle had made preparations for two separate missions, but still found himself in Calcutta. Perhaps he would have to wait for the Panchen Lama to raise the matter with the Emperor in person. That would postpone the journey by as much as a year. Gradually Bogle's habitual optimism must have ebbed away. But at least he could find comfort in the thought that he had sent Purangir on ahead. Over the years Bogle had come to rely increasingly on the *gosain*'s diplomatic *savoir faire* and ability to travel both unobtrusively and freely. Purangir could be relied on to grasp the political nuances of a situation and give a full account of his dealings. Until now, the *gosain* had simply retraced his steps between Bengal and Tibet. The journey to Peking was the most ambitious expedition that he had ever undertaken. He would accompany the Panchen Lama thousands of miles into the unknown rituals and complex politics of the imperial court.

In September Bogle was distracted from his preoccupation with China by a new development. Hastings was at last in a position to offer him a lucrative appointment. The post of resident and collector of Rangpur had fallen vacant. Bogle had passed through the district of Rangpur on his way to and from Bhutan. A frontier region bordering Bhutan and Nepal, it was notorious to the British for the bands of *sannyasis* or armed monks who frequented the area. It was a marshy, fertile plain, ideal for the cultivation of rice, tobacco, indigo and opium. Threaded through with rivers, half the district was regularly inundated during the rainy season. It was unremittingly flat, although in the cold season the mists cleared to reveal a view of the Himalayan foothills. The malarial marshlands may have held few attractions, but the town of Rangpur was within five days' journey of Bhutan. The town was the destination of trade caravans from Bhutan, and the site of an annual fair that attracted Bhutanese and Tibetan traders. A number of merchant houses were based in Rangpur, including that of Mirza Settar, the Kashmiri trader who had accompanied Bogle on his travels. There would be plenty of opportunities to develop the commercial links that Bogle had fostered on his mission. But what persuaded him to accept the position were the financial incentives.

Bogle's appointment was his long-awaited chance to make enough money to pay off his father's debts. The duties of resident and collector combined the maintenance of order and administration of justice with the collection of taxes. In addition to the basic salary there was a commission on all revenue collected. Since the resident was also in charge of the district courts and gaols, imprisonment was frequently used as a coercive measure to enforce the payment of taxes. So handsome were Bogle's prospects that the Assistant Collector at Rangpur offered him 110,000 rupees (more than £10,000) to resign the post immediately in his favour.[20] As a contemporary observed: 'His appointment is a very good one & it is thought he may make a fortune in a few years.'[21]

For several months Hastings held out hope that something might come of the Panchen Lama's promises. 'I wish you and I could manage this Affair with the Lama,' he wrote to Bogle, now in Rangpur, in November.[22] But by the new year Bogle seems to have accepted the situation. In a letter to his brother Robin in January 1780, he explained that the Panchen Lama had left for China, but that he could not join him: 'as I had not passports I could not go'.[23] By then,

Bogle seems to have been settling into the routine of life in a small settlement. He was concerned to increase the tax revenue of the district and was thinking of establishing a land register. The boredom with his fellow Europeans was starting to show. 'We are a small society of half a dozen here,' he grumbled to his sister Bess. 'We are always together and make it out as well as we can.'[24] The distance from Calcutta was also beginning to tell. 'We have the News and Politics of Calcutta only in Scraps,' he complained to Robin.[25]

What saved the place was its proximity to the border. 'It is close to the Foot of my Bootan Mountains, which you know is my Hobby Horse,' he told his brother. 'I am surrounded with great Parcells of Booteeas [Bhutanese], and am like to be ruined by the quantity of Brandy they drink.'[26] He had in mind a trip to the hills but, as he wistfully observed to Robin, could not quite reconcile himself to the difference he would find. For Bogle the region would always be associated with the Panchen Lama. 'I shall if I go, regret the Absence of my Friend the Teshoo Lama, for whom I have a hearty liking, and should be happy again to have his fat hand on my Head.'[27]

THE MEETING BETWEEN THE TWO

Four months into his progress to the imperial court, the Panchen Lama's retinue arrived at the great monastery of Kumbum in the province of Amdo, the far north-east of Tibet. Surrounded by ridged hills and more distant mountains, the monastery stretched like a town before them. Courtyard upon courtyard of low, whitewashed buildings spread along the lower slopes of a wide valley. To greet the Panchen Lama, three thousand monks lined the approach. From the roof tops, banners streamed, horns sounded and drums beat out a welcome.

The Panchen Lama's safe arrival was indeed cause for celebration. To reach Kumbum, his train had followed the strenuous trail over the dizzying Tang-La pass and Burhan Budai mountains. The traditional route taken by Mongol pilgrims and traders, the track passed through the most inhospitable regions. The Panchen Lama's entourage numbered some 1,500 troops and followers, supported by thousands of pack animals. Like all caravans, they would have travelled in relay, with the beasts of burden leaving the camp at night, and the horsemen overtaking them in the course of the day. Yaks, mules, horses and camels crawled over successive snowy ridges. At 17,000 feet, the Tang-La pass induced breathlessness and giddiness; the traditional remedy for the poisonous mountain vapours was to chew garlic and face backwards on one's mount, away from the wind. Equally hazardous were the icy river crossings. Fording the upper reaches of the Yangtze, the horses might have to swim with the riders clinging on to their backs. Weeks were spent trailing over stony steppes where the interminable expanse was broken only by the dust clouds raised by herds of galloping *drong*s, or wild yaks. Skirting the salt marshes of Tsaidam, the travellers finally encountered the intense blue waters of Lake Kokonor to reach Kumbum before the start of winter.

For the Panchen Lama the journey to Kumbum was a pilgrimage to the origins of his order. The monastery marked the birthplace of Tsongkhapa, the revered founder of the Gelugpas. A golden-roofed shrine was built around the miraculous sandalwood tree that sprang from the spot where the placenta that had nourished Tsongkhapa touched the ground. One of the main monastic centres in Tibet, Kumbum served as a seminary with colleges devoted to religious dance, medicine and Tantric studies. In visiting the monastery, the Panchen Lama was following the example set by the Fifth Dalai Lama, who had stayed at Kumbum over a century before. Received with equal honour, he was accommodated in the same building as the Great Fifth. Throughout the winter season, while the snow fell outside, the Panchen Lama led the monks in rituals and religious discussions. At New Year, he officiated at the festivities and laid on a banquet for monastic officials. He bestowed gifts, ordinations and benedictions by the thousand.

The monks were not the only people to feel blessed by his presence. All along the route, nomads came to do him homage, proffering incense, silver and flowers. As the Panchen Lama's chief minister, the Sopon Chumbo, later wrote to Hastings,

those who sojourn in tents, and those who live in cities, came, and were received according to their degrees, and their stations. And the chief princes of the land, and the pillars of the state, and the great leaders, came forth to meet and to guard him on the high road: and they were waiting his arrival with eager expectation; and they obtained admission to the honours of audience in crowds, crowd after crowd, and they presented their gifts, and their offerings: and he laid his hand, conferring blessings, upon their heads, and made them joyful: and this was the established practice all the way.[1]

Such was the demand for his sacred touch that, when camp was struck, a raised wooden platform was erected, draped in rich brocade and furnished with a cushion. Here the Panchen Lama would sit, cross-legged, while the faithful filed past for a touch of his foot on the forehead. The most fortunate would leave with a copy of the Panchen Lama's handprint, made in saffron upon paper, to treasure as a relic.[2]

By imperial order, local officials greeted the Panchen Lama's train along the way with food and fodder, fresh horses and pack animals. The Panchen Lama wrote to thank the Qianlong Emperor for his 'unending and most great grace' in supplying a palanquin, provisions and 'camels, wagons, horses, mules, bulls, and such beasts of burden by the hundreds'.[3] The Emperor and Chankya, the chief Lama at Peking, both dispatched representatives to do homage to the Panchen Lama. 'Now Panchen Erdeni,' the Emperor wrote to the Lama at Kumbum, 'your coming to the celebration next year on the day of my seventieth birthday makes me very happy within. I am hoping and praying that you yourself may come quickly . . . I am now learning the Tibetan spoken language; when we shall meet face to face we shall engage in a great conversation.'[4] To accompany his letter the Emperor sent a deluge of gifts: a pearl rosary, a highly wrought gold saddle and harness, silver teapots, fine satin brocades and 'a high stepping horse with an excellent mane'.[5]

To Kumbum, Purangir, the indefatigable *gosain*, finally made his way. Having set out from Tashilhunpo months behind the Panchen Lama, he managed to catch up with the party only at the monastery. Although able to travel more swiftly than the official caravan, he would have had to cope with deteriorating weather conditions. At Kumbum he had the chance to recuperate, to deliver the letters and gifts from Hastings and Bogle, and brief the Panchen Lama on the concerns of Calcutta. Given leave to join the entourage, Purangir was once again at the heart of Tibetan political affairs. He could take advantage of messengers carrying official correspondence to Tashilhunpo to send his own letters to Bogle at Rangpur.[6] As the party prepared to head towards the seat of Qing power, the British had their informant placed securely within the inner circle.

The date for departure from Kumbum was set for 14 April 1780 when 'the planets and stars were in perfect and auspicious conjunction'.[7] The onward journey led through Inner Mongolia, across the deserts of Alashan and Ordos. In these regions of shifting sand, the party was entirely dependent on the supplies provided by the Emperor. The only forage available was thorny shrubs and tough, spiked grass. Water, too, was in short supply, with muddy ponds and cisterns at intervals along the route. But these natural hazards preoccupied the Panchen Lama's advisers less than the danger that awaited them in the populated areas of China. The northern border zone was notorious for smallpox infection. Travellers and invaders regularly fell victim to the disease. Would it be wise for the Tibetans to subject themselves to the Chinese practice of inoculation? Should the Panchen Lama himself undergo the procedure? In China it was customary to inoculate children in the spring by plugging the nose with wads of cotton soaked in camphor, herbs and powdered smallpox scabs. The infant contracted a mild form of smallpox that lasted between two and three weeks. But it was not clear how an adult might respond. After long debate and divination, it was determined that those members of the party who were not immune should retire to a monastery to be inoculated. Having read the lots, the Panchen Lama decided that he alone would not go.

When the imperial officials were informed of this decision, their anxiety was palpable. It was their duty, they said, both to attend to the Panchen Lama's needs and to report his every action to the Emperor. What the Panchen Lama was proposing broke with all custom and precedent. How would the Emperor react if anything went wrong with the inoculation? As the responsible officials, they would bear the brunt of imperial displeasure; indeed they feared for their necks. But the lots he had cast boded no ill, the Lama insisted reassuringly. If tragedy should strike, he added, he himself would stand between them and the Emperor's anger.[8]

With his entourage reduced to around fifty, the Panchen Lama continued on his way. The attendants who had left to be inoculated would catch up upon recovery. In towns, Muslim and Chinese residents lined the streets alongside Mongol devotees to pay their respects. At the request of local people, the Panchen Lama performed ceremonies to regulate the weather. According to his Tibetan biography, he tamed a gale that had raged for five days with the ritual

'Vanquishing of the Wind'. In a drought-stricken region, he summoned a gentle rain, and the people were 'renewed in hope'.[9] After
weeks of riding, the harsh conditions of the Ordos plateau at last gave
way to the green of the Mongolian grasslands. The landscape that they
now entered would have been deeply refreshing. In the words of a
sixth-century folk saying: 'The sky is blue and white, the earth is flat
and vast, the grasses bow before the sweeping winds, and innumerable
sheep and cattle are seen.'[10]

Every stage of the Panchen Lama's progress was relayed to
the Qianlong Emperor. A highly efficient courier system allowed
the Emperor to receive regular reports from officials stationed
along the route. These dispatches he would read during his morning
office hours. His afternoons were dedicated to artistic and intellectual
pursuits: to poetry, painting, calligraphy or reading. The imperial
routine never varied, even when the Emperor was on tour. From
February to June 1780, he travelled through the southern provinces of
China, seeking warmer weather and scenic spots, visiting temples,
inspecting public works and interrogating officials in a demonstration
of his concern for the people. A man of considerable intellectual and
physical vigour, Qianlong did not slacken as he approached seventy.
Gifted with a prodigious memory and an appetite for paperwork, he
oversaw all aspects of government. He had of course long been
accustomed to absolute command and was supremely confident in
his abilities. No project was too grand, no detail too small for his
consideration. Under his watchful eye, the Panchen Lama's visit was
finely choreographed. The Sixth Prince and the chief Lama, Chankya,
were deputed to meet the Panchen Lama en route at the monastery of
Taska, a month's journey from the summer palace.[11] The Emperor
sent frequent letters to the Panchen Lama, and regularly dispatched
gifts: precious ritual artefacts, fur coats from his own wardrobe, and –
on one occasion – an immense fresh fish.

The most extravagant of the Emperor's gestures was the construction of the temple in the Panchen Lama's honour at Chengde. The
architecture and landscape of Chengde, the imperial resort founded by
his grandfather, numbered among Qianlong's great enthusiasms. The

Emperor was involved in every aspect of the garden's design. Following the example of his grandfather, he identified thirty-six views at Chengde which he commemorated in verse in the illustrated *Album of Imperial Poems* that was distributed to members of the imperial family and tributary princes. His poems, often in multilingual translation, were inscribed on stone tablets set near buildings or at viewing spots around the grounds. In verses delighting in the garden's beauty, reflecting on the imperial condition or the history of the Qing, the Emperor wrote himself into the landscape. Hills, lakes, pavilions and temples all celebrated the achievement of the empire, the variety of its scenery and cultural traditions. Like Louis XIV at Versailles, the Qianlong Emperor turned Chengde into a grand monument to Qing artistry and power.[12]

In less than a year and at vast expense, the Xumifushou miao or 'Temple of Happiness and Longevity of Mount Sumeru' spread over a hillside at Chengde. Supposedly modelled on the Panchen Lama's residence, the Xumifoushou miao resembled Tashilhunpo only in the red of the exterior walls.[13] A pair of marble elephants knelt, forelegs improbably outstretched, on either side of the main gateway. Filling most of the central court was an ornate temple with curved copper-gilt roof, topped by writhing golden dragons. The Panchen Lama's lodgings were located just behind. The complex ended near the hill's summit in a yellow and turquoise ceramic pagoda, seven storeys high.

The most opulent of all the Chengde temples, the Xumifoushou miao was a dazzling display of imperial piety. To ensure that all his subjects should appreciate this act of devotion, the Qianlong Emperor composed an inscription for the temple, translated into Chinese, Manchu, Mongol and Tibetan. A special pavilion was built to house the imperial word, carved on a pillar and mounted on the back of a massive marble tortoise. In the dedication, the Emperor paid scant regard to the actual sequence of events leading to the temple's foundation. The Panchen Lama's travels, the Emperor claimed, were 'not in response to Our summons but came from his own desire to visit the capital in order to witness the flourishing of the Gelukpa sect, [Our] nurturing and teaching, the ubiquitous peace and happiness, and the plenitude of goods in China'. Equally disingenuously, the Emperor asserted that he 'had not intended to allow extravagant ceremony' to mark his seventieth birthday, but could not hinder the Panchen Lama's wish to honour him. The Xumifoushou miao, wrote Qianlong, had been modelled on Tashilhunpo to give the Panchen Lama 'a restful place for meditation'.[14]

By ignoring the repeated earlier invitations sent to Tashilhunpo, the Emperor suggested that it was his virtue alone that attracted the Panchen Lama. In the imperial version of events, designed for posterity, the Panchen Lama's visit testified to the thriving state of the empire under Qianlong. When the Fifth Dalai Lama had come to Peking at the invitation of Qianlong's great-grandfather, the Shunzhi Emperor, the empire had been troubled by Mongol resistance. But now, the Emperor continued, the Mongol tribes had been brought to obedience, and there was 'complete peace and harmony'. At the news of the Panchen Lama's visit, the Mongols 'rejoiced and all wanted to serve him and adore him'. The erection of the Xumifoushou miao, the Emperor concluded, marked the pacification and protection of the realm, and celebrated the 'absolutely sincere desire of the vassal peoples to become civilised'.[15] Even before he arrived, the Panchen Lama was assigned a role in court politics and imperial mythology. Under the Emperor's exacting eye, the stage was set for a triumphant display of Qing power and piety.

By mid-August, the Panchen Lama had reached the imperial hunting grounds of Mulan, the final stage of his journey. At night, the camp was alive with shouts and blazing fires, as the sentries warded off the leopards and tigers that lived in the forests. These beasts were reserved for the court's sport on the annual hunting trip. For a few weeks every year nobles, princes, government officials, Bannermen (soldiers of the hereditary imperial army) and members of the imperial household – including consorts and children – descended on Mulan. With around thirty thousand participants, imperial hunts were elaborate exercises in 'the simple life'. Following the traditions of the Emperor's Manchu forebears, the hunters stayed in Mongol tents, ate plain fare and shifted camp in pursuit of their quarry. But this year the wild beasts were spared the slaughter in deference to the Panchen Lama.

A day's journey further south brought the Panchen Lama's party to the environs of Chengde. The official welcome began at a distance: successive bands of mounted ministers, sporting peacock feathers in their hats, galloped up to the Panchen Lama's sedan chair. They dismounted and prostrated themselves thrice, before galloping back to make way for the next group. At the sight of this unfamiliar escort-by-relay, the Tibetans found it hard not to laugh. Teams of bearers provided by the Emperor carried the Panchen Lama's sedan chair for the last leg of the journey, up a hill to the small pass that led to Chengde. After more than a year on the road, the travellers could finally look down on their destination.

Spread below was the court's summer resort, an entire valley devoted to imperial pleasure. Pine-covered hills surrounded eight artificial lakes, an archipelago of islands, mountains and open prairie. To the south was the palace, and all around were dotted pavilions, kiosks and temples. 'From a distance they saw the wondrous great country,' related the Panchen Lama's biography. 'The mountains and valleys were dyed emerald with fresh grass, young sprouts, green trees, fruit trees loaded with beautiful fruit, cultivated fields of various grains, streams of cool fresh water which flowed quietly along, and were filled with many pleasing houses.'[16]

Descending into this idyll, they were greeted by massed Mongols and Bannermen, ministers and monks. As a mark of respect, the Panchen Lama was invited to make his entry in one of the sedan chairs reserved for the Emperor's personal use. 'I am a very low ranking monk,' the Panchen Lama courteously protested, 'I cannot use the Manjushri emperor's daily sedan.'[17] But, the officials responded, the Emperor wished to honour him and the sedan chair itself would be blessed by his presence. Politely acquiescing, the Panchen Lama settled himself in the chair, accompanied by fifty horsemen and a band of 'big drums, small strings, bamboo flutes, flat drums, round drums, long trumpets, horns, and many different cymbals – fantastic, beautiful and fearful looking'.[18]

Modest and unadorned, at least by the grandiose standards of Qing architecture, the palace was conceived as a rural retreat. From the main gateway, the Panchen Lama was conducted through a series of courtyards towards the reception chamber, where he descended to pay his respects. Arrayed in all his splendour, surrounded by ministers, stood the man considered 'the ruler of the earth'.[19]

The Panchen Lama presented a white silk scarf and jewelled statue of the Buddha. 'As the greetings started, the Panchen Lama began to kneel down but the emperor took his hand and made him rise, saying in Tibetan, "Lama, please do not kneel." '[20] Or so the Tibetan story goes. The Manchu version of events is strikingly different. Here the Panchen Lama not only knelt, but prostrated himself before the Emperor. 'For this Old Buddha, I would perform the rites of bowing,' the Panchen Lama declared in the official *Rehe Gazetteer*.[21] In a note to a poem that he composed on the Panchen Lama's visit, the Emperor observed, 'Our dynasty's family laws rule that when lamas come for an imperial audience, they only have to kneel . . . not kowtow . . . to the emperor.' But the Panchen Lama insisted on performing the full kowtow, which demonstrated his 'respect and sincerity'.[22]

The act of obeisance disappeared entirely in the account of the meeting that Purangir later gave to Hastings. It was at the Panchen Lama's particular request, Purangir claimed, that he was one of the six attendants to accompany the Lama into the reception chamber. According to Purangir, the Emperor received the Lama some forty paces from his throne, and 'immediately stretching forth his hand, and taking hold of the Lama's, led him towards the throne, where, after many salutations, and expressions of affection and pleasure, on both sides, the Lama was seated by the Emperor upon the uppermost cushion with himself, and at his right hand'.[23]

The moment of greeting played a central role in establishing the precise nature of the relationship between the Panchen Lama and the Emperor. In the highly symbolic encounter, every comment, every gesture was laden with religious and political meaning. For the Tibetans, the Panchen Lama was the Emperor's spiritual superior. In preventing the Panchen Lama from kneeling, the Emperor was paying due respect to the Lama as his religious teacher. But, to the Manchus, the Emperor was the supreme lord, and the Panchen Lama his inferior. By voluntarily performing the kowtow, the Panchen Lama was willingly submitting himself to the Emperor's authority. And in addressing Qianlong as an 'old Buddha', he was acknowledging the Emperor's status as a bodhisattva, or living enlightened being.[24] For Purangir, by contrast, the relationship between Emperor and Panchen Lama appeared free from hierarchical constraint. Taking the Panchen Lama by the hand, the Emperor acted the part of the amicable host, welcoming an honoured guest. It would of course have been in the interests of Purangir, reporting back to the British, to stress the strength and intimacy of the Panchen Lama's relations with the Emperor.

If the accounts agree on little else, they at least concur that the encounter was truly momentous. All parties seemed set to gain from the meeting of these two great figures. There was more than enough religious and political prestige to go round. In the Panchen Lama's biography, Chankya, chief Lama of Peking, declared that 'the meeting between the Two, Lama and Patron', was 'a great joyous occasion unlike any other'.[25] The Emperor himself, in a poem composed that very day, claimed to be making history:

> By honouring one person, I've made tens of thousands happy
> Both your name and mine will mark history.[26]

Without a doubt, the meeting was a monumental act of political theatre. Drawing on his immense resources, Qianlong could set the stage, provide the scenery and transport the cast hundreds of miles. But not even he could dictate the plot.

THE PURE LIGHT OF THE VOID

For the first few months of the Panchen Lama's visit, all went according to the imperial plan. Lodged in his newly built monastery, the Panchen Lama fulfilled his ceremonial functions with dignity and grace. He blessed shrines and buildings throughout the palace, attended banquets in the vast yurt erected in the Garden of Ten Thousand Trees, granted titles and officiated at the rituals for the Long Life of the Emperor. His presence sanctified the imperial birthday celebrations and gratified the audience of Mongolian dignitaries.

Between public appearances, there were opportunities for the Panchen Lama to meet the Emperor more intimately. In the months leading up to the Panchen Lama's visit, Qianlong had mastered conversational Tibetan, but still needed Chankya to interpret when the talk turned to theology. Between the three of them, the Panchen Lama imparted religious instruction and conferred Tantric initiations. He also bestowed blessings on the Emperor's children, paying particular attention to the six-year-old Gurun Hexiao, whom Qianlong had recommended as especially pious. 'This princess,' the Emperor informed the Lama, 'is very interested in the dharma. I treat her equally with my sons in gifts and love. This daughter's good tendencies must be a result of her devotion to Buddhism in her previous life. So she has strong faith in you, and is very interested in visiting you.'[1]

Invited to tea, the well-drilled Princess insisted on kneeling throughout, despite the Lama's suggestion that she sit cross-legged; she had to kneel before her father, she explained, and the Panchen Lama deserved equal respect. Such courtesy in one so young suggested that she was a bodhisattva like her father, declared the Panchen Lama. Then he proceeded to instruct her (at her own wish), bestowed gifts and a sacred name on her. As they parted, the Princess removed her own rosary and presented it to the Lama, requesting that he act as her guide in future lives.

How far the Panchen Lama touched on matters political in his conversations with the Emperor is hard to determine. The Manchu records and the Panchen Lama's Tibetan biography concentrate on the ceremonial and religious aspects of the encounter. From them we learn nothing explicit about political discussions. But accounts of the meeting that reached the British focus on the possibility of direct contact between the Emperor and Calcutta – that elusive goal so dear to Bogle and Hastings. The Panchen Lama 'took several occasions of representing, in the strongest terms, the particular amity which subsisted between the Governor General and himself', the Panchen Lama's brother and chief minister reported.[2] So great was the Panchen Lama's influence, they continued, that the Emperor had resolved to open a correspondence with Hastings, through the Lama's mediation.

Purangir substantiated these assertions in his report to Hastings, detailing the conversation between the Panchen Lama and the Emperor. 'In the country of Hindostan, which lies on the borders of my country,' the Lama told the Emperor, 'there resides a great prince, or ruler, for whom I have the greatest friendship. I wish you should know and regard him also; and if you will write him a letter of friendship, and receive his in return, it will afford me great pleasure, as I wish you should be known to each other, and that a friendly communication should, in future, subsist between you.' The Lama's request 'was a very small one indeed', the Emperor replied, 'but that this, or any thing else he desired, should be readily complied with'. Purangir himself then entered the narrative, as the expert summoned to answer the Emperor's questions on Hindostan. The Governor was called Mr Hastings, Purangir informed Qianlong, 'the extent of the country he governed was not near equal to that of China, but superior to any he knew', and the mounted forces at his command numbered over three hundred thousand.[3]

Some historians have doubted whether this conversation ever took place, arguing that Purangir, the Panchen Lama's brother and his minister were only reporting what Hastings wanted to hear (particularly in the light of the expensive gifts that the British had invested in the venture).[4] But Purangir and the Tashilhunpo officials do not seem any more or less unreliable than the other sources. As we have already seen, all the interested parties interpreted the meeting of the Emperor and the Panchen Lama in the light of their own concerns. There was too much at stake in the encounter for the accounts ever to agree. At some stage in the visit, the Panchen Lama may well have raised the issue of the British with the Emperor. After all, the plan to open a correspondence between Peking and Calcutta had initially been his, suggested five years previously to Bogle at Tashilhunpo. The Panchen Lama had been careful to keep the relationship with the British alive over the years, and it would have been in his interest to do what he could for his allies. During the course of his journey, he had written to Bogle and Hastings at least once.[5] He was not averse to intervening on behalf of others, and had confidence in the extent of his influence. Whether that confidence was well placed was another matter.

The month-long festivities at Chengde culminated in the celebration of the Emperor's birthday. Towards the end of September, with the last banquet consumed, the final firework spent, the great yurt dismantled and put into storage, the entire entourage took to the road again. The imperial party made its way to Peking by a roundabout route, stopping at the Eastern Tombs to allow the Emperor to worship at the ancestral mausoleums, while the Panchen Lama headed south-west for the capital. There were two well-maintained roads between Chengde and Peking, one reserved for the Emperor's sole use, the other for his attendants and guests. Descending from the mountains, they took the most direct – and sometimes steepest – route for the 150 miles down to the North China plain. With lodges and guard posts at frequent intervals, the final leg of the Panchen Lama's journey would certainly have been the most luxurious.

On 29 September 1780, the Panchen Lama made his grand entry into Peking, 'this capital of my vast dominions', as Qianlong termed the city.[6] Monks by the thousand lined the streets to do him reverence. The Yellow Temple was now ready to receive the Panchen Lama. Ever alert to the power of historical parallel, Qianlong hoped to gain further glory from the temple's association with the Fifth Dalai Lama and his own great-grandfather, the Shunzhi Emperor. Under Qianlong's patronage, Peking's population of Tibetan Buddhist monks had grown to some four or five thousand, with over forty temples in both palace and city. Ambitious to turn Peking into a centre of Tibetan Buddhist learning to rival the great monasteries of Tibet, Qianlong had converted an imperial mansion into the monastic college of Yonghegong. The Panchen Lama's visit to his capital would crown the Emperor's achievement in fostering the faith.

With Chankya and the Sixth Prince as his guides, the Panchen Lama went sightseeing. Peking was a highly compartmentalised city, divided into concentric rings separated by massive walls. Crossing the city to visit temples, the Panchen Lama's sedan chair would have had to pass through successive fortified gates. Each part of the city had a particular function or racial designation. The Chinese population lived in the southern Outer City, devoted to commercial activity and popular entertainment. Manchu Banner families occupied the Inner City, while the central Imperial City contained government offices and royal gardens. And at the very core stood the imperial palace, the Forbidden City itself. Ringed by a wide moat and impressive walls, guarded by six hundred soldiers, the Forbidden City was the monumental expression of imperial authority. The massive halls and courtyards, residences and shrines were arranged symmetrically. Their red walls and roofs of imperial yellow added to the sense of grandeur and uniformity. The sheer scale and consistency of design were intended to induce awe; this, after all, was the symbolic centre of the world.

The Panchen Lama made his way to the Forbidden City to attend a banquet thrown in his honour at the Hall of Preserving Harmony.

Compared to the relative informality of Chengde – where banquets were held in the yurt to set Mongolian chiefs at their ease – the occasion would have called for the full panoply of imperial hospitality. Life in the Forbidden City was governed by the ceremonial demands of state. Here the Emperor enacted his ritual role as Son of Heaven. To escape these formal constraints, Qianlong spent most of his time at Yuanming Yuan, an extensive garden palace, twelve miles to the north-west of Peking. In the course of his tour, the Panchen Lama was invited to sample the refined charms of the garden residence.

At Yuanming Yuan, the Qing had created a world of water, islands and hills. The imperial residence was built around a lake, on nine islands connected by bridges. Here the Emperor could play the aesthete: fashion landscapes to replicate paintings, supervise the artists of the Painting Academy, and watch the sun sink behind the hills in a special sunset-viewing chamber. His consorts could amuse themselves shopping in a staged market, staffed by court eunuchs trained in the arts of crying wares, bargaining and thieving. For more exotic diversion, the court could repair to the European fantasyland, designed by Jesuits, where elaborate fountains spouted in front of Baroque palaces. These fountains made a particular impression on the Panchen Lama's chief minister, the Sopon Chumbo, who later recalled the water clock 'with figures of a gigantic size, representing the signs of the zodiac; each figure, as the sun entered its corresponding sign, becoming a fountain of water, which continued to play until his passage to the next'.[7] At the nearby Kunming Lake, the visitors were treated to a display of naval power. The Emperor 'had ordered a ship to be constructed on a large lake, and armed with guns, to resemble a first rate man of war', recounted the Sopon Chumbo. 'The guns were discharged on board this ship, to give them an idea of a sea engagement' – a novel sight for the visitors from landlocked Tibet.[8]

Even the most private parts of the palace were open to the Panchen Lama, Purangir reported. With the Emperor's special permission, the Lama was allowed to approach the women's quarters. Qianlong had more than forty consorts, ranked in strict hierarchy according to imperial favour, attended by a staff of some three hundred maids and two thousand eunuchs. Once they had entered the Emperor's household, these consorts stayed within the palace for life, leaving only if fortunate enough to accompany the Emperor on his visits to Chengde or tours of the empire. According to Purangir, many of the consorts were impatient to see the Panchen Lama and receive his blessing. To gratify their wishes, the Lama was invited to sit opposite a doorway to their quarters, screened off with yellow gauze. The imperial consorts:

> approached it, one by one, and having just looked at the Lama, through the gauze, each, according to her rank, and abilities, sent her offering, or present, by a female servant, who delivered it to one of the Lama's religious companions, that were allowed to continue near him; and upon the present being delivered to him, and the name of the person announced, he repeated a prayer, or form of blessing, for each; all the time bending his head forward, and turning his eyes directly towards the ground, to avoid all possibility of beholding the women.[9]

Returning to the Yellow Temple, the Panchen Lama continued with his round of religious duties. Much of the Panchen Lama's time was occupied in bestowing blessings. From the imperial family down, Peking's inhabitants streamed to do him reverence. Purangir explained that the form of benediction was graduated according to the recipient's rank. Only princes and members of the ruling family received the Lama's hand directly on their heads. For nobles, he wrapped his hand in silk; for commoners, he used a wooden rod. The Panchen Lama also officiated at temples, initiated monks, taught at the college of Yonghegong and lectured at the Yellow Temple to mixed Mongolian and Chinese Buddhist congregations.

During his stay in Peking, there were regular opportunities for more private discussions with the Emperor. On one of these occasions, Purangir recounted, the Lama reverted to the subject of the British, repeating his request that the Emperor should engage in a friendly correspondence with Mr Hastings. Qianlong was more than happy to comply with his wishes, Purangir reported, 'and to convince him of his sincerity, he would, if the Lama desired it, cause a letter to be immediately written to the Governor, in such terms as the Lama would dictate; or, if the Lama thought it would be more effectual, towards establishing the friendship he wished, that the letter should be in readiness, when the Lama took his departure from China; and that he should take it with him, and have the care of forwarding it, in such manner as he thought best, to the Governor of Hindostan.'[10] Having secured this undertaking, the Lama did not think it necessary to request the letter at once. He would carry it with him when he left. The British dream of communication between Calcutta and Peking was, apparently, within grasp.

Outside the weather grew colder. By mid-November, it was snowing heavily. On the lake in the Western Park, Bannermen engaged in skating competitions (including acrobatics and archery on ice). The Tibetans had never seen anyone skate before; the Sopon Chumbo would later recall his amazement at the sight of a race between a skater and a horseman, which the skater won.[11] As the winter took hold, the Panchen Lama pressed on with his duties. According to Purangir, whole days, and sometimes part of the night, were taken up 'conferring his blessings upon all ranks of people, who continually crowded to him for that purpose'. Indeed it seemed to Purangir that 'there was not a man, of any denomination whatever, in the extensive city of Pekin, who did not, during the time of the Lama's living there, come to him, and receive his blessing.'[12]

On 20 November, the Panchen Lama confided in the Sopon Chumbo that he did not feel well. He had a headache and no appetite. But it was nothing, he added. After two days, the Sopon Chumbo insisted on consulting Chankya. As an incarnation of Amitabha, Chankya said, the Panchen Lama should not be susceptible to any serious disease. His pulse seemed normal, but, given the change in climate, water and environment, he should take care. He should ask the Emperor to postpone his engagements. 'I am not seriously ill,' the Panchen Lama replied. 'Please do not tell the emperor.'[13]

Later that day, the Panchen Lama attended a banquet held by the Sixth Prince, conducted an initiation rite for the Emperor and exchanged gifts with him. According to his Tibetan biography, the Panchen Lama turned to Chankya at the end of the ceremony and said with a smile, 'I feel released and happy. All my work is done.' Alarmed, Chankya replied that he should not say such things. There should be no talk of dying. His work was far from over. While the

Emperor's wishes may have been fulfilled, there was still much to be done in Tibet. What Chankya said was true, conceded the Lama, 'I just made a kind of joke.'[14]

But then the rash started. It was the Sopon Chumbo who first noticed the red spots on the Lama's palms and the soles of his feet. There could be no mistaking the symptoms. Spreading through the Panchen Lama's body was the disease that they had dreaded from the outset, the disease that lurked along China's northern borders, the disease that many of the Tibetans had been inoculated against, the disease that only the Panchen Lama seemed not to fear: smallpox.

The news of the Panchen Lama's condition spread quickly. Throughout the city, thousands of monks started to recite prayers for him. The Lama's attendants distributed quantities of silver to the monasteries and alms to the poor on his behalf. Abandoning cere-monial, Qianlong visited the sickroom, accompanied by his own physicians. The Emperor sat by the Lama's bed, related Purangir, 'took him by the hand; and for a considerable time, did not cease to encourage him, with the most soothing and affectionate language, assuring him that his prayers should be constantly sent forth for his speedy recovery'.[15] He then enjoined the assembled doctors and clerics to take the utmost care of the Lama, and instructed the Sixth Prince and Chankya to stay in constant attendance. He ordered that paintings depicting the stages of smallpox infection be hung around the room, perhaps as an aid to prognosis. According to Chinese medicine, the four stages of the disease – fever, the emergence of spots, pustules and scabs – each lasted three days. Smallpox, a physician wrote, 'changes one's appearance as snakes shed their skins, and as dragons change into bones'.[16] The location, colour and shape of the spots could be read for auspicious or ominous signs. As he left, the Emperor declared that 'nothing, which could be procured in China, should be wanting, that might tend to mitigate, or ease his pain'.[17]

For Qianlong, this was the worst possible turn of events. Whether or not he was personally afflicted, he would have regarded the Panchen Lama's illness as inauspicious in the extreme. It threatened to wipe out all the religious and political prestige that the Emperor had ac-cumulated over the course of the visit. On his return to the palace, Qianlong distracted himself with painting. It was to be a picture of a

Sal tree, the tree that shaded the Lord Buddha at his birth and death. He would send it as a present to the Lama. But, before it was sent, a copy of the painting was carved in stone, with an accompanying multilingual inscription in Chinese, Tibetan, Manchu and Mongolian. The stone engraving would allow rubbings to be distributed to all the interested parties (see plate 12).[18] As always with Qianlong, it is impossible to disentangle the private gesture from the imperial act; the painting was at once a get-well gift and a public statement of concern.

As his condition worsened, the Panchen Lama devoted himself to prayer. 'From time to time,' according to his biography, 'he would gaze into the sky and joining his palms together he seemed repeatedly to gaze upon the faces of the gods.'[19] He continued to discuss philosophy with Chankya and bless the stream of visitors. Four days into his illness, the Panchen Lama called for six or seven of his closest attendants, including Purangir. He told them that 'he found his disorder so much more than he could support, that he considered their prayers as the comfort he could now enjoy'.[20] They prayed with him all day, the Lama seated cross-legged, propped between two large cushions, against the wall. Towards sunset, without shifting from his position of prayer, he died.

'He became in truth the pure light of the Void, and for a while his body became absorbed into the breast of the Buddha Amitabha,' the Tibetan biography relates.[21] At the moment of his death, the Panchen Lama's body glowed with an unearthly luminescence and gave off a sweet fragrance. Intersecting rainbows arched through the sky and a rain of flowers fell from the clouds. His attendants, 'like blind men in a fearful desert and wilderness separated from their guide', broke down and cried, 'the hidden waters of their hearts bubbled over and welled forth as drops of tears'.[22]

20

THE TANK

News of the momentous events in China had not yet reached Bogle in Rangpur. He last heard from the Panchen Lama and his party on the journey towards Chengde. The letters were long delayed in transit and had suffered a ducking when the bullock carrying them had stumbled at a river crossing. Bogle knew that he could not expect a regular correspondence. 'I have no late Accounts of Teshoo Lama,' he told his father in April 1780. 'Indeed, as he is now in the Middle of Tartary I can hardly expect to hear of him during the Winter.'[1] Reconciled to the silence, Bogle continued to place his trust in Purangir. The *gosain* could be relied on to act as his ears and eyes at the imperial court.

In return, Bogle did his best to protect Purangir's interests in Bengal. When Purangir's guru, Sukhdeogiri, died in 1780, Bogle became involved in a wrangle over the inheritance. Sukhdeogiri had built up a great fortune over a lifetime's trading to and from Tibet. He left property in Patna and assets worth 'not less than a Lack & a half of Rupees', Bogle imagined.[2] Having fallen out with Purangir, the old man had adopted another disciple. This new disciple, Bogle feared, might inherit in Purangir's place. To find the best method to lay claim to Purangir's share of the fortune, Bogle wrote to his friend David Anderson in Calcutta, requesting him to make enquiries of the Hindus of his acquaintance, then to take the necessary legal steps through the Governor General to secure the estate. 'I am anxious about Poorungeer's story as it is so great an object to him,' he told Anderson.[3] Hastings would not take exception to such a request, he reassured Anderson, 'the Governor has already favoured Poorangeer too much to be displeased with the Trouble you will give him.'[4] For his own part, Bogle justified his request to Anderson in terms of his duty to Purangir: 'it behoves me,' he wrote, 'as much as possible to support Poorin.'[5]

If Bogle's hopes of the Panchen Lama's trip to China had yet to materialise, he could at least see the fruits of his commercial negotiations with Bhutan. During his first year at Rangpur, the annual fair attracted 'a great Concourse of Bootea Merchants', he told his father. The traders were no longer required to pay duty on Bhutanese goods entering Bengal and, 'left to the freedom of their own Will in buying and selling', they had 'gone away very well satisfied'.[6] While Rangpur's proximity to Bhutan facilitated trade, the province's border with Nepal was more problematic. As collector of a frontier district, Bogle was charged with the maintenance of law and order, and had an armed force at his disposal. Troubled by reports of Gurkha-backed raids along the border, he dispatched a division of sepoys to the area, confiding in Anderson that he was 'half threatened with a little war' himself.[7] But Bogle seems to have adapted quickly to his new authority. No longer drawing up policy recommendations or conducting political negotiations, Bogle was now in the position to impose Company rule on the ground. He did not flinch from using force. When the Raja of Bycuntpore could not meet increased revenue demands, Bogle sent an armed party to seize and imprison him. He dealt even more summarily with 'the Chief Decoyt' (brigand) in the district. 'He gave me a monstrous deal of plague, and I was obliged to set People on him,' Bogle reported to Anderson, adding in an alarmingly offhand aside, 'His Head was this Moment brought to me.'[8]

As a distraction from the brutal realities of Company power, Bogle botanised. He sent seed collectors to Bhutan, amassed specimens of the flora and compiled descriptions of plants and their uses for Hastings. Bundles of seeds, carefully wrapped, were sent to and from Calcutta. At Hastings's request, he attempted to introduce new plants to the

region, notably that most lucrative of species, the tea plant. In March
1780, he reported to Hastings that he had forwarded packets of tea
seeds to Tashichodzong, and shown samples to the Bhutanese Governor of Buxaduar. 'When I showed them to the Buxa Soobah,' he told
Hastings, 'he got up and danced round them like David. He says they
are worth to his Country a Lack of Rupees considering how much
money goes annually out of it for Tea brought overland from China.'[9]
Clearly Hastings's enthusiasm for the scheme was also driven by
economics. If the plant could be grown in the Himalayan foothills,
then Britain would be spared its draining dependence on China. This
early (failed) attempt to introduce tea to the Himalayan region was a
precursor of that nineteenth-century experiment which would result
in the extensive tea plantations of Assam – and succeed in weaning the
British palate off Chinese tea.

For Bogle, horticulture could also be a matter of sentiment. In
March 1780 Bogle wrote to tell his sister Bess that he was collecting
Bhutanese seeds for the garden at home. Could she send him seeds in
return? Transplanting species across the globe, exchanging the exotic
for the familiar, Bogle sought to unite the family through gardening.
At the same time, he remitted money to his brother John, specifying
that the sum of £30 'be laid out in any scheme of Planting &c, that
you and my sisters may think fit towards beautifying Daldowie',
adding, 'Be sure Bess be consulted.'[10] Rarely in his correspondence did
Bogle set sums aside for a particular purpose other than named
amounts for his siblings (£100 for John, £20 each for his sisters);
most of the money went directly to service his father's debt. But
Daldowie represented both the family's past and future for Bogle.
While he was prepared to countenance the sale of other property, such
as the outlying estate of Whiteinch, Daldowie itself should remain
intact. By sending seeds and laying out sums to beautify the gardens,
Bogle was not only investing in the estate, he was cultivating the
dream of return.

But when would that homecoming be? His sister Mary began to
despair of it: 'it's nine years since you left us, what a long time that is,
and we never hear a syllable of your coming home again, indeed
George if you are not clever we will be old antiquated Sisters, & won't
have Spirit to hear all your adventures or enjoy your agreeable

conversation as we would wish to do'.[11] Bogle's father, now approaching eighty, did not expect to see his youngest son again. For years his letters had anticipated his own death in the rounded rhetoric of his Presbyterian faith. The news of George's good health, he wrote in wavering script in January 1780, 'is to me like Marrow to my old Bones, and is no small comfort to me even amidst the increasing natural infirmity of my advanced years and tends to lighten it and aleviate the irksome reflections of my approaching Exit from all sublunary Enjoyments'. Praising his son's 'natural affection and filial generosity', he thanked him for his part in reducing the debts incurred by the estate in 'that fatal year 1772'.[12] But writing was irksome to him these days, and his letters no longer covered page upon page of foolscap.

The correspondence between George and his favourite brother Robin in Grenada had become erratic in recent years. 'I don't know when I had a Letter from you,' mused George in August 1780, 'I suppose your Letters miscarry as well as mine.' Although situated at opposite ends of the empire – one in the East, the other in the West Indies – the two brothers remained connected, George insisted. Whatever the vagaries of the postal system between the marshy flatlands of Rangpur and the slave-worked plantations of Grenada, they were united in feeling. 'Although we are so disconnected by Time and Space, let us preserve that fine but sensible bond of Affection that binds us together,' George wrote in sentimental vein. 'It is our Interest to do so in expectation of meeting one day again.' In a final flourish, he signed off, 'Farewell my Dearest Brother – believe me blind or dead or anything, but never suspect me of want of affection, or of Forgetfulness of what I owe you.'[13]

But even as his letter professed the strength of fraternal love, it also demonstrated the gulf of 'Time and Space' between the two brothers. George wrote in ignorance of the fact that the previous year, Grenada had been captured – or rather recaptured – by the French. Grenada, like many of the Caribbean islands, had long been a casualty of European rivalries, suffering repeated invasions. In 1762, towards the end of the Seven Years' War, the British had snatched the island from the French; in 1779, a year after France entered the American Revolutionary War, the French claimed Grenada back. For British plantation owners in Grenada, the early years of the American war had been unexpectedly profitable; despite the problems caused by the conflict, scarcity had driven up the price of sugar. But, with the French capture of the island, they were subjected to severe restrictions and steep taxation. For the Bogle family, like many others, this turn of events dealt 'a most unreasonable blow' to their expectations from the plantation.[14]

In January 1781 Bogle received a new proposal from the Governor General. A Committee of Revenue was being formed in Calcutta to oversee tax collection in the provinces. Would Bogle care to join the board? 'If you are pleased with your appointment to it, come immediately to Calcutta,' wrote Hastings. 'If you are not, stay where you are, and I will nominate another; but I should be sorry to lose you.'[15] Bogle was ever alert to his patron's bidding, and the offer must have represented a step up the Company hierarchy. Perhaps he did not relish his new role as the tough frontier collector, or maybe he had grown weary of the limited European society on offer at Rangpur. Whatever the reason, after only fifteen months in post, Bogle was heading back to the capital.

Hastings evidently wanted Bogle close at hand. The past years had been punishing ones for the Governor General, and he may have felt the lack of one of his trusted 'Scotch guardians'. He was beset by military problems: in the west, the Marathas threatened Bombay, and in the south, the forces of Mysore harried Madras. Even more alarming was the prospect of an alliance between these two powers against the British. The defeats inflicted on the Company by the Marathas in 1779 and by Mysore in 1780 were more than humiliating; they raised the spectre that the British could actually be forced out of India (as appeared to be happening in America). With Britain once more at war with France, there were rumours too of a French expeditionary fleet heading for India.

Faced with these military crises, the Governing Council did not close ranks. Philip Francis continued to obstruct Hastings's proposals. A tenacious and intensely ambitious man, Francis aimed at the office of governor general himself. He was not averse to taking risks; indeed he had gained his financial independence through gambling for high stakes (on one occasion reputedly winning £20,000 at whist in a single night).[16] Francis was opposed to Hastings on both intellectual and personal grounds. The government of Bengal, he believed, was ripe for reform. The Company's administrative responsibilities should be devolved on to local Indian institutions and sovereignty handed over to the British crown. There should be no further territorial expansion. Standing in the way of Francis's proposed reforms were just two men: Hastings and his close associate Richard Barwell.[17]

In 1779 Francis's position on the Council was suddenly strengthened when Barwell announced his intention to return to Britain. On Barwell's retirement, Francis would be the most senior Councillor, second only to the Governor General himself. Barwell's departure would also consign Hastings to the minority on the Council once again. For Hastings, this was insupportable; he could not contemplate the suspension of his authority at a time of heightened military tension. In January 1780, he was driven to negotiate a deal with his great rival. Francis undertook not to obstruct Hastings in military matters; in exchange, he was granted the right to exercise his patronage over a number of profitable posts. This so-called 'accommodation' – tellingly described by Francis as an 'armed truce' – did not last long.[18]

By the summer, Francis was insisting that Hastings limit his military activities to Bengal. Hastings considered this a breach of their pact and a provocation that he could not ignore. On 15 August 1780, five years of mutual frustration and hostility reached boiling point. At a Council meeting, Hastings condemned Francis's conduct as dishonest and dishonourable. There was only one possible response for a gentleman to make to such a charge: Francis challenged Hastings to a duel. Francis spent the next day burning private papers and putting his affairs in order, 'in case of the worst'.[19] Hastings, who had provoked the duel quite deliberately, now set about composing a letter of farewell to his wife. The duel, he claimed, was unavoidable. 'I shall leave nothing which I regret to lose but you,' he told Marian.[20] Once set in motion, nothing could stop the descent into ritualised violence – the very custom that Bogle had condemned in the account of Europe written for the Panchen Lama.

At dawn the following morning, the two men met at Alipore, to the south of the city. Neither had fought a pistol duel before, but both had experienced military men as seconds. After three false starts, the order was given to fire. Francis's shot missed, but Hastings's ball pierced Francis's right side. Rushed to town, Francis was attended by Hastings's surgeon, who managed to extract the ball. The wound was not life-threatening, and within a month Francis was back in the Council chamber. He may have mended soon enough, but for years Francis would nurse a grudge that would be satisfied only with his rival's downfall.

On his return to the Council, Francis was soon locked in confrontation with Hastings over the conduct of the war against Mysore. Hastings wanted to send troops from Bengal to aid the forces of Madras, but Francis steadfastly opposed the motion. Then Hastings managed to win round Edward Wheler, Francis's key supporter on the Council. Outraged by what he saw as the desertion of his ally, Francis resigned, and booked his passage home. His departure in December 1780 was more than welcome to Hastings, but any relief that it afforded was transitory. Over the following years, Francis would work assiduously in London to bring his adversary low. Hastings would be denounced in print and to Select Committees of the House of Commons. Francis's reports would influence parliamentary debate and feed into legislation on the government of India. His efforts would culminate in 1788 with the start of one of the most celebrated trials of the century. In association with Edmund Burke, Francis would draft the charges for the impeachment of Warren Hastings.

Bogle arrived in Calcutta in January 1781, towards the end of the party season. Like London, Calcutta had its winter season of balls and dinners, performances and recitals. With his new appointment, Bogle would have found himself advanced a rung up the social ladder, for Europeans in Calcutta carefully observed the gradations of Company rank. At the height of the rivalry between Hastings and Francis, social circles had been defined along strictly partisan lines. With Francis's departure the previous month, there would have been a reduction of tension. But throughout the upheavals of Calcutta politics Bogle had not attracted personal animosity. 'I am not a disliked Man, in spite of all the warm Party work,' he claimed to his brother Robin. 'You will ask me how I managed this. Why only by not speaking ill of People.'[21] Bogle's instinctive diplomacy had stood him in good stead, working equally well in the offices of Calcutta and the monasteries of Tibet. He would be more than capable of surviving the bouts of Company infighting, Robin had predicted years before. 'I am not uneasy about George,' Robin had reassured Annie during the first round of conflict on the Council, 'he will not stick in the World as he told Matty when he was learning to read.'[22]

Indeed George had not stuck. As befitted his rising status, he established himself in one of the garden houses outside the city. The white neo-Palladian villas were by far the most attractive residences in Calcutta. There was room for Bogle's library, and space to keep nine dogs and four horses – a grey pair to pull the phaeton, and two Tanyans to remind him of his time in the hills. Whether there were any other occupants of the house, we do not know. It is difficult to establish anything conclusive about Bogle's private life or domestic arrangements. Later generations of the Bogle family seem to have censored the family archive, but stray references to women and offspring remain.

In the late 1770s Bogle sent a daughter to London to be raised by Maria Stewart, the widow of his friend John Stewart, who had died en route to India in 1778. Bogle presumably entrusted his daughter to Mrs Stewart on her passage home. The family, it appears, were not informed of her existence. The only surviving trace of the girl is a brief reference in a letter of 1780 from Maria Stewart to Bogle where she is not named (though a note in a different hand on the letter identifies her as 'Mary Bogle from Bengal'): 'The present you sent me Home is a fine Creature, I shall regret my inability, if I cannot Educate her in the manner I could wish, what is in my power I will do for her, with the most Heart felt satisfaction for the sake of him she belongs to. She often mentions you, and whenever any thing goes not quite to her wish, she says she will go back to Bengal, to her Papa Bogle.'[23] The little girl's reported wish to return to her father – rather than her mother – is telling. Mixed-race children were encouraged to identify with the British rather than Indian side of their family. And indeed we know even less of the mother than the daughter. She may have shared

Bogle's domestic arrangements or have maintained a separate establishment. Her daughter's frequent references to Papa Bogle suggest at the least that Bogle showed some paternal interest, but whether he was an occasional visitor or a constant presence in the family is hard to determine. Bogle does, however, seem to have been concerned with his daughter's welfare – after the manner of the time. While we may find the idea of separating mother and child repugnant, a British education was considered a great advantage to mixed-race children. British fathers quite regularly sent their children to Britain to improve their social standing and marriage prospects.[24]

Children did not generally undertake the voyage to Britain before the age of six, so this little girl was probably born either before or during Bogle's mission. Her mother may have formed a connection with Bogle at Calcutta. If a Tibetan woman accompanied Bogle down to Bengal, as his descendants believed, she was unlikely to have been his only female companion. Like most Company servants, Bogle kept at least one *bibi* or mistress. He had a number of children: five are named in existing documents. There were two Georges, two Marys and a Martha. The fact that Bogle gave two of his sons and daughters the same name suggests that he maintained two or more separate families.[25] It was not uncommon for Company servants to keep a number of *bibi*s – either at the same time or in succession – or to maintain several women in a *zenana* or harem. Whether any of the women or children associated with Bogle shared his house, either at Calcutta or at Rangpur, is not clear. Company servants generally provided *bibi*s with their own establishments so that they could follow their own religious observances and social customs. Most of the women who became *bibi*s were of Muslim origin and lived in seclusion. It is perhaps significant that listed among Bogle's household goods were six *purdah*s or screens, used to partition off women's quarters.

Like all the garden houses, the villa was set in extensive grounds and equipped with its own tank or reservoir for rainwater. Every morning, Bogle would follow doctor's orders and bathe in the tank. Medical opinion recommended bathing for a number of ailments, but most gentlemen did not actually know how to swim. Bogle's health had not been as good as his letters home suggested. At least twice in the previous year he had been laid up with a 'severe fit of the Bile'. For these liver complaints, he was prescribed 'Phisic & warm water' and banned alcohol. The origins of his ill health remained mysterious: 'I don't know how it happens neither, for I take a good deal of Exercise, live soberly,' he protested to Anderson.[26]

On the morning of 3 April 1781, Bogle went to bathe as usual. But when he arrived at the tank, he found that it was dirty. Contemporaries often grumbled that the tanks of Calcutta attracted all kinds of vermin, particularly pariah dogs, to drink or swim. Complaining to the servants, Bogle set out for a tank near by. He did not want to miss out on the benefits of his daily bath. With steps leading down to the water's edge, it would have been easy enough to enter the water. But this was an unfamiliar pool, and Bogle soon found himself out of his depth. Thrashing, struggling for breath, he desperately tried to keep afloat.

Then he went under.

The surgeon was called immediately, but could offer no assistance. He pronounced Bogle dead, and concluded that he had drowned, after suffering a haemorrhage. He was thirty-four years old.

The tank had claimed the life of the most promising of East India Company servants, a man of rare personal and intellectual qualities. Sunk beneath the water were Bogle's charm and penetration, his curiosity and ambition, his talent for friendship and diplomatic flair. 'The loss is a public, as well as a private misfortune,' mourned the *India Gazette*. 'Few possessed a better share of abilities, or were more faithful; He was generous to a fault; a kind, affectionate Son, and a warm Friend.'[27] As far as Hastings was concerned, Bogle was irreplaceable. For 'Temper, Patience and understanding', declared Hastings to the Council, 'I never hoped to meet with any Person equal to M[r] Bogle.'[28]

Like many Company servants, Bogle died far too young. Most historians have assumed that he went the way of scores of Europeans, succumbing to one of the common killer diseases – cholera, malaria or dysentery. But Bogle's death was as distinctive as his life. For some reason, the newspaper account of his death by drowning has been largely ignored, perhaps because it robs Bogle of a dignified ending – but then he was never one to take himself too seriously.

Bogle was buried in South Park Street Cemetery, surrounded by the ostentatious memorials to the British dead. Funerals were generally conducted at sunset to avoid the heat of the day. Most of the Company servants would have followed his coffin down the avenues of obelisks and mausoleums; attendance at funerals was one of the social obligations of the settlement. 'Our happiness depends upon others & even those who have an applauding Conscience, have their Mind torn by exterior Misfortunes,' wrote Thomas Law to David Anderson, 'when friends unite in honest bewailing, there is a softening Sensation in Sorrow which cannot be termed disagreeable.'[29] To mark Bogle's grave, Anderson and Claud Alexander erected a great stone sarcophagus inscribed 'In Sincere Attachment to the Memory of Mr. George Bogle Late Ambassador to Tibet who died the 3rd of April, 1781'.

Bogle and the Panchen Lama died within four months of each other. Bogle never learnt that his friend had succumbed to smallpox. As Bogle's coffin was being lowered into the ground at South Park Street Cemetery, the Panchen Lama's body, encased in a golden shrine donated by the Qianlong Emperor and attended by a great train, was slowly progressing to its final resting place at Tashilhunpo. With the sad coincidence of their deaths, the British dream of gaining access to Peking through Tibet seemed as remote as ever. Two of the prime movers of the alliance between Tashilhunpo and Calcutta were gone; but Hastings had not altogether abandoned the scheme, and Purangir, the master diplomat, remained in his service.

THE GOLDEN URN

In December 1783, at the monastery of Terpaling, twenty-five miles south-west of Tashilhunpo, Purangir found himself once more bowing low at the feet of the Panchen Lama. The sacred infant sat enthroned on a cushioned dais, an expression of rapt attention on his face. Seven months earlier Purangir had set out from Calcutta to guide a new British delegation led by Lieutenant Samuel Turner to Tibet. Following prolonged talks, he had managed to arrange an audience for the Company servants with the new Incarnation. The sight of the infant Lama would have been more than welcome to Purangir after the double loss that he had recently suffered. The deaths of both the Third Panchen Lama and George Bogle had deprived him of two of his most significant patrons. With the rebirth of the Panchen Lama, his own career as intermediary had revived.

The infant Lama directed a steadfast gaze at the men before him. First they presented the ceremonial white scarf, then laid before him gifts of pearl and coral. He gestured to his attendants to replenish the guests' cups of tea and offer sweetmeats. The time had come for the British envoy's formal address. 'I found myself, though visiting an infant, under the necessity of saying something,' Turner later recalled.[1] Improvising bravely, he delivered his speech: 'the Governor General, on receiving the news of his decease in China, was overwhelmed with grief and sorrow, and continued to lament his absence from the world, until the cloud that had overcast the happiness of this nation, was dispelled by his reappearance.' Warming to the theme, Turner continued: 'The Governor anxiously wished that he might long continue to illumine the world by his presence, and was hopeful that the friendship, which had formerly subsisted between them, would not be diminished, but rather that it might become still greater than before; and that . . . there might be an extensive communication between his votaries, and the dependents of the British nation.'[2] Listening carefully, the Panchen Lama nodded slowly, as if in approval of all that was said. Although accustomed to sleep at this hour, he remained courteous and attentive throughout: a remarkable achievement for a child of eighteen months.

The Fourth Panchen Lama had been discovered in a minor aristocratic family in Panam in the province of Tsang. Of the four boys tested, only he could select the personal possessions of the Third Panchen Lama from an array of similar objects. With this confirmation of his identity, in 1782 the infant Lama had taken up residence with his parents at the monastery of Terpaling, under the regency of the Third Panchen Lama's brother. To greet the new Incarnation, Hastings had decided to send a second mission to Tibet under the guidance of Purangir. In 1783 he chose Samuel Turner, one of his own relations serving with the Company army, as his envoy. He was accompanied by Robert Saunders, a surgeon, and Samuel Davis, a draughtsman and surveyor. Purangir's mediation was crucial to the success of the expedition. While the British party remained stalled in Bhutan, Purangir once again negotiated the mission's entry into Tibet, but Tashilhunpo stipulated that the British deputation could not exceed two (the size of Bogle's party), so Davis was left behind painting watercolours in Bhutan.

The infant Lama was not yet able to speak but, as Turner was advised by monastic officials, 'it is not to be inferred that he cannot understand'.[3] The toddler was to be addressed as the Third Panchen Lama in a new body. Even as he played along, Turner found that he could not dismiss the scene as a complete charade. The more that he studied the child, the more exceptional the young Lama appeared. His attention never wavered, and he seemed to comprehend all that was going on. Or was he simply well drilled? 'I must own,' wrote Turner, 'that his behaviour, on this occasion, appeared perfectly natural and spontaneous, and not directed by any external action or sign of authority.'[4] Arrested between wonder and scepticism, between gravity and ridicule, Turner scrutinised the conduct of the child and those around him. 'The scene, in which I was here brought to act a part, was too new and extraordinary, however trivial, or perhaps preposterous, it may appear to some, not to claim from me great attention, and consequently minute remark.'[5]

In his account, Turner marvelled at the 'astonishing dignity and decorum' of the child, the quality of his concentration and singular beauty; 'altogether,' he concluded, 'I thought him one of the handsomest children I had ever seen.'[6] For the Tibetans, such wonder revealed inner conviction. In the Fourth Panchen Lama's biography, the visitors were awed into reverence by the sight of the infant Lama. 'In such a little body there are activities of body, speech and mind so greatly marvellous and different from the others!' they exclaimed. The encounter spontaneously ignited British belief. 'Although they were not knowers of the niceties of religion, by merely gazing . . . an irrepressible faith was born in them.'[7]

The audience certainly made a deep impression on Turner, but it was no conversion experience. What it actually produced was a new theory of Anglo-Tibetan relations. The doctrine of incarnation could be used to bolster the alliance between Tashilhunpo and Calcutta, Turner argued. 'The usual proof of the identity of a regenerated Lama, is an early recognition of the possessions, acquaintances, and transactions of his pre-existence,' Turner reported to Hastings. 'I am therefore of the opinion that the new Lama will be taught to recur to the connections of the former Teshoo Lama, as one of the strongest marks that can denote his identity, and facilitate his acceptation. And here I ground my hope on presumptions built upon the tenets of their faith, which is the basis on which their government itself is constructed.'[8] With Purangir acting as translator, the monk officials had assured Turner that they would remind the Panchen Lama of his former friendship with the Governor General. Should the Lama, 'when he began to speak, happen to have forgotten it, they would early teach him to repeat the name of Hastings'.[9] Tashilhunpo would not alter the pro-Company policy of the Third Panchen Lama, Turner argued, for fear of undermining the very principle of incarnation itself. Turner's theory was in fact rooted in a profound scepticism: 'Were they to adopt a different conduct, they would necessarily abandon the most sacred and immutable positions of their religion, and expose it to every degrading imputation, which is calculated to rob it of its honours, and lay it open to the reproach, or derision, attendant on detected imposition.'[10]

Turner's audience with the Panchen Lama provided the finale to his mission. He stayed at the monastery of Terpaling for a couple of days en route for Bengal. In his previous talks at Tashilhunpo with the Regent and the chief minister, he had ascertained that little could be done at present to foster relations with Peking. The friendship between Tashilhunpo and Calcutta would best be nurtured through trade, he maintained. In 1784 Hastings proposed a duty-free trading venture to Tibet for Bengali merchants. A list of suitable goods included cloth (not of the best quality), coarse cottons, cheap watches, clocks, snuff-boxes, pocket knives, conch shells, coral and large, flawed pearls. A rather more alluring set of items was available for purchase in Tibet: gold dust, silver, wool, musk and yak tails (for fly whisks).[11] To oversee the venture, Purangir was once again appointed to travel to Tashilhunpo in early 1785.

One of Hastings's final acts as governor general was to entrust Purangir with gifts and letters for the Regent of Tashilhunpo and the infant Panchen Lama. Shortly after, Hastings embarked for Britain, bringing to an end his twelve years' service as governor general. Following him were living souvenirs of his decade-long enthusiasm for Tibet. Turner made arrangements for a pair of yaks to be shipped to Britain. One survived the voyage, to take up residence with two shawl goats in a Berkshire field. Robust but bad-tempered, the yak lived comfortably on Hastings's estate; he fathered many calves, gored a coach horse and had his portrait painted by George Stubbs.

Hastings had finally decided to leave India when he learnt of the conditions imposed on the Company by the India Bill passed by parliament in 1784. A new government Board of Control in London would oversee and approve all correspondence between the Company and Asian powers. The Company could no longer forge diplomatic

Warren Hastings' yak, engraving after George Stubbs

alliances, wage war or make peace on its own account. For Hastings, the India Act of 1784 seriously undermined both the authority of the governor general and that of the Company Proprietors. But, at least with respect to the Council, the position of the governor general was strengthened. The damaging years of partisan conflict were at an end. The Council was reduced in size from five to three members and, following an Act of 1786, the governor general would have the power to overrule the Council. But these reforms came too late for Hastings. The years of opposition in both Calcutta and London had taken their personal toll and, weary of his office, he was now eager to be home. But if he imagined that he would enjoy a peaceful retirement in Britain, he was sadly mistaken. Two and a half years after his return, impeachment proceedings would begin against him.

The trading venture that Hastings had proposed for Tibet met with some success. Purangir reported that the Tashilhunpo markets that he encountered in 1785 were well stocked with British and Bengali goods. Purangir was granted easy access to all the high-ranking officials. After a decade in the Company's service, he was accepted at Tashilhunpo as the official envoy of the government of Bengal. He had of course become intimately acquainted with all the significant figures at court during the journey to and from Peking. One of the most remarkable aspects of Purangir's career was the degree of respect that he commanded in both the Tibetan and British camps. The British were well aware of their indebtedness to him, and Turner – like Bogle before him – was quick to defend his rights. On Purangir's return to Bhot Bagan, he found that a neighbouring landholder had encroached on some of the monastery's land in his absence. Writing to John Macpherson, the acting Governor General, on Purangir's behalf, Turner requested that Macpherson intercede 'in favour of one who has rendered various useful services to this government'.[12]

Few of the Company's agents could compare with Purangir as negotiator, intelligence-gatherer and long-distance traveller. Five years later, the Company thought once again to harness his skills in a renewed search for that elusive botanical prize: the tea plant. The indefatigable Purangir was planning 'another Journey to Lassa on his own account', and was given the difficult and possibly risky 'Commission of obtaining the seed or the plant of Tea with promise of suitable reward if it can be delivered in a state of vegetation to the Chief of Rungpoor and if possible with a native practised in the cultivation'.[13] Sadly, nothing is known of the outcome of this journey. At the same time Purangir was also requested 'to deposit with the Board, the original Diary which he possesses of his several Journies into Tibet and China'.[14] Even more regrettably, the Sanskrit journal has long since been lost. The last time that we hear of Purangir engaged on official business is in 1792. His final task, before he was forced to retire through ill health, was to carry correspondence from Tibet to Calcutta. But these letters were far from the expressions of amity of the previous decades. By 1792 the friendship between Tashilhunpo and Calcutta – fostered through correspondence and visits, conversation and gifts by the Third Panchen Lama, Hastings, Bogle and Purangir himself – was on the verge of collapse.

The deterioration in relations can be attributed to the activities of Nepal. For years Tibet had regarded with concern the expansionist ambitions of its neighbour. In 1788 Nepal turned its attentions to Tibet itself.

Looking for a cause to back, the Regent of Nepal had lighted upon a quarrel within the deceased Panchen Lama's family. The Shamar Trulku was one of the Third Panchen Lama's brothers and a high incarnation within the Karma Kagyu school, an older, rival sect to the Panchen Lama's order of the Gelugpa. On the death of the Third Panchen Lama, the Shamar Trulku had become locked in an inheritance dispute with his other brother, now Regent of Tashilhunpo. Finding it impossible to pursue his claims to the Third Panchen Lama's property, the Shamar Trulku had sought refuge in Nepal. There he found a ready backer in Bahadur Shah, the Regent of Nepal.

Bahadur Shah could exploit several other areas of contention with Tibet. There were complaints about the quality of the salt exported to Nepal, and concern over the treatment of Gurkha merchants in Tibet. More significant was the issue of the currency that the two countries shared. For centuries, Nepal had been responsible for minting the money that circulated in Tibet. The Gurkhas now wished to introduce a new currency to replace the existing, debased coinage, but the Tibetan government resisted the change. To enforce acceptance, Bahadur Shah ordered the Gurkha army to cross the Tibetan border.

By the summer of 1788, Gurkha forces occupied a number of Tibetan frontier districts and were in command of the routes leading to Tashilhunpo. The six-year-old Panchen Lama and his entourage fled to Lhasa. The authorities at Lhasa and Tashilhunpo appealed for military aid in different directions. The Dalai Lama and *ambans* looked to Peking, while the Tashilhunpo Regent wrote in secret to Calcutta. The Regent urged the Company to send forces to see off the invading Gurkhas. If Company troops could settle the matter before imperial forces arrived, then Tibet might be spared the consequences of a large Qing military presence. But on no account should the Company reveal this request, the Regent insisted. Should Peking ever learn of the Regent's correspondence with a foreign power, his punishment would be as swift as it was extreme.

But the new Governor General, Lord Cornwallis, had no intention of getting involved. The British had no argument with the Gurkhas, he replied to the Tashilhunpo Regent. The Company could not contemplate the expense of a war. Nor did Cornwallis want to anger the Qianlong Emperor by intervening in the conflict for fear of the possible consequences for trade at Canton. Of course, had the Company been able to establish diplomatic communication with Peking, as Hastings and Bogle had wished, he might have been able to consult the Emperor in advance. But, in the present circumstances, all that Cornwallis could promise was Company neutrality.

The Qianlong Emperor, by contrast, immediately dispatched troops to Tibet. The arrival of imperial forces in Lhasa promptly caused the Nepalese to seek terms. No fighting was necessary. On the payment of a large annual sum, the Nepalese agreed to withdraw from the occupied border regions. The Tibetans had to accept a devaluation of the old currency and confer various trading privileges on Nepalese merchants. To acknowledge Qing authority, the Gurkhas had to agree to send a tribute mission to Peking.

But the peace between Tibet and Nepal did not last long. In 1789 the Tibetans duly paid the levy demanded by Nepal. But the following year they failed to do so. In 1791 Bahadur Shah decided to exact payment by military means, and once more ordered his army into Tibet. This time, his forces set their course straight for Tashilhunpo, and the Panchen Lama, now nine years old, again had to flee. By the end of October, Tashilhunpo was in Gurkha hands. And so were all the monastic treasures that Bogle had recorded in his journal: the jewelled images, ornaments and ritual items accumulated over centuries of lavish donation – not least by the Qianlong Emperor himself. Every temple and mausoleum, every shrine and hall offered up its contents to the Gurkhas. The great monastic city was soon stripped and gutted, plundered and desecrated.

Reports of the outrage sped to Peking, strengthening the Qianlong Emperor's resolve to show the Gurkhas the full force of imperial disapproval. Manchu authority had to be asserted uncompromisingly, whatever the cost. He dispatched an army, some 17,000 strong, with orders to encounter the Gurkhas as soon as possible. Funds were poured into the campaign to ensure its speed and efficiency. Special lightweight leather cannon were supplied for easy manoeuvrability. Force-marched through the harshest of conditions, across deserts and high mountain passes deep in snow, the army somehow managed to reach Tibet by midwinter. In a two-pronged attack, one detachment entered Tibet by Sining in the north-east, the other by Tachienliu in the east. Hearing of their arrival, the Tashilhunpo Regent gave no thought to secret alliances with the British. His concern now was only that the Company might intervene in support of Nepal. The Tashilhunpo Regent joined with the Dalai Lama and Manchu commander in writing to Cornwallis to request British neutrality. These were the letters entrusted to Purangir on his final journey between Tibet and Bengal. His first mission, some eighteen years previously, had been to sue for peace from the British; now his task was to avert Company involvement in a war.

Cornwallis had no interest in entering the conflict, but the Tibetan and Manchu authorities were not mistaken in their belief that the Company had established closer relations with Nepal. The British were now looking to Nepal as an alternative route to regenerate trans-Himalayan trade. They maintained a Bengali representative in Kathmandu, and were in the process of concluding a trade agreement with Nepal. The Gurkhas did indeed request military assistance from the Company – but to no avail. Cornwallis tendered his services as a mediator, but none of the parties took him up on the offer. The Manchu commander had his own way of settling matters.

By the time that Qing forces stormed into central Tibet, the Nepalese army was slowly heading home, laden with sacred loot. In June 1792 the imperial and Tibetan armies pursued the Gurkhas across Himalayan passes, devastating the retreating forces. The Nepalese finally conceded defeat in 1793 just twenty miles from their capital of Kathmandu. For an imperial army to venture so far and so fast into the Himalayan region was a triumph of military logistics. To Qianlong, the campaign was the last of the ten great victories (or 'Ten Perfections') of his reign. The long arm of imperial authority had reclaimed the spoils of Tashilhunpo. A hundred porters were required to carry the treasure back. As a sign of their submission to the Qing, the Gurkhas were compelled to send a tribute mission to Peking every five years. The Manchu authorities judged the Tashilhunpo Regent responsible for the outbreak of war and confiscated his property. He disappears from the records and may have been taken captive to China. The Qing also suspected the Company of secretly backing Nepal. Cornwallis, they felt sure, was insincere in his pledge of neutrality and offer of mediation. It is possible that the Tibetans shared this conviction; the Company had certainly proved a very lukewarm ally to Tashilhunpo. No direct punishment could be meted out to the Shamar Trulku, whom many blamed for the Gurkha invasion. By the time that imperial forces entered Nepal, he had poisoned himself. Lhasa took possession of his estates and monastery, and outlawed his reincarnation line in perpetuity.

While the Qing army was still engaged in Nepal, a sixty-four-gun British warship dropped anchor off Canton. Nearly two decades after Hastings and Bogle had first envisaged it, a British mission had arrived in China. It was far from the modest deputation that Hastings and Bogle had planned. The 1793 mission was a scheme initiated in London by the Home Minister, Henry Dundas, President of the Company's Board of Control. The undertaking was financed by the Company, and was designed to show off the very best in British arts, technology and manufacturing.

On board the man-of-war was Lord Macartney, 'Ambassador Extraordinary and Plenipotentiary from the King of Great Britain to the Emperor of China'. He was attended by Sir George Staunton, and an entourage of nearly a hundred soldiers, scientists, musicians, artists and interpreters. The magnificence of the mission was an attempt to match the imagined splendour of the imperial court. With its many specialists, the mission also aspired to gather knowledge of China. But its main purpose was to demonstrate British ingenuity and workmanship. Docking alongside the warship were two vessels laden with gifts: scientific instruments, timepieces, a planetarium, firearms, a carriage, Wedgwood chinaware, cloth, tapestries and paintings of all aspects of British life. It was hoped that some item in the tempting cache would catch the Emperor's eye, that some artefact would prise open the gates of the Chinese market. No expense had been spared in the attempt to impress Qianlong. The mission to China was the most costly and elaborate that Britain had ever mounted.

The aims of the embassy were correspondingly high. The British wanted an ambassador stationed at Peking, and an end to the restrictive practices at Canton. They sought access to other Chinese ports, a decrease in trading duties and the right to establish a British settlement on Chinese territory. But, to get round the officials at

Lord Macartney

Canton, Macartney announced that the purpose of the embassy was to honour Qianlong on his eighty-third birthday. Masquerading as a tribute mission, the British were permitted to sail north to Tianjin, where the delegation unloaded its great train of gifts and headed inland.

As was his custom during the summer, the Qianlong Emperor had decamped to Chengde. On the journey towards the hills, imperial officials tried to instruct Macartney in the all-important matter of court ritual. But the Ambassador persisted in his refusal to compromise his own dignity and that of his monarch by performing the kowtow before the Emperor. All that he was prepared to do was to kneel on one knee, as he would before his own king (two knees being reserved for God alone). Arriving at Chengde in mid-September, Macartney was ravished by the valley, which appeared surprisingly familiar to him, as if Capability Brown had been at work in the hills of Manchuria. At every turn, he was reminded of the landscaped gardens of England, 'the magnificence of Stowe, the soft beauties of Woburn or the fairy-land of Painshill'.[15]

On the morning of 14 September 1793, the embassy was finally granted an audience with Qianlong. Accompanied by guards and musicians, Macartney and Staunton rode in palanquins to the Garden of Ten Thousand Trees. Macartney was wearing his full court dress – a velvet suit, and the cloak and diamond star of the Order of the Bath. Staunton had to make do with the red robes of academic dress (to which he was entitled as an Oxford doctor of law). At Qianlong's entrance, Macartney went down on bended knee, while all around courtiers prostrated themselves. He then approached the imperial throne, bearing a casket of gold and diamonds, containing a letter from King George III. The Emperor received the golden box and, in return, presented Macartney with a *ruyi* or baton of imperial favour.

Qianlong treated the British envoys with customary courtesy – feasting them and exchanging gifts – but remained resolutely unimpressed by their wares. Despite his private fascination with European technology, he would never publicly suggest that the Qing Empire needed such goods. 'As your Ambassador can see for himself,' Qianlong wrote to George III, 'we possess all things. I set no value on objects strange or ingenious, and have no use for your country's manufactures.'[16] Some of the gifts were returned. The Celestial Empire produced everything that it required, and conducted trade with less favoured European nations only from motives of benevolence.

Qianlong went on to reject every one of the British requests, point by point. The proposals were 'not consistent with our dynastic usage'.[17] To concede any of the articles would be to set a bad example to other nations trading at Canton. The British could be excused their ignorance of Qing custom, situated as they were at the edge of the globe: 'I do not forget the lonely remoteness of your island, cut off from the world by intervening wastes of sea.'[18] But now that the situation had been explained to the King, the Emperor had a right to absolute obedience. Should British merchants land at any other port than Canton, they would be instantly expelled. 'Do not say that you were not warned in due time!' Qianlong cautioned King George. 'Tremblingly obey and show no negligence!'[19]

The 1793 mission proved an expensive and unmitigated failure. There was never any possibility of finding common ground. The British delegation and Qing court held entirely incompatible notions of foreign relations and trade. For the British, both diplomacy and trade were conceived in terms of mutually advantageous exchange. But, for the Qing, foreigners came to the imperial court only to pay tribute, and commerce was a bestowal of imperial grace.[20] Whether Bogle would have fared any better than Macartney, had he been able to reach Peking, is questionable. He would not have been constrained by the protocol of an official government mission. And he was certainly endowed with a greater degree of cultural sensitivity than Lord Macartney. But even Bogle's ingenuity, adaptability and charm would have found it hard to make any impression on the Emperor. Qianlong believed that he had no reason to pay any attention to the demands of a tiny island state, situated so far from the centre of the world.

With little comprehension of the gulf between British and Qing views, Macartney blamed the failure of the mission on Manchu suspicions that the British had backed Nepal. On arrival in China, Macartney knew nothing of the invasion of Tibet, but during his stay he was questioned repeatedly on the degree of British involvement. For Macartney this could be the only explanation for his singular lack of success; it also conveniently absolved him of personal responsibility.

Following the débâcle of the mission, it was easy to believe that the Qing harboured deep misgivings about the British. A rumour, originating with the Company's representative in Nepal, seemed to offer a convincing explanation of recent events. The story was reproduced in the account that Staunton published of the embassy to China. The Qianlong Emperor, it was said, had heard of the Third Panchen Lama's correspondence with the East India Company and of the visit of a British envoy to Tashilhunpo. So angered was the Emperor by this contact that he summoned the Lama to Peking, 'with intentions different from those which he had expressed in his invitation'. Once the Lama was within his power, the Emperor yielded 'to the suggestions of a policy practised sometimes in the East'.[21] Far from succumbing to smallpox, the Panchen Lama had been poisoned.

Although the story could not explain why the Emperor had gone to such enormous lengths and expense to lure the Panchen Lama to

Peking, it did satisfy a number of needs. The poisoning plot explained the Lama's untimely death, confirmed stereotypes of oriental perfidy and gave the British an inflated sense of their own significance. It demonstrated that the Manchu Emperor was prepared to go to extremes to frustrate the Company. Inevitably, in the passage from rumour to print, the story gained credence. It was repeated over and over again in subsequent histories throughout the nineteenth century.[22] The legend conferred a tragic ending to the narrative of Bogle and the Panchen Lama. In this version, the Lama sacrificed his life in the cause of friendship and British trade.

The story of the Panchen Lama's murder suited the new conditions imposed on Tibet by the Qing. Following the campaign of 1792, the political landscape of the region was changed irrevocably. After such a resounding demonstration of Manchu military might, the Qianlong Emperor tightened his grip on Tibet and the Gelugpa order. Any ambiguity over the status of the country was at an end; Tibet was to be fully integrated into the empire. Indeed the events of 1792 were often used to justify later Chinese claims of sovereignty over Tibet. The imperial *amban*s stationed in Lhasa were endowed with enhanced powers, and the authority of the Dalai and Panchen Lamas significantly curtailed. In future, the Qianlong Emperor pronounced, the *amban* would supervise the selection of great incarnates. To prevent the concentration of power within certain families, the names of all candidates would be placed inside a golden urn, and the *amban* would draw one out (although, in practice, this method was rarely used). Qianlong now justified his support of the Gelugpas solely in terms of political expediency: his patronage of the order was necessary to maintain peace among the Mongols. In apparent disavowal of the honours bestowed on the Third Panchen Lama, Qianlong stated that the Qing dynasty had never revered lamas as spiritual teachers. The Emperor was to be the source of all power, both religious and secular.

Never again would it be possible for a high lama to conduct his own foreign relations as the Third Panchen Lama had done. Following the defeat of Nepal, there was deep distrust of the British in the region. After the war, the Manchu authorities determined to sever all links between Tibet and Bengal. The year 1793 saw an end to all written communication between Tashilhunpo and Calcutta. Manchu officials now guarded the frontier between Tibet and Bhutan, and prevented the entrance of traders or pilgrims from Bengal. Even *gosain*s, previously welcome at Tashilhunpo, were turned away, on suspicion of being spies. The era of Purangir and Bogle, of border-crossings and missions, of trade and cultural exchange, was incontrovertibly over.

As for Purangir himself, he met his end in the defence of the Panchen Lama's monastery. One night, early in 1795, Bhot Bagan was attacked by armed robbers. Purangir set about the intruders with a sword, but was himself gravely injured in the fight. As he lay dying, robbers plundered the monastery of its wealth amassed through trade and of the treasures donated by the Panchen Lama. The *gosain* who had undertaken so many great journeys, who had negotiated with rulers and brokered friendship between nations, was, in the end, murdered in his own home. A tomb was erected within the precincts of Bhot Bagan by Purangir's successor, Daljitgir. The Bengali inscription enjoined all people – Hindu, Muslim and followers of any other religion – to worship at the shrine: a fitting tribute to a monk who had travelled thousands of miles in the service of masters of different faiths.

And Bogle's legacy? He died without making a will. His possessions were auctioned off for the benefit of the estate. There were diamond earrings, strings of pearls, 'Moorish jewels' and 'nabob's elegant bracelets'.[23] Among the suits of flowered silk, white breeches and hookahs were eight yak tails, two chess sets and a print of Warren Hastings. Sold too were various items of Tibetan and Bhutanese clothing: two pairs of boots, five hats and eight jackets. Although Bogle died intestate, he did make provision for a monthly allowance of twenty rupees to be paid to a female companion, one 'Bebee Bogle'. The family's records show that Bibi Bogle in Calcutta continued to receive the allowance for fifty-seven years after George's death.[24]

With the death of their father, Bogle's children were considered orphans, and placed under the protection of his two friends, Anderson and Alexander. The fact that their mother may have been alive was immaterial. His eldest son, George, survived his father by only a year.

'I am sorry to tell you,' Alexander wrote to Anderson on 3 May 1782, 'that the Eldest boy Mister George Bogle Esquire died suddenly on the last day of April. The acct. I have of his Death is that he was very well in the morning but was seized with a violent Headach in the Evening & afterwards a vomiting. He expired during the Night. I am told several of the Black people have gone off so.' The boy's marginal status was reflected in the manner of his burial. 'I had the Corps buried next to his Father but not being a Christian the Funeral Service was not read over him.'[25] Young George's sudden death left Alexander anxious that he and Anderson should be appointed legal guardians to the remaining children. They had 35,000 rupees to provide for their welfare. What, Alexander asked Anderson, were they to do 'with the Money in case they should all die'?[26]

But at least two of Bogle's children did survive. On 10 February 1784, George, Martha and Mary, 'natural children of the late Mr. George Bogle', were baptised – the first step towards British assimilation.[27] What became of George is unclear, but by the end of the year Martha and Mary were on board a ship, the *Southampton*, sailing for Britain. The two girls finally made it to Daldowie – the mansion that their father's fortune had helped to save. Crossing cultures and continents, they ended their journey at their father's childhood home. Martha and Mary were bought up by their aunts and Uncle Robert, who inherited the estate in 1784. It was not uncommon for the children of Company servants to be accepted by their fathers' families, and to find a place in British society (particularly if they happened to be fair-skinned). Martha and Mary grew up as Scottish gentlewomen, with a governess and maid of their own, and a special carriage to drive them to Glasgow.[28] To amuse themselves, they 'used to rummage in big boxes in the attics and dress up in old-fashioned silks and brocade dresses, so rich and stiff they could almost stand alone'.[29] It was part of family lore that their mother was 'Tichan, sister of the Teshoo Lama'.[30] In due course, the two sisters made respectable marriages to local men, as no doubt their father would have wished.

Besides his children, Bogle's most significant legacy was his writing. Anderson sent all of Bogle's papers, including his Tibetan diaries, to his family at Daldowie. Robert had long advocated the publication of George's journal, but now that the papers were in his care he could see just how much work remained to be done. Although the Company had granted Robert permission to proceed with publication, the project remained stalled for many years. The 'principal cause of delay has been a Difficulty in meeting with any Person qualified to correct & arrange them properly for the Press', Robert explained more than a decade after his brother's death.[31] But in 1792 Alexander Dalrymple offered his services as editor. The former maritime explorer (who in 1763 had chosen the island of Balambangan as an alternative site to Canton for the China trade) now occupied the post of hydrographer to the East India Company. Although officially in charge of compiling navigational charts, Dalrymple was as excited by commerce as by unmapped waters and, so many years after the failure of the Balambangan settlement, was still keen to find ways to circumvent the restrictions that remained in place on trade at Canton. Little wonder, then, that he was interested in Bogle's Tibetan venture. But even such an enthusiast found the task beyond him. In 1795 Dalrymple was appointed first hydrographer to the Admiralty and, with his new duties, found little time for the Tibetan journals. For the next eighty years, Bogle's papers would remain unedited, and his exploits fade from memory.

Tibet remained officially closed to the British for more than a century. During this time, the country would acquire its European reputation as a forbidden land, a place of mountains and mystery. It would be variously imagined as the source of occult knowledge and the realm of degenerate religion. Theosophists would exalt Tibet as home to the Mahatmas, the Great Souls who preserved the secret wisdom of Atlantis. Missionaries would condemn it as the abode of superstition and darkness.[32] It would have been difficult to conceive how a friendship could ever have existed between a Scotsman and a Tibetan lama.

EPILOGUE

It was while he was browsing in the library of Becca Hall, his family seat in Yorkshire, that Clements Markham first came across a manuscript fragment of Bogle's diary. Markham's grandfather had worked as Hastings's private secretary during the period of Bogle's proposed second mission to Tibet, and had carefully preserved all the papers. The manuscript could not have fallen into more capable hands. By the 1870s Markham was a dominant figure in British geographical circles. An inveterate traveller himself, he was in charge of the geographical section of the India Office. He was also secretary to the Royal Geographical Society, and honorary secretary to the Hakluyt Society, a body devoted to the publication of early travel texts. His interest ignited, Markham followed the trail of the manuscript to Bogle's great-niece, Martha Brown, who presented him with a large box of journals, memoranda, correspondence and minutes, 'judiciously sorted and arranged' – and probably censored – by one Mr Gairdner of Kilmarnock.[1] From these diverse sources, Markham pieced together a narrative of Bogle's mission, juxtaposing journal entries and letters, reports and instructions. He made marginal comments and crossed out unwanted sections on the original manuscripts, standardised Bogle's spelling, corrected his grammar, compiled exhaustive notes and wrote a substantial introduction for his edition of 1876.[2]

Markham's interest in Bogle was more than merely scholarly. During the 1870s, the British saw Tibet as a vast potential market for the now flourishing Assamese tea industry, and as a possible supplier of wool to the British textile industry.[3] Markham looked forward enthusiastically to the advent of a new era of 'unfettered intercourse through all the Himalayan passes'.[4] Familiar as he was with the India Office's archives, he was aware that the records of Britain's earlier attempts to develop trade with Tibet had been buried beneath the crushing piles of paper produced by the Raj. The 'knowledge that was then acquired with so much care, the lessons of experience that were taught, instead of being carefully stored up and made available as a point of departure for future efforts, have been totally disregarded', he lamented.[5]

With his own publication of Bogle's journals, Markham aimed to supply these gaps in knowledge for the policy-makers of his own day. 'It is believed that the present volume . . . will be useful to those who are officially entrusted with the conduct of these grave and important measures,' Markham declared, a touch pompously.[6] The passage of a century seemed to make little difference when it came to dealing with Tibet. Markham, like many nineteenth-century European writers on the East, regarded the orient as essentially unchanging. Since he could not imagine that there would have been significant developments in the region, Markham assumed that Bogle's experience would still be relevant. His introduction closed with the prediction that British India would soon move on the Tibetan front; Bogle's writing would then become highly topical, and his edition would 'enable a large circle of readers, who are interested in the welfare and progress of India, to form a sound judgment on momentous questions which may not improbably be under discussion in the near future'.[7]

It was not only the commercial and political utility of Bogle's journal that excited Markham; he was touched also by the warmth of Bogle's expressions of devotion to his family and, in particular, by his description of the friendship with the Lama. He wove a few passages from Bogle's letters to his sisters into his narrative as evidence of Bogle's sincerity and depth of feeling. Among these extracts was Bogle's heavy-hearted account to Bess of his departure from Tashilhunpo and final meeting with the Lama. The letter of farewell concluded with the Rousseauesque vision of the contented people of Tibet, living in peace and simplicity, free from the taint of greed or ambition. The reverse of the manuscript of Bogle's letter is annotated in Markham's hand, 'Affection for Lama/a beautiful Letter'.[8] Markham was particularly taken by Bogle's winning combination of adventurous youth and sentiment. At the heart of Bogle's mission, of course, lies the story of a friendship between men.

Bogle's valedictory image of Tibet as a mountain stronghold of innocent happiness would prove of lasting appeal. It was the earliest expression of the most enduring of Western fantasies of Tibet. Once it had made its way into print, Bogle's letter would pave the way for the later myth of Shangri-La.[9] A place of Himalayan peace and contentment, Shangri-La was imagined by James Hilton in his 1933 novel *Lost Horizon*. In creating his mountain idyll, Hilton drew on the Tibetan tradition of Shambhala, the perfect mythical land encircled by snowy peaks – to which the Third Panchen Lama had written a guidebook.[10] The fantasy of a Tibetan Shangri-La, a timeless refuge from the problems of modernity, would continue to haunt the Western imagination on page and screen right up to the present day.

One of the most avid early readers of Markham's edition was Sarat Chandra Das, a young Bengali headmaster of a boarding school for boys of Tibetan descent in Darjeeling. Das received the volume of Bogle's writing soon after its publication as a gift from the British Deputy Commissioner for Darjeeling. He read it 'over and over again', he recalled in his *Autobiography*. 'It kindled in my mind a burning desire for visiting Tibet and for exploring its unknown tracts.'[11] In true *Boys' Own* fashion, the book transformed Das from sedentary schoolmaster into intrepid adventurer.

Das managed to secure an invitation to study at Tashilhunpo through the intercession of a lama who taught him Tibetan. Entering Tibet disguised as a pilgrim in 1879, he became an elite member of the group of 'pandit surveyors' employed from the 1860s by the British. To expand their geographical knowledge of the Himalayan region and to evade the prohibitions against European travel, the British trained a select band of hill men in the arts of subterfuge and surveying. Dressed as Buddhist pilgrims, with sextants hidden in trunks, travel logs secreted inside prayer wheels, and rosaries reduced to a convenient 100 beads to record the length of a day's march, the pandit surveyors painstakingly counted their strides across vast tracts of Tibet. As an educated Bengali, Das was an unlikely recruit. He was more intellectually curious than his fellows, but less precise in his methods of surveying.[12]

It seems that Das modelled his methods on Bogle. Like his Scottish predecessor, he concentrated on cultivating friendships at court and gathering political and cultural intelligence. During his two-month stay at Tashilhunpo, he acquired quantities of Sanskrit and Tibetan texts. But he lacked Bogle's circumspection, and managed to excite the suspicions of the Fifth Panchen Lama. Das had a single audience with the Panchen Lama, and noted the cold and independent bearing of the twenty-five-year-old Incarnate (in implicit contrast with the warmth of Bogle's descriptions of the Third). But Das did manage to grow intimate with the Sengchen Lama, the head of the Tantric College at Tashilhunpo, who showed an eager interest in European science and technology, and received lessons from him in the rudiments of photography.

Building on these contacts, Das made a return trip to Tibet two years later, on this occasion with the official backing of the Survey of India. His brief was to make friends in high places, to pursue his cultural investigations and, like Bogle, to keep a detailed journal (rather than the bare records of routes produced by other pandit surveyors). By this time, the Sengchen Lama was the Chief Minister, and managed to arrange for Das to travel through a smallpox epidemic to Lhasa where he was received by the six-year-old Thirteenth Dalai Lama. But, on his return to Tashilhunpo, Das found that the smallpox had again claimed a Panchen Lama as its victim. In such unsettled circumstances, facing rumours that he was a British spy, Das was forced to beat a hasty retreat to India.

Das's lack of discretion had tragic consequences for the Sengchen Lama. In 1887, amid mounting Tibetan suspicions of the British, the government at Lhasa found the Sengchen Lama guilty of divulging secrets to a foreign power and condemned him to death by drowning. Many of his followers were likewise executed, imprisoned or tortured.[13] Das, by contrast, earned a reputation as one of British India's leading Tibetan experts. In 1890 his reports were declassified and these, together with his autobiography, were later published. Das received a clutch of medals in recognition of his services, including an award from the Royal Geographical Society (where Clements Markham held the post of honorary secretary).

Among the manuscripts that Das translated were passages of the Tibetan biography of the Third Panchen Lama. Published in the *Journal of the Asiatic Society of Bengal*, these extracts rendered the Tibetan account of Bogle's visit to Tashilhunpo into English for the first time. Unfortunately for Das, the Tibetan original was somewhat reticent on the nature of the relationship between the Panchen Lama and Bogle. As a later scholar has pointed out, Das was not altogether faithful in his translation techniques and sometimes 'inserted his own opinions without distinguishing them as such'.[14] In an act of homage to his hero, Das seems to have expanded the original to celebrate the friendship between the Panchen Lama and Bogle. It is only in Das's translation that we get a sense of the Lama's affection for Bogle. 'The Panchen often entered into long discourses with Bogle Saheb and evinced great delight at his answers and questions,' Das's translation reads. 'His Holiness's kind attachment to Bogle Saheb resembled that of a spiritual guide to his disciple or of a Lama to his almsgiver.'[15] In figuring the mutual devotion of Lama and Sahib as the relation between guru and disciple, Das produced an image that would prove most compelling to the British imagination.

If he was a little too imaginative as a translator, Das was himself subject to the process of creative transformation. The chronicler and bard of British India, Rudyard Kipling, took Das as the model for the Bengali agent Hurree Chunder Mookerjee in his novel *Kim*. The ingenious yet ridiculous 'Babu' is a key player in Kipling's story of Great Game espionage. Published in 1901, *Kim* became one the most memorable literary celebrations of imperial boyhood. For generations of British schoolchildren, it *was* India. The story of spying, disguise and adventure has at its centre the unlikely friendship between Kim, an orphaned Irish boy raised in Lahore, and the aged Teshoo Lama, who had travelled from Tibet in search of enlightenment. Gifted with uncanny skills of impersonation, Kim can slip between races, roles and cultures at will. He is at once a young recruit to the Great Game and a devoted disciple to the unworldly Lama.

Kipling appears to have borrowed the name of his lama – the 'Teshoo Lama' – from the version of the Tibetan title used by the British for the Panchen Lama. Throughout their accounts, Bogle and Turner refer to the Panchen Lama by this name. More significantly, the story of the friendship of Bogle and the Third Panchen Lama may have figured among Kipling's various sources.[16] While much transformed, Bogle's account seems to have fed into *Kim*; as the critic Laurie Hovell McMillin observes: 'it is as if the novel has swallowed Bogle whole.'[17] Kipling's Lama may be elderly and have left his monastic seat to go wandering, and Kim may be a child of the Lahore streets, but the relationship between the two seems indebted to Bogle's account. The energy and playfulness of Bogle's writing may have contributed to his youthful reincarnation, and Bogle's willingness to adapt to Tibetan customs and clothes may lie behind Kim's capacity for mimicry and disguise. It is notable too that, in his translation of the Tibetan biography of the Third Panchen Lama, Das had already recast the relationship between the Lama and Bogle as that between guru and disciple. In *Kim*, Bogle's account was reborn as late imperial romance.

Two years after the publication of *Kim*, the British Empire embarked on its last great military venture, played out on the heights of Tibet. In July 1903, Sikh troops under British command crossed into Tibet, trespassing half a day's march over the border. After repeated Tibetan refusals to engage in negotiations, British India had determined on a show of force. If there was one thing that the Raj could not brook, it was being ignored. The act of aggression, the British claimed, would make the Tibetan authorities see sense. The Sikh troops struck up camp at Khamba Dzong, the first settlement on the road into Tibet, just ten miles from the frontier with the British-protected kingdom of Sikkim.

For their part, the Tibetans had no inclination whatsoever to engage in talks. Tibet's policy of isolation may have been initiated by the

Qing more than a century before, but now the Tibetan authorities themselves wanted to have nothing to do with the imperial power to the south. Over the course of the nineteenth century, the British had shown themselves ever more ruthless in their dealings with China. They had achieved all the aims of the Macartney mission – and much more besides – through the use of force. At terrible human cost, the two Opium Wars (1839–42, 1856–60) had blown apart the restrictions on trade at Canton – and wantonly destroyed the beauties of Yuanming Yuan, the opulent garden palace outside Peking. Ports all along the Chinese coast were now open to British commerce, operating under a fixed customs tariff, and traders and missionaries, once they had obtained the necessary passports, could travel around the interior. The British had secured possession of the island of Hong Kong, and now had an ambassador stationed at Peking.

Qing authority throughout the empire had been drastically undermined by a combination of external aggression, economic decline and popular unrest. For much of the nineteenth century, the Qing had little effective power in Tibet. By the turn of the twentieth, the Thirteenth Dalai Lama was well aware of the weakness of the dynasty. But in the attempt to assert his autonomy the Dalai Lama had precipitated the present crisis. He had resisted a treaty on trade and the definition of the border agreed between the Qing and the British, on the grounds that the Tibetan authorities had not been consulted. The Dalai Lama had also started to investigate diplomatic links with Russia, in the hope that St Petersburg might function as an alternative source of support. As far as the British in India were concerned, these exploratory talks were a most alarming development.

For many years the Viceroy, Lord Curzon, had been obsessed by the threat that Russia posed to British India. The second half of the nineteenth century saw Russia's relentless advance into Central Asia, and it seemed obvious to many Raj officials that the Czar's ultimate goal was India itself. Tibet took on a new strategic importance as a buffer against Russian aggression. When news reached India of the negotiations between the Thirteenth Dalai Lama and Czar Nicholas II, the government decided that the time had come to act. If the Dalai Lama were on speaking terms with the Czar, then the British would find ways of making him talk to the Viceroy.

The leader of the missionary force was Francis Younghusband, an ambitious forty-year-old who had caught Curzon's eye. Like the Viceroy, Younghusband burned with the conviction that the Russians were laying plots in Tibet. He was less confident of his knowledge of the region, and to prepare for his role as negotiator had hurriedly purchased all the volumes on Buddhism and Tibet that he could find on sale in Calcutta. The initial weeks at Khamba Dzong were spent in unsatisfactory encounters with representatives of the Dalai Lama who were under orders to deflect and delay all attempts at dialogue, in the hope that the British would simply withdraw. In the periods between fruitless meetings, Younghusband turned to his books. On 27 July, after composing a letter and cipher telegram about the Russians and Tibet, he picked up one of the volumes. The more that he read, the more excited he grew. 'I have the feeling I am doing something really big,' he wrote to his wife Helen that evening. 'I have been working up today all about Warren Hastings' attempts to send an envoy up here in 1774 and I am the next since then to come on an official Mission. It is a great thing.'[18]

The book that filled Younghusband with such a sense of his own importance was the edition of Bogle's journals and letters prepared by Clements Markham in 1876. Caught up in the romance of Bogle's travels, Younghusband fondly imagined himself to be the first British envoy to follow in Bogle's footsteps – conveniently forgetting Turner's 1783 mission in a characteristic moment of self-aggrandisement. But his sense that he was Bogle's successor was a fantasy in more ways than one. Bogle's descriptions of intimate conversations with the Panchen Lama could not have been further from Younghusband's current impasse. And as for the means of persuasion, Bogle had charm, while Younghusband had firepower.

Nevertheless, Younghusband picked up practical hints from his study of earlier missions. Two days later, envoys from the Sixth Panchen Lama arrived at Khamba Dzong to demand an explanation of the British forces' presence in Tibet and to seek their immediate withdrawal. In an attempt to conciliate the Tashilhunpo delegate, Younghusband had recourse to the strategy outlined by Turner when he had visited the infant Panchen Lama. Like Turner, Younghusband attempted to turn the principle of reincarnation to British advantage.

'I told his Deputy to thank the Lama for the very great kindness he had shown to the two Englishmen who had visited,' he wrote to his wife. 'The Deputy looked very surprised: I said that possibly His Holiness might have forgotten these Englishmen as he did it 130 years ago in one of his former existences: but the British Government had not forgotten his kindness, and I desired on their behalf to thank him for it.' Then, taking credit for the idea, he boasted: 'This is a great piece of diplomacy on my part! You know theoretically these great Lamas never die and it is supposed to be the same person merely in different bodies. And as two Englishmen had been sent on an Embassy to the Lama by Warren Hastings and had been well-received by him I thought this was an appropriate way of reminding these Tibetans that an English mission was no new thing.'[19] Incongruously pressing Bogle and Turner to his service, Younghusband attempted to justify the presence of a British army on Tibetan soil.

To reinforce the message, Younghusband's interpreter, Frederick O'Connor, produced textual evidence of the earlier British missions. On their next visit, the Tashilhunpo delegates were shown copies of Bogle's and Turner's accounts. O'Connor pointed out the plates in the books with engravings of familiar landmarks and a letter in Tibetan script sent to Turner. But to complement this exhibition of former friendship, O'Connor laid on a rather more chilling display. 'While they were in camp,' O'Connor noted in his diary, 'Captain Bethune worked the Maxim gun which excited their utmost astonishment and evidently gave them an increased respect for the power of modern armaments.'[20] Well might the Tashilhunpo envoys wonder at the Maxim gun. Rattling off a thousand rounds every ninety seconds, it was one of the British army's most effective killing machines.

After five months of stalemate at Khamba Dzong, Younghusband withdrew only to return in force that winter. An army of Sikhs and Gurkhas, backed by a Royal Artillery Mountain Battery and Maxim gun detachment – not to mention thousands of porters and camp followers, yaks, bullocks and mules – trailed over the mountain passes from Sikkim. Never before had the British Indian army been exposed to such altitudes or to the rigours of the Tibetan winter.

When news of the British invasion reached Lhasa, a force of between two and three thousand Tibetan troops – many of them irregular –

assembled at the village of Guru, south of Gyantse, to defend the route that led to the capital. Armed with matchlock guns, swords and spears, the Tibetan soldiers set about preparing fortifications. They built a six-foot-high wall running some hundred yards across the plain below Guru, near the hot springs of Chumi Shengo. A potent symbol of resistance, the wall was but a flimsy barrier to Younghusband's invading forces.

On the morning of 31 March 1904, with six inches of snow on the ground, the British army advanced slowly on Chumi Shengo. As the lines of invaders approached, neither side fired. Pressing ever closer, the British forces managed to surround the wall almost entirely. With Maxim guns and rifles trained directly on them, the Tibetans had no option but to concede defeat. It was only after the surrender that a scuffle broke out. And then the firing began. 'As soon as my guns got to work the slaughter was terrible,' the commander of the Maxim guns wrote home to his father, 'the Tibetans fell in heaps where the maxims struck them. I got so sick of the slaughter I ceased fire.'[21] By eleven o'clock that morning, over five hundred Tibetans lay dead. There were no fatalities on the British side. In an official telegraph, Younghusband laid the blame for the carnage on the victims themselves. 'The result was wholly caused by the complete inability of the Tibetans, even when our troops absolutely surrounded them, to take in the seriousness of the situation,' he wrote in a grotesque attempt to excuse the massacre.[22]

Fighting and looting their way north-east, British forces took four months to reach the famously inaccessible city of Lhasa. The Dalai Lama had fled and, try as they might, the British could find no trace of Russian armaments. Younghusband forced the remaining monk officials to agree to the punitive terms of the Lhasa Convention. Tibet was banned from entering into treaties with foreign powers, and obliged to open two trade marts and accommodate a British trade agent. The British would receive a massive indemnity of seven and a half million rupees and the right to occupy the frontier district of the Chumbi Valley for seventy-five years. The Lhasa Convention had cost the lives of nearly three thousand Tibetans. Its excesses were apparent even to the British government in London, which reduced the indemnity imposed on Tibet by two-thirds and shortened the occupation of the Chumbi Valley to three years.

Younghusband, who felt betrayed by the British government, continued to defend his and Curzon's policy to the last. In 1910 he published *India and Tibet*, an idiosyncratic history of relations between British India and Tibet which argued that the 1904 expedition was 'merely the culmination of a long series of efforts to regularize and humanize' relations between the two powers.[23] The first chapter was devoted to Bogle and Hastings. Like Markham, Younghusband was much taken by Bogle's youth, 'good breeding and . . . great natural kindliness of disposition'.[24] Hastings he praised for his foresight and decisiveness. He was eager to point out that it had been the Panchen Lama who had initiated the contact with the British. 'We were not the interferers. It was the Tibetans themselves who made the first move.'[25] Above all, Younghusband wanted to establish that he was only picking up where Bogle had left off. The same perfectly reasonable request to trade had motivated Bogle's mission and the 1904 invasion. 'Not a very aggressive request to make or a very great favour to ask, especially as the Tibetans had begun their intercourse by asking a favour from us,' Younghusband wrote in self-defence. 'But it was not for a century and a quarter, and not till we had carried our arms to Lhasa itself, that that simple request was answered.'[26]

Younghusband was by no means the last to use Bogle in unlikely justification of an invasion of Tibet. In recent years China has had recourse to Bogle (among many other sources) to substantiate its claim that Tibet is an inalienable part of its territory. In 2000 the British Foreign and Commonwealth Office issued a report on human rights that stated that the UK did not recognise Chinese sovereignty over Tibet (although – in a classic diplomatic fudge – neither did it recognise Tibet's independence).[27] As part of its response, the Chinese Ministry of Foreign Affairs posted a statement on its website that outlined its version of British relations with Tibet from the eighteenth century on: 'each time the Tibet issue was raised between Britain and the Qing imperial court, it was on the basis of Tibet being a part of Chinese territory.' When Bogle sought to establish trade links with Tibet without reference to Peking, the website stated, the Panchen Lama replied: 'The Chinese emperor controls and supervises Tibet through the prince regent and commissioner whom he has appointed and stationed in Tibet . . . I am merely a lama who chants sutras, so I cannot conclude any convention with foreign countries.' Bogle similarly asserted that Tibet was 'under the jurisdiction of the Chinese emperor'.[28] The dynamic nature of the Panchen Lama's relations with the British was completely erased – a minor but telling act of amnesia in the vast official project to rewrite the historical record.

With such deeply contested territory as Tibet as his subject, it is inevitable that Bogle has been much used and abused. Readers have mined his account according to their various ideological, commercial and literary needs, and the afterlife of his journals and letters is as important as the original venture. Bogle is particularly susceptible to selective reading since he was a writer of many voices and modes – by turns playful and scholarly, pragmatic and philosophical. He has featured in various accounts of European travellers in Tibet, in histories of trade and international relations. Markham's edition has been reprinted several times, and in 2002 Alastair Lamb published a scholarly edition of Bogle's journals and official letters.[29] But this is the first book to set Bogle in a wider historical and cultural context. I have tried to restore the ambiguity and complexity of the man, of his writing and his political world. I wanted to show the internal and external power struggles in Calcutta, Tashilhunpo and Peking, and to investigate Bogle's own contradictory commercial and intellectual impulses: to view him as the product at once of the East India Company and of the progressive ideals of the Enlightenment.

But Bogle was not my only subject. As Younghusband was fond of pointing out, it was the Panchen Lama who initiated contact with the British. Here was a leader at the heart of Central Asian networks of influence and power, a figure who could negotiate peace treaties with the East India Company and broker deals with the Qing Empire. Like Hastings, the Panchen Lama was intellectually curious and prepared to back speculative ventures. Both leaders exercised autonomy in the matter of foreign relations (although both were subject to certain constraints: the Panchen Lama had to deal with Lhasa and the *ambans*, Hastings with the Council majority and London). The Third Panchen Lama was by no means a pawn in the Company game, but rather a player in his own right. He saw the alliance between Tashilhunpo and

Calcutta as a means of extending Gelugpa influence, and acquiring his own monastery on the banks of the Ganges. Hastings's gains were less concrete. There was a brief revival of trans-Himalayan trade, but Tibet never became a major market for Bengali goods and the dream of gaining access to the Qing court died with the Panchen Lama.

Keeping the lines of communication open between Tashilhunpo and Calcutta fell to Purangir: guide, negotiator and traveller extraordinaire. From the beginning, Purangir was crucial to the encounter between the Tibetans and the British. He carried the Panchen Lama's original letter to Calcutta and gained Bogle admission to Tibet. He reported on the Panchen Lama's visit to Peking and ran the first Gelugpa monastery to be founded in India for many centuries. As a *gosain* or trading monk, he united both commerce and religion, making him the perfect intermediary between a trading company and a religious hierarch. Endlessly crossing between Bengal and Tibet, Purangir was uniquely placed to act as cultural interpreter. Trusted by both sides but owned by neither, he managed to carve an independent diplomatic career out of his wandering vocation.

Purangir accompanied my story on all its travels. Indeed there would have been no book without him. I found myself writing the narrative of two journeys: the first, Bogle's mission to Tashilhunpo, the second, the Panchen Lama's progress to Peking. The book's horizon inevitably expanded beyond Bengal and Tibet to China. The Company always looked beyond Tibet to the vast Chinese market, and valued the Panchen Lama primarily for his connections with the Qianlong Emperor. In the scheme to advocate the British cause at the Qing court, the Company sought to invest the Panchen Lama with the role of intermediary (after the manner of Purangir). For the Panchen Lama was far more accessible than the Qianlong Emperor. His long conversations with Bogle indicated a polite sociability – one of the key attributes of an eighteenth-century British gentleman. He seemed to share British notions of the reciprocal advantages of diplomacy and trade – something that could not be said of Qianlong. Inevitably, Bogle constructed the Panchen Lama in his own image, highlighting his commercial interests at the expense of his religious concerns.

But, for all the distortions of emphasis, Bogle's account remains remarkable as a record of cultural encounter. Tutored by Purangir,

Bogle managed to enter into surprisingly close relations with the Panchen Lama. Both parties evidently felt that they benefited from the exchange. Such reciprocity was indeed rare in the Company's dealings with other states. Bogle's mission is perhaps the exception that proves the rule. Unusually for this period, the Company did not back its commercial proposals with threats or the use of arms. Faced with a barrier the size of the Himalayas, the British were obliged to play a more courteous diplomatic game. Bogle was able to pioneer a new mode of Company diplomacy that operated through personal alliances and cultural understanding.

Reading Bogle today, we can still sense the thrill of the encounter with Tibet. But our enjoyment is tinged with a sense of loss, for we inevitably read his account in the knowledge of the tragic destruction of Tibetan culture in our own time. Bogle's vision remains as fresh and his wit as sharp as they were for his original readers. It is as if he never quite got over the surprise of being on intimate terms with the Panchen Lama. It still seems delightfully incongruous that the young Glaswegian should have struck up a friendship with the incarnation of Amitabha, the Buddha of Boundless Light. Bogle boasted in a letter to his brother Robin of 'enjoying advantages which no European traveller before me ever possessed'.[30] With the passage of more than two centuries, we might add that few Europeans after Bogle would ever possess such advantages again.

NOTES

Chapter 1: The Panchen Lama's Letter

1 George Bogle to Mary Bogle, Calcutta, 24 March 1774, Bogle Collection [BC], Mitchell Library [ML].

2 C. A. Bayly, *Rulers, Townsmen and Bazaars: North Indian Society in the Age of British Expansion 1770–1870* (Delhi: Oxford University Press, 2003) 126–7, 143, 183–5. John Clark, 'Hindu Trading Pilgrims', in Alex McKay, ed., *Pilgrimage in Tibet* (London: Curzon, 1998) 52–71.

3 'Memorandum on Trade', H/Misc/118, f. 377, Asia, Pacific & Africa Collections [APAC], British Library [BL].

4 Gaur Dás Bysack, 'Notes on a Buddhist Monastery at Bhot Bágán', *Journal of the Asiatic Society of Bengal* 59: 1 (1890) 87.

5 C. A. Bayly, *Empire and Information: Intelligence Gathering and Social Communication in India, 1780–1870.* (Cambridge: Cambridge University Press, 1996) 18.

6 C. A. Bayly, *Rulers, Townsmen and Bazaars* 143.

7 The title Panchen Lama combines Sanskrit and Tibetan words to mean 'great scholar'. It is the title first bestowed by the Fourth Dalai Lama on his teacher in 1601. Subsequent reincarnations of the teacher also bore the title Panchen Lama. To the Tibetans, Lobsang Palden Yeshé is the Third Panchen Lama. The Chinese recognise earlier incarnations and refer to Lobsang Palden Yeshé as the Sixth Panchen Lama.

8 Toni Huber, *The Holy Land Reborn: Pilgrimage and the Reinvention of Buddhist India in the Tibetan Tradition* (Chicago: University of Chicago Press, forthcoming).

9 A. R. Field, 'A Note Concerning Early Anglo-Bhutanese Relations', *East and West* 13 (1962) 344.

10 Luciano Petech, *Selected Papers on Asian History* (Rome: Istituto Italiano per il Medio ed Estremo Oriente, 1988) 55.

11 Schuyler Cammann, *Trade through the Himalayas: The Early British Attempts to Open Tibet* (Princeton: Princeton University Press, 1951) 26.

12 Field, 344.

13 Samuel Turner, *An Account of an Embassy to the Court of the Teshoo Lama in Tibet* (London: G. & W. Nicol, 1800) xiii.

14 H/Misc/117, f. 15, APAC, BL.

15 MSS Eur E226/1, APAC, BL.

16 S. K. Bhuyan, *Anglo-Assamese Relations, 1771–1826* (Gauhuti: Department of Historical and Antiquarian Studies in Assam, 1949) 71–6.

17 *Calendar of Persian Correspondence 1772–5*, vol. iv (Calcutta: Government of India, 1925) 170.

18 *Calendar of Persian Correspondence 1772–5* 171.

19 MSS Eur E226/77(c), APAC, BL.

Chapter 2: Private Commissions to Mr Bogle

1 George Bogle to Robert Bogle, 19 January 1774, Calcutta, BC, ML.

2 See Romolo Gandolfo, 'Bhutan and Tibet in European Cartography (1597–1800)', *Proceedings of the First International Seminar on Bhutan Studies*, Thimphu: Centre for Bhutan Studies, 2004, 90–136.

3 George Bogle to Robert Bogle, 25 August 1774, Tashichodzong, BC, ML.

4 MSS Eur E226/7, APAC, BL.

5 Hastings and Bogle seem to have been unaware of the existence of the map of the borders of Bengal published in 1773 by James Rennell, the first Surveyor-General of Bengal. See Alastair Lamb, *Bhutan and Tibet: The Travels of George Bogle and Alexander Hamilton 1774–1777* (Hertingfordbury: Roxford Books, 2002) 1: 60, footnote.

6 John MacGregor, *Tibet: A Chronicle of Exploration* (London: Routledge & Kegan Paul, 1970) 104.

7 MSS Eur E226/7, APAC, BL.

8 MSS Eur E226/7, APAC, BL.

9 John Riddy, 'Warren Hastings: Scotland's Benefactor?', in Geoffrey Carnall and Colin Nicholson, eds, *The Impeachment of Warren Hastings: Papers from a Bicentenary Commemoration* (Edinburgh: Edinburgh University Press, 1989) 35.

10 Carolyn Marie Peters, 'Glasgow's Tobacco Lords: An Examination of Wealth Creators in the Eighteenth Century' (PhD thesis, Glasgow University, 1990) 47, 81.

11 John Moore in a biographical preface to 1797 *Works of Tobias Smollett*, quoted in T. M. Devine and Gordon Jackson, eds, *Glasgow: Beginnings to 1830* (Manchester: Manchester University Press, 1995) 1: 318.

12 Charles Morehead, ed., *Memorials of the Life and Writings of the Rev. Robert Morehead* (Edinburgh: Edmonston & Douglas, 1875) 43.

13 George Bogle to Robert Bogle, 27 March 1770, the ship *Vansittart*, BC, ML.

14 George Bogle to George Bogle (senior), 1 December 1769, London, BC, ML.

15 T. S. Ashton, *Economic Fluctuations in England 1700–1800* (Oxford: Clarendon Press, 1959) 107.

16 Cited in Julian Hoppit, *Risk and Failure in English Business 1700–1800* (Cambridge: Cambridge University Press, 1987) 130.

17 Ashton, 128.

18 Robert Bogle to George Bogle, 19 November 1772, London, BC, ML.

19 Robert Bogle to George Bogle, 19 November 1772, London, BC, ML.

20 Robert Bogle to George Bogle, 19 November 1772, London, BC, ML.

21 George Bogle to Robert Bogle, undated, BC, ML.

22 George Bogle to Robert Bogle, 12 November 1773, Calcutta, BC, ML.

23 Eliza Fay, *Original Letters from India (1779–1815)*, ed. E. M. Forster (London: Chatto & Windus, 1986) 181.

24 George Bogle to Robin Bogle, undated, BC, ML.

25 Thomas Williamson, *East India Vade-Mecum; or, Complete Guide to Gentlemen intended for the Civil, Military, or Naval Service of the Hon. East India Company* (London: Black, Parry & Kingsbury, 1810) 1: 414.

26 Indrani Chatterjee, 'Colouring Subalternity: Slaves, Concubines and Social Orphans in Early Colonial India', *Subaltern Studies* 10 (1999) 57–8, Durba Ghosh, 'Colonial Companions: *Bibis, Begums*, and Concubines of the British in North India 1760–1830' (PhD thesis, University of California, Berkeley, 2000) 30.

27 Robert Bogle to George Bogle, 15 April 1773, London, BC, ML.

28 James N. M. Maclean, *Reward is Secondary: The Life of a Political Adventurer and an Inquiry into the Mystery of 'Junius'* (London: Hodder & Stoughton, 1963) 188–90.

29 Warren Hastings to John Stewart, January 1776, quoted in Maclean, 320.

30 George Bogle to Elizabeth Bogle, 24 March 1774, Calcutta, BC, ML.

31 George Bogle to Robert Bogle, 19 January 1774, Calcutta, BC, ML.

32 Warren Hastings to George Bogle, 13 May 1774, Fort William, Add. 29117, f. 56, BL.

33 Ghulam Hussain Khan, *A Translation of the Seir Mutaqharin; or View of Modern Times, being an History of India* (Calcutta: James White, 1789) 402.

34 Warren Hastings to George Bogle, 16 May 1774, Fort William, Add. 29117, f. 59, BL.

35 Warren Hastings to George Bogle, 16 May 1774, Fort William, Add. 29117, f. 59, BL.

36 Warren Hastings to the Court of Directors, May 1774, MSS Eur E226/3, APAC, BL.

Chapter 3: Lazy, Lolling Palankins

1 George Bogle to George Bogle (senior), 25 August 1774, Tashichodzong, BC, ML.

2 Quoted in P. J. Marshall, *Bengal, the British Bridgehead: Eastern India 1740–1828* (Cambridge: Cambridge University Press, 1987) 13.

3 Marshall, 14, 6.

4 Jan Splinter Stavorinus, *Voyages to the East-Indies* (London: G. G. & J. Robinson, 1798) 1: 528–30.

5 Stavorinus 1: 515.

6 George Bogle to Robert Bogle, 26 December 1770, Calcutta, BC, ML.

7 George Bogle to Robert Bogle, 25 August 1774, Tashichodzong, BC, ML.

8 George Bogle to Robert Bogle, 25 August 1774, Tashichodzong, BC, ML.

9 Charles Acland, *A Popular Account of the Manners and Customs of India* (London: John Murray, 1847) 40–1.

10 Marshall, 10–12.

11 *Gentlemen's Magazine* 41 (1771) 402–4; *London Magazine* (1771) 469–71; *Annual Register* (1771) 'Appendix to the Chronicle' 205–8.

12 George Bogle to Robert Bogle, 5 September 1770, Calcutta, BC, ML.

13 K. M. Mohsin, 'Murshidabad in the Eighteenth Century', in Kenneth Ballhatchet and John Harrison, eds, *The City in South Asia: Pre-Modern and Modern* (London: Curzon Press, 1980) 81.

14 Ghulam Hussain Khan, *A Translation of the Seir Mutaqharin; or, View of Modern Times, being an History of India* (Calcutta: James White, 1789) 403.

15 George Bogle to Robert Bogle, 26 December 1770, Calcutta, BC, ML.

16 Ghulam Hussain Khan, 591.

17 William Scott to George Bogle, 18 November 1773, London, BC, ML.

18 P. J. Marshall, *East Indian Fortunes: The British in Bengal in the Eighteenth Century* (Oxford: Oxford University Press, 1976) 215.

19 T. M. Devine, *Scotland's Empire 1600–1815* (London: Allen Lane, 2003) 268–9.

20 William Bolts, *Considerations on Indian Affairs* (London, 1772) 1: 84, quoted in Peter Marshall, 'Masters and Banians in Eighteenth-Century Calcutta', in Blair B. King and M. N. Pearson, eds, *The Age of Partnership: Europeans in Asia before Dominion* (Honolulu: University of Hawaii Press, 1979) 192–3.

21 George Bogle to Robert Bogle, 11 April 1771, Calcutta, Letterbook f. 147, BC, ML.

22 Lucy S. Sutherland, *The East India Company in Eighteenth-Century Politics* (Oxford: Clarendon Press, 1952) 223–60.

23 George Bogle to Mrs Brown, 10 December 1772, Calcutta, BC, ML.

24 George Bogle to Mrs Brown, 10 December 1772, Calcutta, BC, ML.

25 George Bogle to Mrs Brown, 10 December 1772, Calcutta, BC, ML.

26 Khan Mohammad Mohsin, *A Bengal District in Transition: Murshidabad 1765–1793* (Dacca: Asiatic Society of Bangladesh, 1973) 162–4.

27 Committee of Circuit Proceedings, 11 July 1772, p. 43, quoted in Mohsin, 163.

28 Marshall, *Bengal, the British Bridgehead*, 97.

29 I am indebted to Alastair Lamb for this suggestion.

30 MSS Eur E226/8, APAC, BL.

31 George Bogle to George Bogle (senior), 25 August 1774, Tashichodzong, BC, ML.

Chapter 4: Perpetual Ascending and Descending

1 Add. MS 29233, f. 389r, BL.

2 MSS Eur E226/8, APAC, BL.

3 MSS Eur E226/8, APAC, BL.

4 Add. MS 29233, f. 388v, BL.

5 Add. MS 29233, ff. 388r–388v, BL.

6 MSS Eur E226/76 APAC, BL.

7 Kathleen Wilson, *The Island Race: Englishness, Empire and Gender in the Eighteenth Century* (London: Routledge, 2003) 59–62.

8 Warren Hastings to George Bogle, 8 September 1774, Add. MS 29117, f. 63v, BL.

9 MSS Eur E226/8 APAC, BL.

10 MSS Eur E226/8, APAC, BL.

11 MSS Eur E226/8, APAC, BL.

12 Samuel Turner, *An Account of an Embassy to the Court of Teshoo Lama in Tibet* (London: G. & W. Nicol, 1800) 44–5.

13 MSS Eur E226/8, APAC, BL.

14 Peter Bishop, *The Myth of Shangri-La: Tibet, Travel Writing and the Western Creation of Sacred Landscape* (London: Athlone Press, 1989) 39.

15 MSS Eur E226/77(c), APAC, BL.

16 MSS Eur E226/77(c), APAC, BL.

17 MSS Eur E226/77(c), APAC, BL.

18 MSS Eur E226/77(c), APAC, BL.

19 MSS Eur E226/78, APAC, BL.

20 MSS Eur E226/77, APAC, BL.

21 MSS Eur E226/78, APAC, BL.

22 Add. MS 45421, f. 30v, BL.

23 Philip Edwards, ed., *The Journals of Captain Cook* (Harmondsworth: Penguin, 1999) 272.

24 Add. MS 29117, f. 61r, BL.

25 Turner, 140.

26 Michael Aris, *Views of Medieval Bhutan: The Diary and Drawings of Samuel Davis, 1783* (London: Serindia Publications, 1982) 74.

27 MSS Eur E226/78, APAC, BL.

28 George Bogle (senior) to George Bogle, 24 April 1773, Daldowie, BC, ML.

29 MSS Eur E226/78, APAC, BL.

30 Janet Gurkin Altman, *Epistolarity: Approaches to a Form* (Columbus: Ohio State University Press, 1982) 15.

31 MSS Eur E226/78, APAC, BL.

Chapter 5: The First European in These Parts

1 George Bogle to Mary Bogle, 25 August 1774, Tashichodzong, BC, ML.

2 Tenzin Chögyel, *Lho'i Chöjung* (1759) f. 66b, cited in Christian Schicklgruber and Françoise Pommaret, eds, *Bhutan: Mountain Fortress of the Gods* (London: Serindia Publications, 1997) 206.

3 Dawa Norbu, 'The Europeanization of Sino-Tibetan Relations, 1775–1907: The Genesis of Chinese "Suzerainty" and Tibetan "Autonomy"', *Tibet Journal* 15: 4 (1990) 38.

4 George Bogle to Anne Bogle, 23 August 1774, Tashichodzong, BC, ML.

5 George Bogle to Anne Bogle, 23 August 1774, Tashichodzong, BC, ML.

6 MSS Eur E226/77(c), APAC, BL, and George Bogle to Anne Bogle, 23 August 1774, Tashichodzong, BC, ML. Two copies of this letter exist, both slightly damaged. I have combined them where necessary.

7 George Bogle to Anne Bogle, 23 August 1774, Tashichodzong, BC, ML.

8 Add. MS 19283, f. 5v, BL.

9 George Bogle to Anne Bogle, 23 August 1774, Tashichodzong, BC, ML.

10 MSS Eur E226/77(c), APAC, BL.

11 George Bogle to Anne Bogle, 23 August 1774, Tashichodzong, BC, ML.

12 Add. MS 19283, f. 6v, BL.

13 Add. MS 19283, f. 7r, BL.

14 Add. MS 19283, ff. 7r–v, BL.

15 Add. MS 19283, f. 8r, BL.

16 H/ Misc /117 f. 16, APAC, BL; H/Misc/219 f. 334, APAC, BL.

17 Add. MS 19283, f. 12r, BL.

18 Add. MS 19283, f. 12v, BL.

19 Add. MS 19283, f. 13v, BL.
20 Add. MS 19283, f. 16r, BL.
21 Add. MS 19283, ff. 16r–v, BL.
22 Add. MS 19283, f. 17r, BL.
23 Add. MS 19283, f. 17v, BL.
24 Add. MS 19283, ff. 17v–18r, BL.

Chapter 6: Monkish to the Greatest Degree

1 MSS Eur E226/9, f. 3v, APAC, BL.
2 MSS Eur E226/9, f. 3v, APAC, BL.
3 MSS Eur E226/77(c), APAC, BL.
4 MSS Eur E226/77(c), APAC, BL.
5 George Bogle to Alexander Elliot, 11 October 1774, Tashichodzong, MSS Eur E226/79, APAC, BL.
6 MSS Eur E226/77(c), APAC, BL.
7 Lt D. Williams to George Bogle, 17 August 1774, Cooch Behar, BC, ML.
8 MSS Eur E226/9, f. 4r, APAC, BL.
9 MSS Eur E226/9, f. 3r, APAC, BL.
10 Michael Aris, *Views of Medieval Bhutan: The Diary and Drawings of Samuel Davis, 1783* (London: Serindia Publications, 1982) 120.
11 John A. Ardussi, 'Bhutan before the British: A Historical Study' (PhD thesis, Australian National University, 1977) 528.
12 George Bogle to Warren Hastings, 17 July 1774, Tashichodzong, BC, ML.
13 MSS Eur E226/9, f. 9v, APAC, BL.
14 MSS Eur E226/77(c), APAC, BL.
15 Robert Crawford, *Devolving English Literature* (Oxford: Oxford University Press, 1992) 17.
16 MSS Eur E226/14, APAC, BL.
17 Add. MS 45421, f. 31r, BL.
18 MSS Eur E226/77(c), APAC, BL.
19 Peter France, 'Primitivism and Enlightenment: Rousseau and the Scots', *Yearbook of English Studies* 15 (1985) 64.
20 Peter France, 'Western European Civilisation and its Mountain Frontiers (1750–1850)', *History of European Ideas* 6: 3 (1985) 308.
21 MSS Eur E226/77(c), APAC, BL; George Bogle to Warren Hastings, 9 June 1775, Beyhar, BC, ML.
22 George Bogle (senior) to George Bogle, 11 December 1770, Daldowie, BC, ML.
23 Keith Stewart, 'Towards Defining an Aesthetic for the Familiar Letter in Eighteenth-Century England', *Prose Studies* 5 (1982) 186–7.
24 MSS Eur E226/78, APAC, BL.
25 MSS Eur E226/13, APAC, BL.
26 MSS Eur E226/77(e), APAC, BL.
27 C. Wessels, *Early Jesuit Travellers in Central Asia 1603–1721* (1924; New Delhi: Asian Educational Series, 1992) 139. For texts see Hugues Didier, *Les Portugais au Tibet: les premières relations jésuites, 1624–1635* (Paris: Editions Chandeigne, 1996).
28 Ardussi, 216.
29 Warren Hastings to George Bogle, 10 August 1774, Fort William, Add. MS 29117, f. 62r, BL.

30 Warren Hastings to George Bogle, 10 August 1774, Fort William, Add. MS 29117, f. 62v, BL.
31 Warren Hastings to George Bogle, 10 August 1774, Fort William, Add. MS 29117, f. 61r, BL.

Chapter 7: Bloody Work

1 Luciano Petech, *Selected Papers on Asian History* (Rome: Istituto Italiano per il Medio ed Estremo Oriente, 1988) 52.
2 George Bogle to Warren Hastings, 27 April 1775, Paro, MSS Eur E226/23, APAC, BL.
3 Samuel Turner, *An Account of an Embassy to the Court of the Teshoo Lama in Tibet* (London: G. & W. Nicol, 1800) 117–18.
4 George Bogle to Robert Bogle, 8 January 1775, Tashilhunpo, MSS Eur E226/80, APAC, BL.
5 George Bogle to Robert Bogle, 8 January 1775, Tashilhunpo, MSS Eur E226/80, APAC, BL.
6 George Bogle to Elizabeth Bogle, 30 December 1774, Tashilhunpo, MSS Eur E226/80, APAC, BL.
7 MSS Eur E226/14, APAC, BL.
8 MSS Eur E226/14, APAC, BL.
9 MSS Eur E226/16, APAC, BL.
10 MSS Eur E226/16, APAC, BL.
11 MSS Eur E226/16, APAC, BL.
12 MSS Eur E226/16, APAC, BL.
13 MSS Eur E226/80, APAC, BL.
14 MSS Eur E226/16, APAC, BL.
15 MSS Eur E226/16, APAC, BL.
16 MSS Eur E226/16, APAC, BL.
17 MSS Eur E226/16, APAC, BL.

Chapter 8: God's Vicegerent

1 George Bogle to the family at Daldowie, 30 November 1774, Dechenrubje, MSS Eur E226/80, APAC, BL.
2 George Bogle to Mrs Morehead, 27 November 1774, Dechenrubje, MSS Eur E226/80, APAC, BL.
3 MSS Eur E226/18, APAC, BL.
4 Thomas Astley, *A New General Collection of Voyages and Travels* (London: Thomas Astley, 1747) 4: 449.
5 Mary Bogle to George Bogle, 4 November 1775, Daldowie, BC, ML.
6 George Bogle to Mr Bayne, Tashichodzong, MSS Eur E226/79, APAC, BL.
7 Add. MS 19283, f. 22r, BL.
8 Add. MS 19283, f. 21r, BL.
9 Add. MS 19283, f. 22r, BL.
10 Add. MS 19283, f. 22v, BL.
11 Add. MS 19283, f. 23r, BL.
12 Add. MS 19283, f. 23v, BL.

13 Add. MS 19283, ff. 23v–24r, BL.
14 Add. MS 19283, f. 26v, BL.
15 Toni Huber, *The Holy Land Reborn: Pilgrimage and the Reinvention of Buddhist India in the Tibetan Tradition* (Chicago: University of Chicago Press, forthcoming).
16 Add. MS 19283, f. 27r, BL.
17 Add. MS 19283, f. 27v, BL.
18 Add. MS 19283, f. 28r, BL.
19 Add. MS 19283, f. 28v, BL.
20 Add. MS 19283, f. 28v, BL.
21 Add. MS 19283, f. 29v, BL.
22 Add. MS 19283, f. 43v, BL.
23 Add. MS 19283, f. 33r, BL.
24 MSS Eur E226/18, APAC, BL.
25 George Bogle to the family at Daldowie, 27 November 1774, Dechenrubje, MSS Eur E226/77, APAC, BL.
26 George Bogle to Mrs Brown, 30 November 1774, Dechenrubje, MSS Eur E226/80, APAC, BL.
27 MSS Eur E226/19, APAC, BL.
28 MSS Eur E226/19, APAC, BL.
29 Add. MS 19283, f. 31v, BL.
30 George Bogle to Mrs Brown, 8 March 1775, Tashilhunpo, MSS Eur E226/77(k) APAC, BL. Sir Samuel Fludyer (1705–68) was lord mayor of London in 1761. He was an extremely rich cloth merchant who also dealt in government finance.
31 George Bogle to Mrs Brown, 8 March 1775, Tashilhunpo, MSS Eur E226/77(k), APAC, BL.
32 George Bogle to Mrs Brown, 8 March 1775, Tashilhunpo, MSS Eur E226/77(k), APAC, BL.
33 George Bogle to Mrs Brown, 8 March 1775, Tashilhunpo, MSS Eur E226/77(k), APAC, BL.
34 Add. MS 29233, f. 388v, BL.
35 Add. MS 19283, ff. 33r, 35v, BL.
36 Add. MS 19283, ff. 35v–36r, BL.
37 J. Hanbury-Tracy, *Black River of Tibet* (London: Frederick Muller, 1938) 58, quoted by Wim van Spengen, 'The Geo-History of Long-Distance Trade in Tibet 1850–1950', *Tibet Journal* 20: 2 (1995) 45.
38 Add. MS 19283, f. 38r, BL.

Chapter 9: To Tashilhunpo

1 George Bogle to Mrs Brown, 8 January 1775, Tashilhunpo, MSS Eur E226/80, APAC, BL.
2 MSS Eur E226/18, APAC, BL.
3 MSS Eur E226/18, APAC, BL.
4 Toni Huber tentatively identifies the Panchen Lama's mother as Nyida Wangmo, probably a princess from Mustang in northern Nepal, whose first marriage was to the Ladakhi king, Dekyong Namgyel. Later marriages resulted in several sons, one of whom was recognised as the Third Panchen Lama. See Toni Huber, *The Holy Land Reborn: Pilgrimage and the Reinvention of Buddhist India in the Tibetan Tradition* (Chicago: University of Chicago Press, forthcoming).

5 'The Latter Part of the Biography called "Rays of the Sun", of the foremost Lama, the Crown Ornament of Samsara and Nirvana, the Omniscient Panchen, the Glorious and Good Losang Belden Yeshe' by Dkon-mchog-'jigs-med-dban-po II (1728–91). I have not been able to consult this text in the original. Portions of the work have been translated by Sarat Chandra Das, 'Contributions on the Religion, History &c of Tibet', *Journal of the Asiatic Society of Bengal*, 51: 1 (1882) 28–43; Margaret M. Shu-yi Loo, 'The Biography of the III Panchen Lama, Blo-bzang-dpal-Ldan-ye-shes-dpal-bzang-po, Examined in the Light of Sino-Tibetan Relations during the Late Eighteenth-Century' (PhD thesis, University of Washington, 1970); and Ya Hanzhang, *Biographies of the Tibetan Spiritual Leaders Panchen Erdenis*, trans. Chen Guansheng and Li Peizhu (Beijing: Foreign Languages Press, 1994).

6 Das, 'Contributions on the Religion, History &c of Tibet' 30.

7 James L. Hevia, 'Lamas, Emperors, and Rituals: Political Implications in Qing Imperial Ceremonies', *Journal of the International Association of Buddhist Studies* 16: 2 (1993) 255.

8 Xiangyun Wang, 'Tibetan Buddhism at the Court of Qing: The Life and Work of lCang-skya Rol-pa'i-rdo-rje (1717–86)' (PhD thesis, Harvard University, 1995) 294.

9 Xiangyun Wang, 'The Qing Court's Tibet Connection: Lcang skya Rol pa'i rdo rje and the Qianlong Emperor', *Harvard Journal of Asiatic Studies* 60: 1 (June 2000) 136.

10 MSS Eur E226/18, APAC, BL.

11 George Bogle to Mrs Brown, 8 January 1775, Tashilhunpo, MSS Eur E226/80, APAC, BL.

12 George Bogle to Mary Bogle, 8 March 1775, Tashilhunpo, MSS Eur E226/77(j), APAC, BL.

13 Add. MS 19283, f. 48r, BL.

14 MSS Eur E226/18, APAC, BL.

15 MSS Eur E226/18, APAC, BL.

Chapter 10: Thibet Vocabulary

1 MSS Eur E226/18, APAC, BL.

2 MSS Eur E226/18, APAC, BL.

3 MSS Eur E226/18, APAC, BL.

4 MSS Eur E226/18, APAC, BL.

5 MSS Eur E226/18, APAC, BL.

6 MSS Eur E226/18, APAC, BL.

7 George Bogle to Mary Bogle, 3 January 1775, Tashilhunpo, MSS Eur E226/80, APAC, BL.

8 MSS Eur E226/16, APAC, BL.

9 MSS Eur E226/16, APAC, BL.

10 MSS Eur E226/80, APAC, BL.

11 MSS Eur E226/80, APAC, BL.

12 MSS Eur E226/80, APAC, BL.

13 MSS Eur E226/80, APAC, BL.

14 MSS Eur E226/80, APAC, BL.

15 MSS Eur E226/80, APAC, BL.

16 William Robertson, 'A View of the Progress of Society in Europe from the Subversion of the Roman Empire to the Beginning of the Sixteenth Century', in *The History of the Reign of Emperor Charles V* (London: George Routledge & Co., 1857) 1: 71.

17 MSS Eur E226/68, APAC, BL.

18 George Bogle to Anne Bogle, 29 December 1774, Dechenrubje, Tashilhunpo, MSS Eur E226/80, APAC, BL.

19 George Bogle to Anne Bogle, 29 December 1774, Dechenrubje, Tashilhunpo, MSS Eur E226/80, APAC, BL.

20 MSS Eur E226/80, APAC, BL.

21 MSS Eur E226/18, APAC, BL.

22 Add. MS 19283, f. 53v, BL.

23 Add. MS 19283, f. 56r, BL.

24 Add. MS 19283, f. 57v, BL.

25 Add. MS 19283, ff. 57v–58r, BL.

26 Add. MS 19283, f. 59r, BL.

27 Add. MS 19283, f. 59v, BL.

Chapter 11: The Business of a Traveller

1 Abraham de Wicquefort's *L'Ambassadeur et ses fonctions* (1681) was translated into English as *The Embassador and his Functions* in 1716. See G. R. Berridge, Maurice Keens-Soper and T. G. Otte, *Diplomatic Theory from Machiavelli to Kissinger* (Basingstoke: Palgrave, 2001) 99.

2 Berridge et al., 99.

3 Add. MS 19283, ff. 59v–60r, BL.

4 Add. MS 19283, f. 60r, BL.

5 See Berridge et al., 114–16.

6 Add. MS 19283, f. 115v, BL.

7 Add. MS 19283, f. 115v, BL.

8 Add. MS 19283, f. 117v, BL.

9 Add. MS 19823, ff. 117v–118r, BL.

10 Add. MS 19283, f. 119r, BL.

11 Add. MS 19283, f. 118r, BL.

12 Add. MS 19283, f. 119r, BL.

13 Add. MS 19283, f. 119v, BL.

14 Add. MS 19283, f. 65v, BL.

15 Add. MS 19283, f. 65v, BL.

16 Add. MS 19283, ff. 66r–v, BL.

17 MSS Eur E226/18, APAC, BL.

18 MSS Eur E226/18, APAC, BL.

19 MSS Eur E226/65, APAC, BL.

20 MSS Eur E226/65, APAC, BL.

21 MSS Eur E226/65, APAC, BL.

22 MSS Eur E226/65, APAC, BL.

23 MSS Eur E226/65, APAC, BL.

24 MSS Eur E226/65, APAC, BL.

25 MSS Eur E226/65, APAC, BL.

26 MSS Eur E226/18, APAC, BL.

27 Add. MS 19283, f. 76r, BL.

28 Albert Grünwedel, *Der Weg nach Śambhala des dritten Gross-Lama von bKra śis lhun po bLo bzan dPal ldan Yeśes* (Munich: Abhandlungen der Königlich Bayerischen Akademie der Wissenschaften, 1915) 44–5.

29 Add. MS 19283, f. 108v, BL.

30 In Bogle's translation the other precepts are: 2. Thou shalt not take anything that is thy neighbours, unless he gives it to thee. 3. Thou shalt not commit adultery. 4. Thou shalt not lye. 5. Thou shalt not slander thy neighbour. 6. Thou shalt not threaten or use angry words towards thy Neighbour. 7. Thou shalt not speak vain & needless words. 8. Thou shalt not covet anything that is thy neighbours. 9. Thou shalt not wish harm to thy neighbour or harbour Evil against him. 10. Thou shalt not be guilty of Disbelief. 'On Religion, Justice and Government', BC, ML.

31 MSS Eur E226/65, APAC, BL.

32 MSS Eur E226/65, APAC, BL.

33 MSS Eur E226/65, APAC, BL.

Chapter 12: Living Like a Thibetian

1 George Bogle to Mary Bogle, 8 March 1775, Tashilhunpo, MS Eur E226/77(j), APAC, BL.

2 MSS Eur E226/18, APAC, BL.

3 MSS Eur E226/18, APAC, BL.

4 MSS Eur E226/18, APAC, BL.

5 MSS Eur E226/18, APAC, BL.

6 MSS Eur E226/18, APAC, BL.

7 MSS Eur E226/18, APAC, BL.

8 MSS Eur E226/18, APAC, BL.

9 MSS Eur E226/80, APAC, BL.

10 MSS Eur E226/80, APAC, BL.

11 MSS Eur E226/18, APAC, BL.

12 MSS Eur E226/18, APAC, BL.

13 MSS Eur E226/18, APAC, BL.

14 MSS Eur E226/78, APAC, BL.

15 MSS Eur E226/80, APAC, BL.

16 MSS Eur E226/18, APAC, BL.

17 MSS Eur E226/18, APAC, BL.

18 MSS Eur E226/80, APAC, BL.

19 MSS Eur E226/18, APAC, BL.

20 MSS Eur E226/18, APAC, BL.

21 MSS Eur E226/18, APAC, BL.

22 MSS Eur E226/18, APAC, BL.

23 George Bogle to Mary Bogle, 8 March 1775, Tashilhunpo, MSS Eur E226/77(j), APAC, BL.

24 MSS Eur E226/18, APAC, BL.

25 George Bogle to Mary Bogle, 8 March 1775, Tashilhunpo, MSS Eur E226/77(j), APAC, BL.

26 MSS Eur E226/18, APAC, BL.

27 George Bogle to Mary Bogle, 8 March 1775, Tashilhunpo, MSS Eur E226/77(j), APAC, BL.

28 MSS Eur E226/18, APAC, BL.

29 MSS Eur E226/18, APAC, BL.
30 George Bogle to Mary Bogle, 8 March 1775, Tashilhunpo, MSS Eur E226/77(j), APAC, BL.
31 MSS Eur E226/18, APAC, BL.
32 MSS Eur E226/18, APAC, BL.
33 George Bogle to Mary Bogle, 8 March 1775, Tashilhunpo, MSS Eur E226/77(j), APAC, BL.
34 Notebook f. 2, BC, ML.
35 Notebook f. 6, BC, ML.
36 Alexander Hamilton to George Bogle, 17 May 1775, Behar, MSS Eur E226/86(b), APAC, BL.
37 H. E. Richardson, 'George Bogle and his Children', *Scottish Genealogist* 29: 3 (September 1982), 76, 80.

Chapter 13: A Last Farewell

 1 Add. MS 19283, f. 109v, BL.
 2 Toni Huber, *The Holy Land Reborn: Pilgrimage and the Reinvention of Buddhist India in the Tibetan Tradition* (Chicago: University of Chicago Press, forthcoming).
 3 MSS Eur E226/85(a), The Panchen Lama to Warren Hastings, received 22 July 1775, APAC, BL.
 4 Add. MS 19283, f. 104v, BL.
 5 Add. MS 19283, f. 51r, BL.
 6 MSS Eur E226/23, APAC, BL.
 7 MSS Eur E226/18, APAC, BL.
 8 'A Necessary Caution', MSS Eur E226/70, APAC, BL.
 9 Add. MS 45421, f. 33r, BL.
10 Add. MS 45421, f. 33r, BL.
11 MSS Eur E226/80, APAC, BL.
12 George Bogle to Elizabeth Bogle, 5 March 1775, MSS Eur E226/25, APAC, BL.
13 George Bogle to Elizabeth Bogle, 5 March 1775, MSS Eur E226/25, APAC, BL.
14 MSS Eur E226/18, APAC, BL.
15 MSS Eur E226/18, APAC, BL.
16 MSS Eur E226/18, APAC, BL.
17 George Bogle to Elizabeth Bogle, 5 March 1775, MSS Eur E226/25, APAC, BL.
18 George Bogle to Warren Hastings, 27 April 1775, Rinjipoo [Paro], MSS Eur E226/23, APAC, BL.
19 George Bogle to Warren Hastings, 27 April 1775, Rinjipoo [Paro], MSS Eur E226/23, APAC, BL.
20 'On Religion, Justice and Government', BC, ML.
21 Add. MS 19283, f. 114r, BL.
22 Add. MS 19283, f. 114r, BL.

Chapter 14: Melancholy Hall

 1 J. P. Losty, *Calcutta: City of Palaces* (London: British Library, 1990) 44.
 2 Alexander Hamilton to George Bogle, 26 December 1775, Kirantee, MSS Eur E226/86(f), APAC, BL.

3 George Bogle to David Anderson, 26 October 1775, Calcutta, Add. MS 45421, f. 45r, BL.

4 Add. MS 19283, f. 165v, BL.

5 George Bogle to Warren Hastings, 9 June 1775, Cooch Behar, BC, ML.

6 Home Misc/219: f. 373, APAC, BL.

7 Warren Hastings to George Bogle, 24 May 1775, Fort William, Add. MS 29117, ff. 68r–v, BL.

8 Quoted in T.H. Bowyer, 'Philip Francis and the Government of Bengal: Parliament and Personality in the Frustration of an Ambition', *Parliamentary History* 18: 1 (1999) 3–4.

9 Lucy Sutherland, 'New Evidence on the Nandakuma Trial', *English Historical Review* 72 (1957) 465.

10 George Bogle to George Bogle (senior), 5 August 1775, Calcutta, BC, ML.

11 George Bogle to Robert Bogle, 4 August 1775, Calcutta, BC, ML.

12 George Bogle to Robert Bogle, 4 August 1775, Calcutta, BC, ML,

13 George Bogle to Robert Bogle, 4 August 1775, Calcutta, BC, ML.

14 George Bogle to George Bogle (senior), 5 August 1775, Calcutta, BC, ML.

15 George Bogle to David Anderson, 26 October 1775, Calcutta, Add. MS 45421, f. 45r, BL.

16 George Bogle to David Anderson, 28 August 1775, Calcutta, Add. MS 45421, f. 44r, BL. Point Palmiras was in the Bay of Bengal.

17 George Bogle (senior) to George Bogle, 4 November 1775, Daldowie, BC, ML.

18 George Bogle (senior) to George Bogle, 19 February 1776, Daldowie, BC, ML.

19 Bruce Redford, ed., *The Letters of Samuel Johnson*, 5 vols (Oxford: Clarendon Press, 1992) 2: 136.

20 G. R. Gleig, *Memoirs of the Life of the Right Hon. Warren Hastings*, 3 vols (London: Richard Bengley, 1841) 2: 19.

21 George Bogle to Robert Bogle, 15 February 1777, Calcutta, BC, ML.

22 Alexander Hamilton to George Bogle, 26 December 1775, Kirantee, MSS Eur E226/86(f), APAC, BL.

23 George Bogle to Mrs Brown, 30 March 1776, Calcutta, BC, ML.

24 George Bogle to Mrs Brown, 30 March 1776, Calcutta, BC, ML.

25 'An Account of the Kingdom of Thibet', *Philosophical Transactions* LXVII, Part II: 468–9.

26 'An Account of the Kingdom of Thibet', *Philosophical Transactions* LXVII, Part II: 479.

27 'An Account of the Kingdom of Thibet', *Philosophical Transactions* LXVII, Part II: 487.

28 Michael Aris, *Views of Medieval Bhutan: The Diary and Drawings of Samuel Davis, 1783* (London: Serindia Publications, 1982) 20.

29 Mildred Archer, *British Portrait Painters in India 1770–1835* (London: Sotheby Parke Bernet Publications, 1979) 440.

30 George Bogle to Robert Bogle, 15 February 1777, Calcutta, BC, ML.

Chapter 15: Tibet Garden

1 *Calendar of Persian Correspondence* (Calcutta: Government of India, 1930) 5: No. 253.

2 Alastair Lamb, *Bhutan and Tibet: The Travels of George Bogle and Alexander Hamilton 1774–1777* (Hertingfordbury: Roxford Books, 2002) 383.

3 Much of the detail about Bhot Bagan is derived from Gaur Dás Bysack, 'Notes on a Buddhist Monastery at Bhot Bágán', *Journal of the Asiatic Society of Bengal* 59: 1 (1890) 50–99.

4 C.A. Bayly, *Indian Society and the Making of the British Empire* (Cambridge: Cambridge University Press, 1988) 41.

5 George Bogle to Warren Hastings, 9 May 1775, Tashichodzong, MSS Eur E226/77, APAC, BL.

6 Wade H. Dazey, 'Tradition and Modernization in the Organisation of the Dasanani Samnyasins', in Austin B. Creel and Vasudha Narayanan, eds, *Monastic Life in the Christian and Hindu Traditions: A Comparative Study* (Lewiston, NY: Edwin Mellen Press, 1990) 308–11.

7 Teshoo Lama to Warren Hastings, received 29 July 1775, MSS Eur E226/85, APAC, BL.

8 Bernard S. Cohn, 'The Role of Gosains in the Economy of Eighteenth and Nineteenth Century Upper India', *Indian Economic and Social History Review* 1: 4 (1963–4) 178.

9 *Calendar of Persian Correspondence* 5: No. 253.

10 *Calendar of Persian Correspondence* 5: No. 436.

11 George Bogle to David Anderson, 4 May 1780, Rangpur, Add. MS 45421, f. 108r, BL.

12 Schuyler Cammann, *Trade through the Himalayas: The Early British Attempts to Open Tibet* (Princeton: Princeton University Press, 1951) 141.

13 For the accounts of Bogle's presents, see MSS Eur E226/60, APAC, BL. The fact that Bogle sent presents to the Panchen Lama's nieces in June 1776 suggests that Hugh Richardson is incorrect in his conjecture that one of the nieces might have become involved with Bogle and accompanied him to Calcutta; see Hugh Richardson, 'George Bogle and his Children', *Scottish Genealogist* 29: 3 (September 1982) 77.

14 MSS Eur E226/85(c), APAC, BL.

15 Toni Huber, *The Holy Land Reborn: Pilgrimage and the Reinvention of Buddhist India in the Tibetan Tradition* (Chicago: University of Chicago Press, forthcoming).

16 MSS Eur E226/60, APAC, BL.

17 Huber, forthcoming

18 George Bogle to Mary Bogle, 27 December 1770, Calcutta, BC, ML.

19 George Bogle to Mary Bogle, 27 December 1770, Calcutta, BC, ML.

20 On colonial drama as a performance of national identity, see Kathleen Wilson, *The Island Race: Englishness, Empire and Gender in the Eighteenth Century* (London: Routledge, 2003) 163.

21 George Bogle to Alexander Hamilton, no date, MSS Eur E226/77(s), APAC, BL.

22 Alexander Hamilton to George Bogle, 1 March 1776, Cantalbary, MSS Eur E226/86(l), APAC, BL.

23 Alexander Hamilton to George Bogle, 6 November 1775, Balatunghee, MSS Eur E226/86(d), APAC, BL.

24 Alexander Hamilton to George Bogle, 6 November 1775, Balatunghee, MSS Eur E226/86(d), APAC, BL.

25 Alexander Hamilton to George Bogle, 1 March 1776, Cantalbary, MSS Eur E226/86(l), APAC, BL.

26 Alexander Hamilton to George Bogle, 7 January 1776, Doonga, MSS Eur E226/86(h), APAC, BL.

27 Alexander Hamilton to George Bogle, 30 May 1776, Tashichodzong, MSS Eur E226/86(o), APAC, BL.

28 Alexander Hamilton to George Bogle, 22 July 1777, Buxaduar, MSS Eur E226/86(v), APAC, BL.

29 Alexander Hamilton to George Bogle, 22 July 1777, Buxaduar, MSS Eur E226/86(v), APAC, BL.

30 India Office Records P/154/58: 165, APAC, BL.

31 'Declaration of the Vakil of the Rajah of Bhutan under his seal, dated Calcutta Bengal style 1185', quoted in Lamb, *Bhutan and Tibet* 428.

Chapter 16: To Adventure for Possibilities

1 George Bogle to George Bogle (senior), 24 November 1777, Calcutta, BC, ML.

2 William Hickey, *Memoirs of William Hickey*, ed. Alfred Spencer, 4 vols (London: Hurst & Blacket, 1913–25) 2: 154.

3 George Bogle to George Bogle (senior), 24 November 1777, Calcutta, BC, ML.

4 George Bogle to George Bogle (senior), 24 November 1777, Calcutta, BC, ML.

5 Bengal General Consultations, 19 April 1779, H/Misc/219: ff. 383–4, APAC, BL.

6 Bengal General Consultations, 19 April 1779, H/Misc/219: f. 384, APAC, BL.

7 MSS Eur E226/85, APAC, BL.

8 MSS Eur E226/85, APAC, BL.

9 See Alastair Lamb, *The Mandarin Road to Old Hué: Narratives of Anglo-Vietnamese Diplomacy from the Seventeenth Century to the Eve of the French Conquest* (London: Chatto, 1970).

10 Bengal General Consultations, 19 April 1779, H/Misc/219: f. 386, APAC, BL.

11 Bengal General Consultations, 19 April 1779, H/Misc/219: f. 386, APAC, BL.

12 Bengal General Consultations, 19 April 1779, H/Misc/219: f. 446, APAC, BL.

13 Bengal General Consultations, 19 April 1779, H/Misc/219: f. 447, APAC, BL.

14 George Bogle (senior) to George Bogle, 19 January 1779, Daldowie, BC, ML.

15 George Bogle to David Anderson, 30 September 1778, Add. MS 45421, f. 78r, BL.

16 George Bogle to Robert Bogle, 18 January 1780, Rangpur, BC, ML.

17 George Bogle to George Bogle (senior), 20 April 1779, Calcutta, BC, ML.

18 George Bogle to George Bogle (senior), 20 April 1779, Calcutta, BC, ML.

19 George Bogle to Robert Bogle, 18 January 1780, Rangpur, BC, ML.

20 George Bogle to Robert Bogle, 18 January 1780, Rangpur, BC, ML.

Chapter 17: The Emperor's Invitation

1 Sven Hedin calculates the distance of the direct route between Tashilhunpo and Peking as 1,800 miles. To take in the major monasteries en route may have added some 600 miles. See Sven Hedin, *Jehol: City of Emperors* (London: Kegan Paul, 1932) 118.

2 The Qianlong Emperor's reign is usually dated 1736–99, although it technically ended in 1796 when he abdicated in favour of his son, the Jiaqing Emperor. But adopting the role of 'Super-Emperor', Qianlong instructed his son and effectively remained in control until his death in 1799.

3 Pamela Kyle Crossley, *The Manchus* (Oxford: Blackwell, 1997) 112.

4 The palace and gardens go under a variety of names: Chengde ('Virtue Bearer') is the name given to the summer palace by the Qianlong Emperor in 1778 and is still the current Chinese name. Rehe ('Warm River') is the earlier name used by the

Kangxi Emperor, and is found in eighteenth-century English texts. Jehol is used by French and German writers of the period. See Philippe Forêt, *Mapping Chengde: The Qing Landscape Enterprise* (Honolulu: University of Hawaii Press, 2000) 16, and James A. Millward, Ruth W. Dunnell, Mark C. Elliott and Philippe Forêt, eds, *The New Qing Imperial History: The Making of Inner Asian Empire at Qing Chengde* (London: RoutledgeCurzon, 2004) 1.

5   See Forêt, 13.

6   See Anne Chayet, 'Architectural Wonderland: An Empire of Fictions', in Millward et al., 40.

7   Alastair Lamb, *Bhutan and Tibet: The Travels of George Bogle and Alexander Hamilton 1774–1777* (Hertingfordbury: Roxford Books, 2002) 255.

8   See James A. Millward, 'Qing Inner Asian Empire and the Return of the Torghuts', in Millward et al., 91–4.

9   See Chia-feng Chang, 'Aspects of Smallpox in Chinese History' (PhD thesis, SOAS, University of London, 1996).

10 James Hevia, 'Lamas, Emperors and Rituals: Political Implications in Qing Imperial Ceremonies', *Journal of the International Association of Buddhist Studies* 16: 2 (1993) 246–7.

11 Xiangyun Wang, 'The Qing Court's Tibet Connection: Lcang skya Rol pa'i rdo rje and the Qianlong Emperor', *Harvard Journal of Asiatic Studies* 60: 1 (June 2000) 153.

12 Wang, 153.

13 MSS Eur E226/34, APAC, BL.

14 MSS Eur E226/83, APAC, BL.

15 MSS Eur E226/34, APAC, BL.

16 Claude Alexander to David Anderson, 13 April 1782, Calcutta, Add. MS 45424, BL.

17 MSS Eur E226/83, APAC, BL.

18 MSS Eur E226/34, APAC, BL.

19 MSS Eur E226/34, APAC, BL.

20 Richard Goodlad to George Bogle, 24 September 1779, Rangpur, BC, ML.

21 Note dated 21 November 1779, BC, ML.

22 Warren Hastings to George Bogle, 18 November 1779, quoted in Evan Cotton, 'A Letter from Warren Hastings to George Bogle', *Bengal Past & Present* 42 (1931) 86.

23 George Bogle to Robert Bogle, 18 January 1780, Rangpur, BC, ML.

24 George Bogle to Elizabeth Bogle, 20 January 1780, Rangpur, BC, ML.

25 George Bogle to Robert Bogle, 18 January 1780, Rangpur, BC, ML.

26 George Bogle to Robert Bogle, 18 January 1780, Rangpur, BC, ML.

27 George Bogle to Robert Bogle, 18 January 1780, Rangpur, BC, ML.

Chapter 18: The Meeting between the Two

1   'Appendix III: Translation of a Letter from Soopoon Choomboo, Mirkin Chassa Lama, Minister to the Late Teshoo Lama, to Warren Hastings. Received 12 February, 1782', in Samuel Turner, *An Account of an Embassy to the Court of the Teshoo Lama in Tibet* (London: G. & W. Nicol, 1800) 454–5.

2   'Appendix IV: Narrative of the Particulars of the Journey of Teshoo Lama and his Suite, from Tibet to China, from the verbal Report of Poorungheer Gosein', in Turner, 458–9.

3 Letter from the Panchen Lama to the Qianlong Emperor, November 26, 1779, translated in Margaret M. Shu-yi Loo, 'The Biography of the III Panchen Lama, Blo-bzang-dpal-Ldan-ye-shes-dpal-bzang-po, Examined in the Light of Sino-Tibetan Relations during the Late Eighteenth Century' (PhD thesis, University of Washington, 1970) 97–8.

4 Loo, 97.

5 Loo, 97.

6 On 30 September 1780, Bogle reported to Warren Hastings that he had received letters from the Panchen Lama, the Sopon Chumbo (the Panchen Lama's Cup Bearer), the Drungpa Trulku (the Panchen Lama's half-brother and Treasurer) and Purangir. The Panchen Lama's letter was sent from Sining. See Warren Hastings Papers, Add. MS 29146, ff. 75–6, BL.

7 Loo, 111.

8 Loo, 112–16.

9 Loo, 115–16.

10 Philippe Forêt, *Mapping Chengde: The Qing Landscape Enterprise* (Honolulu: University of Hawaii Press, 2000) 82.

11 The Sixth Prince was the sixth son of Qianlong, Zhizhuang qinwang Yongrong (1743–89). He was placed in charge of the Imperial Household Department 1772–85. See Xiangyun Wang 'The Qing Court's Tibet Connection: Lcang skya Rol p'i rdo rje and the Qianlong Emperor', *Harvard Journal of Asiatic Studies* 60: 1 (2000) 157.

12 See Forêt, 121–2 for an extended comparison between Chengde and Versailles.

13 Anne Chayet, 'Architectural Wonderland: An Empire of Fictions', in James A. Millward, Ruth W. Dunnell, Mark C. Elliott and Philippe Forêt, eds, *The New Qing Imperial History: The Making of Inner Asian Empire at Qing Chengde* (London: RoutledgeCurzon, 2004) 41–5.

14 Peter Zarrow trans., 'Qianlong's Inscription on the Founding of the Temple of the Happiness and Longevity of Mt Sumeru (Xumifoushou miao)', in Millward et al., *New Qing Imperial History*, 185. See also Peter Zarrow, 'The Imperial Word in Stord: Stele Inscriptions at Chengde', in Millward et al., *New Qing Imperial History*, 156–7.

15 Zarrow, 'Qianlong's Inscription' 186.

16 Loo, 120.

17 Translation from Dkon-mchog-'jigs-med-dban-po II, in Nima Dorjee Ragnubs, 'The Third Panchen Lama's Visit to Chengde', in Millward et al., 189.

18 Ragnubs, 'The Third Panchen Lama's Visit' 189–190.

19 Ragnubs, 'The Third Panchen Lama's Visit' 190.

20 Ragnubs, 'The Third Panchen Lama's Visit' 190.

21 Angela Zito, unpublished paper. 'Hosting and Hierarchy: The Panchen Lama Comes to Dinner', 12.

22 Renqiu Yu, 'Imperial Banquets in the Wanshu Yuan' in Millward et al., 89.

23 Appendix IV, Turner, 462.

24 My account of the divergent versions of the meeting relies heavily on Zito and James Hevia, 'Lamas, Emperors and Rituals: Political Implications in Qing Imperial Ceremonies', *Journal of the International Association of Buddhist Studies* 16: 2 (1993) 246–7.

25 Loo, 123.

26 Renqiu Yu, 'Imperial Banquets in the Wanshu Yuan' in Millward et al., 88.

Chapter 19: The Pure Light of the Void

1 Translation from Dkon-mchog-'jigs-med-dban-po II, in Nima Dorjee Ragnubs, 'The Third Panchen Lama's Visit to Chengde', in James A. Millward, Ruth W. Dunnell, Mark C. Elliott and Philippe Forêt, eds, *The New Qing Imperial History: The Making of Inner Asian Empire at Qing Chengde* (London: RoutledgeCurzon, 2004) 193.

2 'Report delivered to the Hon. Warren Hastings . . . upon the result of my mission to the court of Teshoo Loomboo', in Samuel Turner, *An Account of an Embassy to the Court of the Teshoo Lama in Tibet* (London: G. & W. Nicol, 1800) 362.

3 Appendix IV, 'Narrative of the Particulars of the Journey of Teshoo Lama and his Suite, from Tibet to China, from the verbal report of Poorungheer Gosein' in Turner, 463.

4 Schuyler Cammann, *Trade through the Himalayas: The Early British Attempts to Open Tibet* (Princeton: Princeton University Press, 1951) 71–4

5 George Bogle to Warren Hastings, 30 September 1780, Rangpur, Warren Hastings Papers, Add. MS 29146, ff. 75–6, BL.

6 Appendix I, 'Translation of a Letter from Kienlong, Emperor of China to Dalai Lama', in Turner, 445.

7 Turner, 291.

8 Turner, 291.

9 Appendix IV in Turner, 466.

10 Appendix IV in Turner, 468–9.

11 Turner, 331.

12 Appendix IV in Turner, 469.

13 Ragnubs, 'The Third Panchen Lama's Visit' 197.

14 Ragnubs, 'The Third Panchen Lama's Visit' 197.

15 Appendix IV in Turner, 469.

16 Chia-feng Chang, 'Aspects of Smallpox in Chinese History' (PhD thesis, SOAS, University of London, 1996) 18.

17 Appendix IV in Turner, 470.

18 Chuimei Ho and Bennet Bronson, eds, *Splendors of China's Forbidden City: The Glorious Reign of Emperor Qianlong* (London: Merrell; Chicago: Field Museum, 2004) 133.

19 Translation from Dkon-mchog-'jigs-med-dban-po II, in Margaret M. Shu-yi Loo, 'The Biography of the III Panchen Lama, Blo-bzang-dpal-Ldan-ye-shes-dpal-bzang-po, Examined in the Light of Sino-Tibetan Relations during the Late Eighteenth Century' (PhD thesis, University of Washington, 1970) 140.

20 Appendix IV in Turner, 470.

21 Loo, 142.

22 Loo, 142.

Chapter 20: The Tank

1 George Bogle to George Bogle (senior), 10 April 1780, Rangpur, BC, ML.

2 George Bogle to David Anderson, 4 May 1780, Rangpur, Add. MS 45421, f. 108r, BL. A *lack* is one hundred thousand.

3 George Bogle to David Anderson, 17 May 1780, Rangpur, Add. MS 45421, f. 110r, BL.

4 George Bogle to David Anderson, 4 May 1780, Rangpur, Add. MS 45421, ff. 108v–109r, BL.

5 George Bogle to David Anderson, 4 May 1780, Rangpur, Add. MS 45421, f. 108v, BL.

6 George Bogle to George Bogle (senior), 10 April 1780, Rangpur, BC, ML.

7 George Bogle to David Anderson, 4 May 1780, Rangpur, Add. MS 45421, f. 107v, BL.

8 George Bogle to David Anderson, April 1780, Rangpur, Add. MS 45421, ff. 104v–105r, BL.

9 George Bogle to Warren Hastings, 2 March 1780, Rangpur, Hastings Papers, Add. MS 29144, f. 400, BL.

10 George Bogle to John Bogle, 1 March 1780, Rangpur, BC, ML.

11 Mary Bogle to George Bogle, 19 January 1779, Daldowie, BC, ML.

12 George Bogle (senior) to George Bogle, 13 January 1780, BC, ML.

13 George Bogle to Robert Bogle, 4 August 1780, Rangpur, BC, ML.

14 William Scott to George Bogle, 5 April 1780, Glasgow, BC, ML.

15 Clements R. Markham, *Narratives of the Mission of George Bogle to Tibet, and of the Journey of Thomas Manning to Lhasa* (London: Trübner & Co., 1876) cxlix–cl.

16 T. H. Bowyer, 'India and the Personal Finances of Philip Francis', *English Historical Review* 110: 435 (February 1995) 128.

17 T. H. Bowyer, 'Philip Francis and the Government of Bengal: Parliament and Personality in the Frustration of an Ambition', *Parliamentary History* 18: 1 (1999) 1–21.

18 Sophia Weitzman, *Warren Hastings and Philip Francis* (Manchester: Manchester University Press, 1929) 351.

19 Francis's journal entry for 16 August 1780, cited in Eliza Fay, *Original Letters from India (1779–1815)*, ed. E. M. Forster (London: Chatto & Windus, 1986) 280, n. 30.

20 Keith Feiling, *Warren Hastings* (London: Macmillan, 1954) 228.

21 George Bogle to Robert Bogle, 1 March 1780, Rangpur, BC, ML.

22 Robert Bogle to Anne Bogle, 11 June 1776, Grenada, BC, ML.

23 Maria Stewart to George Bogle, 27 August 1780, London, BC, ML.

24 Durba Ghosh, 'Colonial Companions, *Bibis*, *Begums*, and Concubines of the British in North India, 1760–1830' (PhD thesis, University of California, Berkeley, 2000) 122–3.

25 See H.E. Richardson, 'George Bogle and his Children', *Scottish Genealogist* 29: 3 (September 1982) 73–83. Richardson observes that there were two Mary Bogles – the one sent to London, and one baptised in 1784 – but does not remark that there were also two sons named George Bogle: he mentions the George Bogle who was baptised in 1784, but does not note that the son who died on 30 April 1782 was also named George Bogle. See Claud Alexander to David Anderson, 3 May 1782, Add. MS 45424, f. 77v, BL.

26 George Bogle to David Anderson, 4 May 1780, Rangpur, Add. MS 45421, f. 106r, BL.

27 *India Gazette or Calcutta Public Advertiser*, no. 21, Saturday 7 April 1781.

28 Extract of Bengal General Consultations, 9 January 1783, H/Misc/219, f. 455, APAC, BL.

29 Thomas Law to David Anderson, 15 April 1781, Patna, Add. MS 45434, f. 211r, BL.

Chapter 21: The Golden Urn

1 Samuel Turner, *An Account of an Embassy to the Court of the Teshoo Lama in Tibet* (London: G. & W. Nicol, 1800) 334.

2 Turner, 334–5.

3 Turner, 334.

4 Turner, 335.

5 Turner, 335.

6 Turner, 336.

7 Luciano Petech, 'The Missions of Bogle and Turner according to the Tibetan Texts', *Selected Papers on Asian History* (Rome: Istituto Italiano per il Medio ed Estremo Oriente, 1988) 61.

8 Turner, 337.

9 Turner, 337.

10 Turner, 337.

11 Alastair Lamb, *British India and Tibet 1766–1910* (London: Routledge & Kegan Paul, 1986) 15.

12 Turner, 432.

13 S. C. Sarkar, 'A Note on Puran Gir Gosain', *Bengal Past & Present* 43 (1932) 87.

14 Sarkar, 87.

15 J. L. Cranmer-Byng, *An Embassy to China: Being the Journal kept by Lord Macartney during his embassy to the Emperor Ch'ien-lung 1793–1794* (London: Longman, 1962) 126.

16 'The First Edict, September 1793', in Pei-kai Cheng, Michael Lestz and Jonathan D. Spence, eds, *The Search for Modern China: A Documentary Collection* (New York: W. W. Norton, 1999) 105.

17 'The Second Edict, September 1793', in Cheng et al., 106.

18 'The Second Edict, September 1793', in Cheng et al., 106.

19 'The Second Edict, September 1793', in Cheng et al., 109.

20 See James L. Hevia, *Cherishing Men from Afar: Qing Guest Ritual and the Macartney Embassy of 1793* (Durham: Duke University Press, 1995) for a detailed discussion of these ideas.

21 Sir George Staunton, *An Historical Account of the Embassy to the Emperor of China*, 3 vols (London: John Stockdale, 1797) 2: 215.

22 Schuyler Cammann, *Trade through the Himalayas: The Early British Attempts to Open Tibet* (Princeton: Princeton University Press, 1951) 75–7.

23 'Jewellry left by Mr Bogle with Mr Alexander', BC, ML.

24 H. E. Richardson, 'George Bogle and his Children', *Scottish Genealogist* 29: 3 (September 1982) 77–8.

25 Claud Alexander to David Anderson, 3 May 1782, Add. MS 45424, ff. 77v–78r, BL

26 Claud Alexander to David Anderson, 3 May 1782, Add. MS 45424, f. 78r, BL.

27 Richardson, 79.

28 Richardson, 75.

29 Reminiscence of Amelia Sturrock, Bogle's great-granddaughter, MS Or. Richardson 22 f. 20r, Bodleian Library.

30 Richardson, 76.

31 Robert Bogle to Alexander Dalrymple, 28 January 1792, Daldowie, Add. MS 19283, BL.

32 See Donald S. Lopez Jr, *The Prisoners of Shangri-La: Tibetan Buddhism and the West* (Chicago: University of Chicago Press, 1998) for a detailed discussion of these ideas.

Epilogue

1 Clements R. Markham, ed., *Narratives of the Mission of George Bogle to Tibet, and of the Journey of Thomas Manning to Lhasa* (London: Trübner & Co., 1876) cliv.

2 Markham's edition also contained the journal of Thomas Manning, an independent adventurer who had studied Chinese in France and Canton and managed to enter Tibet in 1810–11. He travelled in disguise and stayed some months at Lhasa, where he was received by the Dalai Lama.

3 Alastair Lamb, *Bhutan and Tibet: The Travels of George Bogle and Alexander Hamilton 1774–1777* (Hertingfordbury: Roxford Books, 2002) 15.

4 Markham, cxx.

5 Markham, xxii.

6 Markham, cxxiii.

7 Markham, cxxiii.

8 George Bogle to Elizabeth Bogle, 5 March 1775, MSS Eur E226/25, APAC, BL; discussed by Laurie Hovell McMillin, *English in Tibet, Tibet in English: Self-Presentation in Tibet and the Diaspora* (New York: Palgrave, 2001) 33.

9 See McMillin, 32–3. For the myth of Shangri-La, see Peter Bishop, *The Myth of Shangri-La: Tibet, Travel-Writing and the Western Creation of Sacred Landscape* (London: Athlone Press, 1989), Donald S. Lopez Jr, *Prisoners of Shangri-La: Tibetan Buddhism and the West* (Chicago: University of Chicago Press, 1998) 181–207, Orville Schell, *Virtual Tibet: Searching for Shangri-La from the Himalayas to Hollywood* (New York: Metropolitan Books, 2000).

10 In his novel Hilton drew on *Shambhala: In Search of a New Era* (1930) by the Russian painter-mystic Nicholas Roerich. See K. Bjoergan, 'Shangri-La and the West: The Myth of Tibet in Western Media and Culture in the Period of Modernity' (Master of Arts thesis, Victoria University, Wellington, 2001). I am grateful to Toni Huber for this reference.

11 Sarat Chandra Das, *Autobiography: Narratives of the Incidents of my Early Life* (Calcutta: R. K. Maitra, 1969) 17.

12 Derek Waller, *The Pundits: British Exploration of Tibet and Central Asia* (Lexington: University Press of Kentucky, 1988) 196, 204–5.

13 For a discussion of the significance of the execution of the Sengchen Lama, see Alex McKay, 'The Drowning of Lama Sengchen Kyabying: A Preliminary Enquiry from British Sources', in H. Blezer, ed., *Tibet Past and Present: Tibetan Studies I. The Proceedings of the 9th International Seminar for Tibetan Studies, Leiden 2000*, Leiden: Brill, 2002.

14 Luciano Petech, *Selected Papers on Asian History* (Rome: Istituto Italiano per il Medio ed Estremo Oriente, 1988) 49.

15 Sarat Chandra Das, 'Contributions on the Religion, History &c of Tibet', *Journal of the Asiatic Society of Bengal* 51: 1 (1882) 35.

16 For an account of Kipling's many sources for *Kim*, see Peter Hopkirk, *Quest for Kim: In Search of Kipling's Great Game* (Oxford: Oxford University Press, 2001).

17 McMillin, 79.

18 Younghusband to his wife, 27 July 1902, Khamba Jong, MSS Eur F197/173, APAC, BL, cited in unpublished paper, Gordon Stewart, 'Can Reincarnated Tibetan Lamas Remember History?'

19 Younghusband to Helen Younghusband, 30 July 1903, Khamba Jong, MSS Eur F197/173, APAC, BL, cited in Stewart.

20 Diary kept by Captain O'Connor during the Tibet Frontier Mission, 3 August 1903, Khamba Jong, cited in Stewart.

21 Lieutenant Arthur C. Hadow, Letter to father, Norfolk Regiment Museum, Norwich, cited in Charles Allen, *Duel in the Snows: The True Story of the Younghusband Mission to Lhasa* (London: John Murray, 2004) 119.

22 *The British Invasion of Tibet: Colonel Younghusband,* 1904 (London: Stationery Office, 1999) 233.

23 Francis Younghusband, *India and Tibet*, ed. Alastair Lamb (Hong Kong: Oxford University Press, 1985) viii.

24 Francis Younghusband, *India and Tibet* (London: John Murray, 1910) 9.

25 Younghusband (1910), 14–15.

26 Younghusband (1910), 21.

27 *Human Rights: Annual Report 2000* (London: Foreign and Commonwealth Office, 2000) 19.

28 'Frequently Asked Questions', *http://www.fmprc.gov.cn/ce/cegv/eng/premade/60544/TibetFAQ7*.HTM, accessed 20 June 2005.

29 See, for example, John MacGregor, *Tibet: A Chronicle of Exploration* (London: Routledge & Kegan Paul, 1970), George Woodcock, *Into Tibet: Early British Explorers* (London: Faber & Faber, 1971), Schuyler Cammann, *Trade through the Himalayas: The Early British Attempts to Open Tibet* (Princeton: Princeton University Press, 1951), Alastair Lamb, *British India and Tibet 1766–1910* (London: Routledge, 1986), Alastair Lamb, *Bhutan and Tibet: The Travels of George Bogle and Alexander Hamilton 1774–1777* (Hertingfordbury: Roxford Books, 2002).

30 George Bogle to Robin Bogle, 8 January 1775, Tashilhunpo, MSS Eur E226/80, APAC, BL.

BIBLIOGRAPHY

Manuscript Sources and Government Proceedings

The Asia, Pacific and Africa Collection at the British Library was previously known as the Oriental and India Office Collection.

Add. MSS 19283, British Library, London

Anderson Papers, Add. MSS, British Library, London

Bengal General Consultations, Asia, Pacific & Africa Collections, British Library, London

Bogle Collection, Mitchell Library, Glasgow

Bogle Papers, MSS Eur E226, Asia, Pacific & Africa Collections, British Library, London

Calendar of Persian Correspondence, 10 vols, Government of India, Calcutta, 1911–59

Fort William – India House Correspondence, 21 vols, National Archives of India, Delhi, 1949–85

Hastings Papers, Add. MSS, British Library, London

Home Miscellaneous Series, Asia, Pacific & Africa Collections, British Library, London

Richardson Papers, MS Or., Bodleian Library, Oxford

Unpublished Manuscripts and Dissertations

Ardussi, John A., 'Bhutan before the British: A Historical Study', PhD thesis, Australian National University, 1977

Bjoergan, K., 'Shangri-La and the West: The Myth of Tibet in Western Media and Culture in the Period of Modernity', Master of Arts thesis, Victoria University, Wellington, 2001

Chang, Chia-feng, 'Aspects of Smallpox in Chinese History', PhD thesis, SOAS, University of London, 1996

Ghosh, Durba, 'Colonial Companions, *Bibis*, *Begums*, and Concubines of the British in North India, 1760–1830', PhD thesis, University of California, Berkeley, 2000

Loo, Margaret M. Shu-yi, 'The Biography of the III Panchen Lama, Blo-bzang-dpal-Ldan-ye-shes-dpal-bzang-po, Examined in the Light of Sino-Tibetan Relations during the Late Eighteenth-Century', PhD thesis, University of Washington, 1970

Peters, Carolyn Marie, 'Glasgow's Tobacco Lords: An Examination of Wealth Creators in the Eighteenth Century', PhD thesis, Glasgow University, 1990

Stewart, Gordon, 'Can Reincarnated Tibetan Lamas Remember History?', unpublished paper

Wang, Xiangyun, 'Tibetan Buddhism at the Court of Qing: The Life and Work of lCang-skya Rol-pa'i-rdo-rje (1717–86)', PhD thesis, Harvard University, 1995

Zito, Angela, 'Hosting and Hierarchy: The Panchen Lama Comes to Dinner', unpublished paper

Website

http://www.fmprc.gov.cn/ce/cegv/eng/premade/60544/TibetFAQ7.htm, accessed 20 June 2005

Contemporary Printed Works

Acland, Charles, *A Popular Account of the Manners and Customs of India*, John Murray, London, 1847

Astley, Thomas, *A New General Collection of Voyages and Travels*, 4 vols, Thomas Astley, London, 1747

Bell, John, *Travels from St. Petersburg in Russia, to Diverse Parts of Asia*, 2 vols, Robert & Andrew Foulis, Glasgow, 1763

Busteed, H. E., *Echoes from Old Calcutta*, W. Thacker & Co., London, 1908

Cranmer-Byng, J. L., *An Embassy to China: Being the Journal kept by Lord Macartney during his embassy to the Emperor Ch'ien-lung 1793–1794*, Longman, London, 1962

Daniell, William, *Views in Bootan: from the Drawings of Samuel Davis*, London, 1813

Das, Sarat Chandra, *Autobiography: Narratives of the Incidents of my Early Life*, R. K. Maitra, Calcutta, 1969

————, 'Contributions on the Religion, History &c of Tibet', *Journal of the Asiatic Society of Bengal*, 51: 1, 1882, 28–43

Edwards, Philip, ed., *The Journals of Captain Cook*, Penguin, Harmondsworth, 1999

Fay, Eliza, *Original Letters from India* (1779–1815), ed. E. M. Forster, Chatto & Windus, London, 1986

Ferguson, Adam, *An Essay on the History of Civil Society*, ed. Fania Oz-Salzberger, Cambridge University Press, Cambridge, 1995

Ghulam Hussain Khan, *A Translation of the Seir Mutaqharin; or View of Modern Times, being an History of India*, trans. 'Nota-Manus', James White, Calcutta, 1789

Gleig, G. R., *Memoirs of the Life of the Right Hon. Warren Hastings*, 3 vols, Richard Bengley, London, 1841

Grünwedel, Albert, *Der Weg nach Śambhala des dritten Gross-Lama von bKra śis lhun po bLo bzan dPal ldan Yeśes*, Abhandlungen der Königlich Bayerischen Akademie der Wissenschaften, Munich, 1915

Hickey, William, *Memoirs of William Hickey*, ed. Alfred Spencer, 4 vols, Hurst & Blacket, London, 1913–25

Hodges, William, *Travels in India during the Years 1780, 1781, 1782 and 1783*, J. Edwards, London, 1793

Huc, Régis-Evariste, and Joseph Gabet, *Travels in Tartary, Thibet and China 1844–1846*, trans. William Hazlitt, 2 vols, George Routledge, London, 1928

Kindersley, Jemima, *Letters from the Island of Teneriffe, Brazil, the Cape of Good Hope and the East Indies*, J. Nourse, London, 1777

Markham, Clements R., *Narratives of the Mission of George Bogle to Tibet, and of the Journey of Thomas Manning to Lhasa*, Trübner & Co., London, 1876

Mémoires concernant l'Histoire, les Sciences, les Arts, les Mœurs, les Usages &c des Chinois par les Missionnaires de Pe-kin, vol. 9, Paris, 1783

Morehead, Charles, ed., *Memorials of the Life and Writings of the Rev. Robert Morehead*, Edmonston & Douglas, Edinburgh, 1875

Redford, Bruce, ed., *The Letters of Samuel Johnson*, 5 vols, Clarendon Press, Oxford, 1992

Roberts, Emma, *Scenes and Characteristics of Hindostan with Sketches of Anglo-Indian Society*, 3 vols, William Allen, London, 1835

Robertson, William, *The History of the Reign of Emperor Charles V*, George Routledge & Co., London, 1857

Stanhope, Philip Dormer, *Genuine Memoirs of Asiaticus*, ed. Walter Kelly Firminger, N. L. Chowdhury, Hugli, 1909

Staunton, George, *An Historical Account of the Embassy to the Emperor of China*, 3 vols, John Stockdale, London, 1797

Stavorinus, Jan Splinter, *Voyages to the East-Indies*, G. G. & J. Robinson, London, 1798

Stewart, John, 'An Account of the Kingdom of Thibet', *Philosophical Transactions*, 67: 2, 1777, 465–92

Turner, Samuel, *An Account of an Embassy to the Court of the Teshoo Lama in Tibet*, G. & W. Nicol, London, 1800

Twining, Thomas, *Travels in India a hundred years ago*, James R. Osgood, McIlvaine & Co., London, 1893

Williamson, Thomas, *East India Vade-Mecum; or, Complete Guide to Gentlemen intended for the Civil, Military, or Naval Service of the Hon. East India Company*, Black, Parry & Kingsbury, London, 1810

Yule, Henry, *Hobson-Jobson: A Glossary of Colloquial Anglo-Indian Words and Phrases*, Rupa & Co., Calcutta, 1986

Secondary Works and Periodical Articles

Allen, Charles, *Duel in the Snows: The True Story of the Younghusband Mission to Lhasa*, John Murray, London, 2004

Altman, Janet Gurkin, *Epistolarity: Approaches to a Form*, Ohio State University Press, Columbus, 1982

Archer, Mildred, *British Portrait Painters in India 1770–1835*, Sotheby Parke Bernet Publications, London, 1979

Aris, Michael, *Bhutan: The Early History of a Himalayan Kingdom*, Aris & Phillips, Warminster, 1979

————, 'India and the British according to a Tibetan Text of the later Eighteenth Century', *Tibetan Studies: Proceedings of the Sixth Seminar of the International Association for Tibetan Studies*, 1, ed. Per Kvaerne, The Institute for Comparative Research in Human Culture, Oslo, 1994, 7–15

————, *Views of Medieval Bhutan: The Diary and Drawings of Samuel Davis, 1783*, Serindia Publications, London, 1982

Aris, Michael, and Michael Hutt, *Bhutan: Aspects of Culture and Development*, Kiscadale Asia Research Publications, 5, Kiscadale Publications, Gartmore, 1994

Ashton, T. S., *Economic Fluctuations in England 1700–1800*, Clarendon Press, Oxford, 1959

Bayly, C. A., *Empire and Information: Intelligence Gathering and Social Communication in India, 1780–1870*, Cambridge University Press, Cambridge, 1996

————, *Indian Society and the Making of the British Empire, The New Cambridge History of India*, II: 1, Cambridge University Press, Cambridge, 1988

————, *The Raj: India and the British 1600–1947*, National Portrait Gallery Publications, London, 1990

————, *Rulers, Townsmen and Bazaars: North Indian Society in the Age of British Expansion 1770–1870*, Oxford University Press, Delhi, 2003

Bernbaum, Edwin, *The Way to Shambhala: A Search for the Mythical Kingdom beyond the Himalayas*, Anchor Books, New York, 1980

Bernstein, Jeremy, *Dawning of the Raj: The Life and Trials of Warren Hastings*, Aurum Press, London, 2001

Berridge, G. R., Maurice Keens-Soper and T. G. Otte, *Diplomatic Theory from Machiavelli to Kissinger*, Palgrave, Basingstoke, 2001

Bhuyan, S. K. *Anglo-Assamese Relations 1771–1826*, Department of Historical and Antiquarian Studies in Assam, Gauhuti, 1949

Bishop, Peter, *The Myth of Shangri-La: Tibet, Travel Writing and the Western Creation of Sacred Landscape*, Athlone Press, London, 1989

Bowyer, T. H., 'India and the Personal Finances of Philip Francis', *English Historical Review*, 110: 435, February 1995, 122–31

————, 'Philip Francis and the Government of Bengal: Parliament and Personality in the Frustration of an Ambition', *Parliamentary History*, 18: 1, 1999, 1–21

Brewer, John, *The Pleasures of the Imagination: English Culture in the Eighteenth Century*, HarperCollins, London, 1997

The British Invasion of Tibet: Colonel Younghusband, 1904, Stationery Office, London, 1999

'The Buddhist Monastery at Ghoosery', *Bengal Past & Present*, 26, 1923, 195–7

Bysack, Gaur Dás, 'Notes on a Buddhist Monastery at Bhot Bágán', *Journal of the Asiatic Society of Bengal*, 59: 1, 1890, 50–99

Cammann, Schuyler, *Trade through the Himalayas: The Early British Attempts to Open Tibet*, Princeton University Press, Princeton, 1951

Chatterjee, Indrani, 'Colouring Subalternity: Slaves, Concubines and Social Orphans in Early Colonial India', *Subaltern Studies*, 10, 1999, 49–97

Chayet, Anne, *Les Temples de Jehol et leurs modèles tibétains*, Editions Recherche sur les Civilisations, Paris, 1985

Cheng, Pei-kai, Michael Lestz and Jonathan D. Spence, eds, *The Search for Modern China: A Documentary Collection*, W. W. Norton, New York, 1999

Cheong, Weng Eang, *The Hong Merchants of Canton: Chinese Merchants in Sino-Western Trade*, Curzon, Richmond, 1997

Clark, John, 'Hindu Trading Pilgrims', in Alex McKay, ed., *Pilgrimage in Tibet*, Curzon, London, 1998, 53–71

Cohn, Bernard S. 'The Role of Gosains in the Economy of Eighteenth and Nineteenth

Century Upper India', *Indian Economic and Social History Review*, 1: 4, 1963–4, 175–82

Colley, Linda, *Britons: Forging the Nation 1707–1837*, Pimlico, London, 1992

Collingham, E. M., *Imperial Bodies: The Physical Experience of the Raj c. 1800–1947*, Polity, Cambridge, 2001

Collister, Peter, *Bhutan and the British*, Serindia Publications with Belitha Press, London, 1987

Cotton, Evan, 'A Letter from Warren Hastings to George Bogle', *Bengal Past & Present*, 42, 1931, 83–9

Crawford, Robert, *Devolving English Literature*, Oxford University Press, Oxford, 1992

Crossley, Pamela Kyle, *The Manchus*, Blackwell, Oxford, 1997

Dalrymple, William, *White Mughals: Love and Betrayal in Eighteenth-Century India*, HarperCollins, London, 2002

Dasgupta, Atis K., *The Fakir and Sannyasi Uprisings*, K. P. Bagchi, Calcutta, 1992

Dazey, Wade H., 'Tradition and Modernization in the Organisation of the Dasanani Samnyasins', in Austin B. Creel and Vasudha Narayanan, eds, *Monastic Life in the Christian and Hindu Traditions: A Comparative Study*, Edwin Mellen Press, Lewiston, NY, 1990

Deb, Arabinda, 'Diarchy in Bhutan: The Dharma Raja-Deb System', *Bengal Past & Present*, 91, 1972, 158–65

————, 'George Bogle's Treaty with Bhutan 1775', *Bulletin of Tibetology*, 8: 1, 1971, 5–14

Devine, T. M., *Scotland's Empire 1600–1815*, Allen Lane, London, 2003

————, *The Tobacco Lords: A Study of the Tobacco Merchants of Glasgow and their Trading Activities c. 1740–90*, John Donald Publishers, Edinburgh, 1975

Devine, T. M., and Gordon Jackson, eds, *Glasgow: Beginnings to 1830*, Manchester University Press, Manchester, 1995

Diskalkar, D. B., 'Bogle's Embassy to Tibet', *Indian Historical Quarterly*, 9, 1933, 420–38

Fairbank, John King, ed., *The Chinese World Order: Traditional China's Foreign Relations*, Harvard University Press, Cambridge, Mass., 1968

Feiling, Keith, *Warren Hastings*, Macmillan, London, 1954

Field, A. R. 'A Note Concerning Early Anglo-Bhutanese Relations', *East and West*, 13, 1962, 340–4

Forêt, Philippe, *Mapping Chengde: The Qing Landscape Enterprise*, University of Hawaii Press, Honolulu, 2000

France, Peter, 'Primitivism and Enlightenment: Rousseau and the Scots', *Yearbook of English Studies*, 15, 1985, 64–79

————, 'Western European Civilisation and its Mountain Frontiers (1750–1850)', *History of European Ideas*, 6: 3, 1985, 297–310

French, Patrick, *Younghusband: The Last Great Imperial Adventurer*, HarperCollins, London, 1994

Gandolfo, Romolo, 'Bhutan and Tibet in European Cartography (1597–1800)', *Proceedings of the First International Seminar on Bhutan Studies*, Centre for Bhutan Studies, Thimphu, 2004, 90–136

Ghosh, Jamin Mohan, *Sannyasi and Fakir Raiders in Bengal*, Bengal Secretariat Book Depot, Calcutta, 1930

Ghosh, Suresh Chandra, *The Social Condition of the British Community in Bengal 1757–1800*, E. J. Brill, Leiden, 1970

Ghurye, G. S., *Indian Sadhus*, Popular Prakashan, Bombay, 1964

Hanzhang, Ya, *Biographies of the Tibetan Spiritual Leaders Panchen Erdenis*, trans. Chen Guansheng and Li Peizhu, Foreign Languages Press, Beijing, 1994

Hasrat, Bikrama Jit, *History of Bhutan: Land of the Peaceful Dragon*, Education Department Bhutan, Thimphu, 1980

Hedin, Sven, *Jehol: City of Emperors*, Kegan Paul, London, 1932

Hevia, James L., *Cherishing Men from Afar: Qing Guest Ritual and the Macartney Embassy of 1793*, Duke University Press, Durham, 1995

————, 'Lamas, Emperors, and Rituals: Political Implications in Qing Imperial Ceremonies', *Journal of the International Association of Buddhist Studies*, 16: 2, 1993, 243–78

Hook, Andrew, and Richard B. Sher, *The Glasgow Enlightenment*, Tuckwell Press, East Linton, 1995

Ho, Chuimei, and Bennet Bronson, eds, *Splendors of China's Forbidden City: The Glorious Reign of Emperor Qianlong*, Merrell, London; Field Museum, Chicago, 2004

Ho, Chuimei, and Cheri A. Jones, eds, *Life in the Imperial Court of Qing Dynasty China: Proceedings of the Denver Museum of Natural History*, 3: 15, 1998

Hopkins, Donald R., *Princes and Peasants: Smallpox in History*, University of Chicago Press, Chicago, 1983

Hopkirk, Peter, *Quest for Kim: In Search of Kipling's Great Game*, Oxford University Press, Oxford, 2001

Hoppit, Julian, *Risk and Failure in English Business 1700–1800*, Cambridge University Press, Cambridge, 1987

Huber, Toni, *The Holy Land Reborn: Pilgrimage and the Reinvention of Buddhist India in the Tibetan Tradition*, University of Chicago Press, Chicago, forthcoming

Human Rights: Annual Report 2000, Foreign and Commonwealth Office, London, 2000

Jasanoff, Maya, *Edge of Empire: Conquest and Collecting in the East 1750–1850*, Fourth Estate, London, 2005

Jasbir Singh, and Amar Kaur, *Himalayan Triangle: A Historical Survey of British India's Relations with Tibet, Sikkim and Bhutan 1765–1950*, British Library, London, 1988

Kahn, Harold L., *Monarchy in the Emperor's Eyes: Image and Reality in the Ch'ien-lung Reign*, Harvard University Press, Cambridge, Mass., 1971

Keay, John, *The Honourable Company: A History of the English East India Company*, HarperCollins, London, 1991

Kolff, D. H. A., 'Sannyasi Trader–Soldiers', *Indian Economic and Social History Review*, 8: 2, 1971, 213–18

Kunwar, Mayura Jang, 'China and War in the Himalayas 1792–1793', *English Historical Review*, 77: 303, 1962, 283–97

Lamb, Alastair, *Bhutan and Tibet: The Travels of George Bogle and Alexander Hamilton 1774–1777*, Roxford Books, Hertingfordbury, 2002

————, *British India and Tibet 1766–1910*, Routledge & Kegan Paul, London, 1986

————, *The Mandarin Road to Old Hué: Narratives of Anglo-Vietnamese Diplomacy from the Seventeenth Century to the Eve of the French Conquest*, Chatto, London, 1970

Lawson, Philip, *The East India Company: A History*, Longman, London, 1993

Lopez, Donald S., Jr, *The Prisoners of Shangri-La: Tibetan Buddhism and the West*, University of Chicago Press, Chicago, 1998

Lorenzen, David N., 'Warrior Ascetics in Indian History', *Journal of the American Oriental Society*, 98, 1978, 61–75

Losty, J. P., *Calcutta: City of Palaces*, British Library, London, 1990

MacGregor, John, *Tibet: A Chronicle of Exploration*, Routledge & Kegan Paul, London, 1970.

McKay, Alex, 'The Drowning of Lama Sengchen Kyabying: A Preliminary Enquiry from British Sources', in H. Blezer, ed., *Tibet Past and Present: Tibetan Studies I. The Proceedings of the 9th International Seminar for Tibetan Studies, Leiden 2000*, Brill, Leiden, 2002

Mackerras, Colin, *Western Images of China*, Oxford University Press, Hong Kong, 1999

Maclean, James N. M., *Reward is Secondary: The Life of a Political Adventurer and an Inquiry into the Mystery of 'Junius'*, Hodder & Stoughton, London, 1963

McMillin, Laurie Hovell, *English in Tibet, Tibet in English: Self-Presentation in Tibet and the Diaspora*, Palgrave, New York, 2001

Marshall, P. J., *Bengal: The British Bridgehead, Eastern India, 1740–1828*, The New Cambridge History of India, 2: 2, Cambridge University Press, Cambridge, 1987

————, *East Indian Fortunes: The British in Bengal in the Eighteenth Century*, Oxford University Press, Oxford, 1976

————, 'Eighteenth-Century Calcutta', in Robert Ross and Gerard J. Telkamp, eds, *Colonial Cities: Essays on Urbanism in a Colonial Context*, Martinus Nijhoff Publishers, Leiden, 1985

————, 'Masters and Banians in Eighteenth-Century Calcutta', in Blair B. King and M. N. Pearson, eds, *The Age of Partnership: Europeans in Asia before Dominion*, University of Hawaii Press, Honolulu, 1979

————, ed., *The Eighteenth Century*, The Oxford History of the British Empire, Oxford University Press, Oxford, 1998

Marshall, P. J., and Glyndwr Williams, *The Great Map of Mankind: British Perceptions of the World in the Age of Enlightenment*, J. M. Dent, London, 1982

Millward, James A., Ruth W. Dunnell, Mark C. Elliott and Philippe Forêt, eds, *The New Qing Imperial History: The Making of Inner Asian Empire at Qing Chengde*, RoutledgeCurzon, London, 2004

Mohsin, Khan Mohammad, *A Bengal District in Transition: Murshidabad 1765–1793*, Asiatic Society of Bangladesh, Dacca, 1973

————, 'Murshidabad in the Eighteenth Century', in Kenneth Ballhatchet and John Harrison, eds, *The City in South Asia: Pre-Modern and Modern*, Curzon Press, London, 1980

Mote, F. W., *Imperial China 900–1800*, Harvard University Press, Cambridge, Mass., 1999

Mukherjee, S. N., *Calcutta: Essays in Urban History*, Subarnarekha, Calcutta, 1993

Mungello, D. E., *The Great Encounter of China and the West 1500–1800*, Rowman & Littlefield, Lanham, 1999

Naquin, Susan, *Peking: Temples and City Life 1400–1900*, University of California Press, Berkeley, 2000

Norbu, Dawa, 'The Europeanization of Sino-Tibetan Relations, 1775–1907: The Genesis of Chinese "Suzerainty" and Tibetan "Autonomy"', *Tibet Journal*, 15: 4 1990, 28–74

Norbu, Thubten Jigme, *Tibet is my Country*, told to Heinrich L. Harrer, trans. Edward Fitzgerald, Rupert Hart-Davis, London, 1960

Petech, Luciano, *China and Tibet in the Early Eighteenth Century: History of the Establishment of Chinese Protectorate in Tibet*, E. J. Brill, Leiden, 1972

————, *Selected Papers on Asian History*, Istituto Italiano per il Medio ed Estremo Oriente, Rome, 1988

Peterson, Willard J., ed., *The Chi'ing Empire to 1800*, The Cambridge History of China, 9: 1, Cambridge University Press, Cambridge, 2002

Pritchard, Earl H., *The Crucial Years of Early Anglo-Chinese Relations 1750–1800*, Research Studies of the State College of Washington, Washington, 1936

Rendall, Jane, *The Origins of the Scottish Enlightenment*, Macmillan, London, 1978

Richardson, H. E., 'George Bogle and his Children', *Scottish Genealogist*, 29: 3, September 1982, 73–83

Riddy, John, 'Warren Hastings: Scotland's Benefactor?', in Geoffrey Carnall and Colin Nicholson, eds, *The Impeachment of Warren Hastings: Papers from a Bicentenary Commemoration*, Edinburgh University Press, Edinburgh, 1989

Rose, Leo E., *Nepal: Strategy for Survival*, University of California Press, Berkeley, 1971
————, *The Politics of Bhutan*, Cornell University Press, Ithaca, 1977

Samuel, Geoffrey, *Civilized Shamans: Buddhism in Tibetan Societies*, Smithsonian Institution Press, Washington, 1993

Sarkar, Jadunath, *A History of Dasnami Naga Sanyasis*, Sri Panchayi Akhara, Allahabad, 1955

Sarkar, S. C, 'A Note on Puran Gir Gosain', *Bengal Past & Present*, 43, 1932, 119–28

Schell, Orville, *Virtual Tibet: Searching for Shangri-La from the Himalayas to Hollywood*, Metropolitan Books, New York, 2000

Schicklgruber, Christian, and Françoise Pommaret, eds, *Bhutan: Mountain Fortress of the Gods*, Serindia Publications, London, 1997

Shakabpa, Tsepon W. D., *Tibet: A Political History*, Potalo Publications, New York, 1984

Smith, E. Gene, *Among Tibetan Texts: History and Literature of the Himalayan Plateau*, ed. Kurtis R. Schaeffer, Wisdom Publications, Boston, 2001

Spengen, Wim van, 'The Geo-History of Long-Distance Trade in Tibet 1850–1950', *Tibet Journal*, 20: 2, 1995, 18–63

Stewart, Keith, 'Towards Defining an Aesthetic for the Familiar Letter in Eighteenth-Century England', *Prose Studies*, 5, 1982, 179–92

Sutherland, Lucy, 'New Evidence on the Nandakuma Trial', *English Historical Review*, 72, 1957, 438–65
————, *The East India Company in Eighteenth-Century Politics*, Clarendon Press, Oxford, 1952

Twitchett, Denis, and John K. Fairbank, eds, *Late Ch'ing, 1800–1911, The Cambridge History of China*, 10: 1, Cambridge University Press, Cambridge, 1978

Waley-Cohen, Joanna, 'Religion, War and Empire-Building in Eighteenth-Century China', *International History Review*, 20: 2, 1998, 336–52
————, *The Sextants of Beijing: Global Currents in Chinese History*, W. W. Norton, New York, 1999

Waller, Derek, *The Pundits: British Exploration of Tibet and Central Asia*, University Press of Kentucky, Lexington, 1988

Wang, Xiangyun, 'The Qing Court's Tibet Connection: Lcang skya Rol pa'i rdo rje and the Qianlong Emperor', *Harvard Journal of Asiatic Studies*, 60: 1, June 2000, 125–63

Weitzman, Sophia, *Warren Hastings and Philip Francis*, Manchester University Press, Manchester, 1929

Wenger, Richard, 'George Bogle 1746–1781, Part I, His Early Years', *The Journal of the Families in British India Society*, 14, 2005, 2–11

Wessels, C., *Early Jesuit Travellers in Central Asia 1603–1721*, Asian Educational Series, New Delhi, 1992

Whelpton, John, *A History of Nepal*, Cambridge University Press, Cambridge, 2005

Wilson, Kathleen, *The Island Race: Englishness, Empire and Gender in the Eighteenth Century*, Routledge, London, 2003

Wong, Young-Tsu, *A Paradise Lost: The Imperial Garden of Yuanming Yuan*, University of Hawaii Press, Honolulu, 2001

Woodcock, George, *Into Tibet: Early British Explorers*, Faber & Faber, London, 1971

Younghusband, Francis, *India and Tibet*, John Murray, London, 1910

————, *India and Tibet*, ed. Alastair Lamb, Oxford University Press, Hong Kong, 1985

Zito, Angela, *Of Body and Brush: Grand Sacrifice as Text/Performance in Eighteenth-Century China*, University of Chicago Press, Chicago, 1997

ACKNOWLEDGEMENTS

This book has been long in the making. Over the years, various institutions and many individuals have made it possible for me to complete the book. I am particularly indebted to Roehampton University for periods of study leave and to the British Academy for a research grant.

At the beginning of the project, I received much help from Hugh Richardson and Michael Aris, two great scholars of Tibet and Bhutan (and George Bogle enthusiasts), both now sadly no longer with us. I was able to develop my ideas in academic papers and articles written at the invitation of John Barrell, Stephen Clark, Rebecca Earle, Felicity Nussbaum, Carolyn Steedman, David Washbrook, Kathleen Wilson and Tim Youngs. It was Linda Colley who suggested that the story might appeal to a wider audience. Clare Brant, John Clark and Nigel Leask have all been generous with their comments. Gordon Stewart and Angela Zito sent me copies of unpublished papers, and Wim van Spengen gave me essential cartographic advice. I have been greatly assisted in my research by the librarians at the British Library, SOAS, the Bodleian Library, and in particular by Hamish Whyte at the Mitchell Library, Glasgow. His Royal Highness The Duke of York kindly allowed me to view Tilly Kettle's painting, reproduced on the cover.

I am extremely grateful to those friends and colleagues who read the manuscript, corrected my errors and suggested improvements. My writing on eighteenth-century India has always benefited from the work of Chris Bayly and Peter Marshall, and they have been the most courteous and helpful of readers. Alastair Lamb was tireless in his interest and inexhaustible in his knowledge. His edition of George Bogle's journal has proved invaluable in the preparation of this book. Alex McKay took the time to answer every troublesome query and seemed to know every scholar working on Tibet. Toni Huber was most incisive in his comments and allowed me a preview of his forthcoming book. John Ardussi kindly put me right on Bhutan, and Tim Barrett did the same for China. John Mullan helped me to identify Bogle's literary and cultural influences. John Carey buoyed me up with his response, and Jenny Uglow presided like a godmother over the book.

I could not have asked for a better agent than Gill Coleridge. Aided by Lucy Luck, she smoothed the path for the book. Gill's tact and advice have always been faultless. Publishing at Bloomsbury has been a great pleasure. With his boundless enthusiasm, Michael Fishwick has been the most generous of editors and the book's constant advocate. Tram-Anh Doan has helped at every turn, and Lisa Birdwood has made the book look beautiful. Sloan Harris found the book a happy American home at Farrar, Straus & Giroux, where it has benefited from the editorial care of John Glusman and Paul Elie.

In the course of my research, I have strayed far from my professional patch. My colleagues at Roehampton University have indulged me in my wayward interests, and my friends have sustained me throughout. I would like to thank Marina Benjamin, Bhaswati Chakravorty, Michael Dobson, Simon Edwards, Christoph Emmrich, Jenny Hartley, Ian Haywood, Nicola Humble, Zach Leader, Susan Matthews, Philippa Park, Laura Peters, Srilata Raman, Jonah Siegel, Francis Spufford, Sarah Turvey, Cathy Wells-Cole and Nancy Yousef. I have received great help from Susy Beltranena, Greice Benedet de Lorenzi Cancellier, Hilda Berrie, Ros Campbell, Andrea Gutt, Doreen Lowe, Lisa Ralph and Emma Yaxley.

My family has offered love and endless support. My first and greatest debt is to Maina and William Teltscher. Together with

Barbara Loose, Peter and Judith Loose, they have excelled in their grandparental roles. My sister, Helen Rigby, has the sharpest pair of copy-editing eyes. Julian Loose has lived with this book, nurtured it, read and reread it – truly a labour of love. Our two sons, Jacob and Isaac, have offered the best possible antidote to the writing life. They have made it all worthwhile.

INDEX

The Index includes the Prologue, Chapters 1 – 21 and the Epilogue but not the Notes. Filing order is word-by-word. The following abbreviations are used: GB for George Bogle; AH for Alexander Hamilton and WH for Warren Hastings. The name 'East India Company' is used as a main entry; all other reference to it are to 'Company'.

A NOTE ON THE AUTHOR

Kate Teltscher is a Reader in the School of Arts at Roehampton University. She studied at the University of York and was a North Senior scholar at St John's College, Oxford. She has published numerous essays in academic collections and journals, and reviewed for the *Guardian* and the *TLS*. Her doctoral research, a study of British and European writing on India in the seventeenth and eighteenth centuries, was published as *India Inscribed* (Oxford University Press, 1995). *The High Road to China* is her first book for a general readership.

A NOTE ON THE TYPE

Linotype Garamond Three – based on seventeenth century copies
of Claude Garamond's types, cut by Jean Jannon. This version
was designed for American Type Founders in 1917, by Morris
Fuller Benton and Thomas Maitland Cleland and adapted
for mechanical composition by Linotype in 1936.